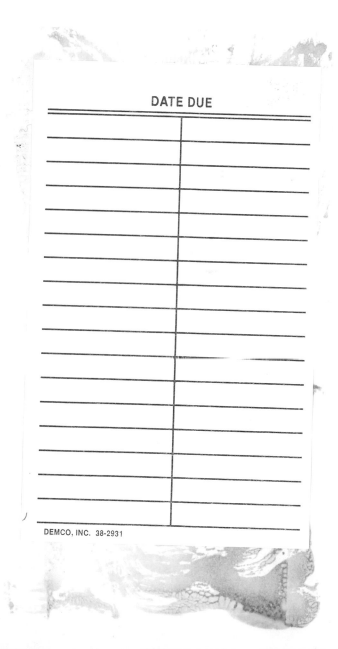

DATE DUE

MARKETPLACE
MEDICINE

MARKETPLACE MEDICINE

The Rise of the For-Profit Hospital Chains

DAVE LINDORFF

BANTAM BOOKS
NEW YORK · TORONTO · LONDON · SYDNEY · AUCKLAND

MARKETPLACE MEDICINE

A Bantam Book / February 1992

Library of Congress Cataloging-in-Publication Data

Lindorff, David E.
 Marketplace medicine: the rise of the for-profit hospital chains
 David Lindorff.
    p.   cm.
 Includes bibliographical references and index.
 ISBN 0-553-07552-7
 1. Hospitals, Proprietary–United States. 2. Medical
corporations–United States.   I. Title.
RA975.P74L56   1992
362.1′1–dc20   91-23353
                                                                                   CIP

Published simultaneously in the United States and Canada

Bantam Books are published by Bantam Books, a division of Bantam Doubleday
Dell Publishing Group, Inc. Its trademark, consisting of the words "Bantam
Books" and the portrayal of a rooster, is Registered in U.S. Patent and
Trademark Office and in other countries. Marca Registrada. Bantam Books, 666
Fifth Avenue, New York, New York 10103.

To my daughter Ariel Mariah Lindorff, who was born at the same time as the idea for Marketplace Medicine, *and who grew up with it. May she reach adulthood in an America that no longer allows one's financial position to determine the medical care one can expect to receive.*

CONTENTS

ACKNOWLEDGMENTS

During the seven years that I was either thinking about, researching, or writing and editing this book, I was aided and abetted by experts, sources, and friends too numerous to mention. I am indebted to them all.

To some, however, I owe a special bow of gratitude. In particular, I wish to thank three friends: Betty Holcomb, with whom I first discussed the idea of a book on the hospital industry and who encouraged me to get on with it; her husband, Michael Waldholz, a health industry reporter at the *Wall Street Journal*, who read and criticized my first draft, offering many needed suggestions for improvement; and economist Marty de Kadt, who generously read and critiqued the sections on the economics and politics of the industry.

Others who were particularly helpful in various stages of the work include the late Robert Lekachman, who encouraged me to pursue the idea and whose always pithy and humorous works remain an inspiration (even if in style they are unattainable); Geri Dallek, who as head of the National Health Law Project in Los Angeles, was a key "source of sources"; and the staff of Health–PAC, another important provider of sources about the industry.

Also providing crucial information and leads were a network of dozens of reporters at daily newspapers across the country, who were always ready and willing to send their clips and share their sources with me, and the newspaper librarians, for whom a proper citation was a point of honor. Without their help, I could never have hoped to get the details on the local stories that tell what is happening to health care nationwide.

Thanks to my editors at Bantam Books, Toni Burbank and Howard Kaplan, to whose incisive (if often painful) pencilwork this work owes whatever stylistic merits it can boast, and to a true "writer's attorney," Sara Goodman. Thanks too to Stephen Rubin, who made the initial decision to buy the book, and who stuck with it through the hard times, and to my agent, Charlotte Sheedy, who kept on my back when the pressing needs of earning a living sometimes compelled me to set the book project aside.

Having given this nod to "management," I must also thank my brothers and sisters in the National Writers Union, without whose experience and encouragement I might never have dared tackle such a large project.

Finally special thanks to my wife Joyce, who often had to take on much more than our idealized role of "50-percent parent" during the course of this project, and who has always been my most valued journalistic critic.

I hasten to add that with all the help I received in putting together this book, its shortcomings remain wholly my own.

FOREWORD

This is a historic moment in the provision of health services in the United States. It is a time of sharply escalating medical-care costs, of over thirty million Americans who are completely uninsured against the cost of services and tens of millions more who are grossly underinsured, of shamefully high numbers of low-birthweight babies and infant mortality rates, of millions of poor preschool children who are not fully immunized, of preventable outbreaks of measles and tuberculosis, and of a dual health-care system—one for middle-class and affluent citizens, another for the poor, near poor, and many members of the working class; one for many of our white citizens, another for millions of people of color.

The 1980s has also been a period of rapid growth of for profit hospitals. The names Humana, Hospital Corporation of America, and American Medical International became symbols of astonishing financial success in the medical profession, in the financial world, and in the minds of many patients, their families, and members of their communities. As the social experiments of the 1960s and 1970s and even the limited government provision of human services have been assailed by the conservative critics of the 1980s and 1990s, many sectors of American society have turned to privatization. Today we see prisons run under contract to public authorities by the private sector, sanitation work increasingly performed by private companies, private security services supplementing or replacing police protection, and even adoption services, once the virtual monopoly of public and voluntary social agencies, now facilitated on a profit-making basis by physicians and lawyers. It is therefore not surprising that hospital care should also be increasingly dominated by the private, profit-making sector.

Money-making has, of course, long been a cornerstone of American medicine. Medical care has been provided largely by physicians in private practice through fee-for-service payment that rewards overutilization of medical services and provision of unnecessary care. Any attempt to alter the configuration of the "sacred doctor-patient relationship" based on "free choice" by the patient and "free enterprise" by the physician has been repeatedly beaten back as virtually un-American. Now, medicine has developed new methods of money-making that are based not only on high fees for services received but also on high profits from investments in hospitals and medical equipment. It is, therefore, little wonder that today we have a multibillion-dollar for-profit hospital industry.

What is the problem, one might ask, of for-profit hospitals accounting for a significant percentage of all U.S. hospitals? In his thoughtful and carefully-researched book *Marketplace Medicine*, Dave Lindorff analyzes the impact of this relatively recent development on the health-care system. He documents the commodification and commercialization of medicine during the 1980s; the growing acceptance of profit making in the care of the sick, a service considered a fundamental human right regardless of ability to pay in much of the rest of the world; and the increasing difficulty that the poor and those without appropriate insurance endure in obtaining decent medical care in rural areas, in our inner cities—in virtually every part of this affluent country.

The United States in the early 1990s continues to experience the greatest gap between rich and poor in its history. In 1989 the richest 20 percent of the population received 46.8 percent of national income, a significantly greater share than in 1979 or 1969, while the poorest 20 percent received only 3.8 percent, a lower share than in the two previous decades. The distribution of wealth in the United States is even more inequitable. By catering to the affluent, by "dumping" the poor and the uninsured, by further legitimizing making profits from the illness and misery of defenseless people, the for-profit hospital system reflects, reinforces, and grows rich from these obscene inequities.

Marketplace Medicine demonstrates with great clarity the venality and bankruptcy of our current health-care system. As the United States moves during the 1990s toward serious consideration of a comprehensive, cost-controlled health-care system available to all, this study of for-profit hospital care will contribute significantly to the discussion. There is hope that by the beginning of the twenty-first century the United States will join virtually all other industrialized nations and move rapidly toward a consistently high-quality, equitable health-care system for all its citizens. That will, indeed, be a historic undertaking.

RUTH SIDEL, Ph.D.,
Professor of Sociology,
Hunter College

MARKETPLACE
MEDICINE

PREFACE

The medical system may not be doing too well at fighting disease, but as any broker will testify, it's one of the healthiest businesses around.
—Barbara and John Ehrenreich
in *The American Health Empire*

Every family must have its medical war stories. There are so many things that can go wrong, so many ways doctors, hospitals, and insurance companies can be insensitive or even incompetent. On top of this, American health care costs so much: well over half a *trillion* dollars in 1990 and rising. In terms of out-of-pocket expenses, this represents 10 percent of the average family budget. This latter figure, moreover, doesn't count hidden costs to the family, such as higher prices of goods and services to cover employee health benefits, higher taxes to finance public health-care programs for the poor and elderly and to fund research and hospital construction, or lower wages to breadwinners because of the diversion of funds by employers to pay for employee health-insurance benefits. Polls have repeatedly shown that a majority of Americans thinks something is seriously wrong with our health-care system, and with costs going up and access to care going down, they are right. Something *is* seriously wrong.

The United States spends over 12 percent of its gross national product on health care, the highest in the developed world, even

1

compared to countries like Canada, Sweden, or Great Britain—all of which have full-scale socialized medicine. Our record on infant mortality, long an indicator of a nation's health, is dismal, and instead of getting better, it's getting worse. We're below not only some of the poorer European countries, but also some Third World countries such as Singapore and Hong Kong.[1] In the poorest parts of this country—the ghettos and some rural regions—infant mortality rates rival those in Bangladesh. But statistics only tell part of the story.

In 1985, shortly after beginning work on this book, my infant daughter had a febrile seizure, a frightening event in itself, since it can cause a child to stop breathing for as long as a minute or two, but which also revealed to me how America's health care was failing us, not just as a family but as a nation.

It wasn't that we didn't get good care for her. The truth is our experience with both doctor and hospital (the pediatric ward of New York University Medical Center) was excellent. It was what came later that disturbed me profoundly.

After the first traumatic episode, during which my wife and I both thought Ariel had died in our arms, whenever Ariel got sick, we would rush her to the doctor, hoping that the cause was something like strep throat, which could be treated with an antibiotic, thus removing the threat of another fever-induced seizure. We had been told that febrile seizures are almost always harmless, but we had also been cautioned that there was a remote possibility of brain damage from a particularly bad episode.

As freelancers, my wife, Joyce, and I had a rather pathetic health insurance plan, with a $1,000 deductible on each insured person. So despite annual premium payments of $3000 or more, every time we brought Ariel to the doctor, it cost us $50, and the diagnosis was invariably a virus, which no prescription can cure. After a while, chronically strapped for cash, we found ourselves wondering whether or not to bring Ariel to the doctor for every sign of illness. I began to get annoyed at myself for worrying about $50 where my daughter's safety was concerned.

If I, as a reasonably successful free-lance journalist who could at least afford *some* health insurance, was taking such risks with my child's health, what, I asked myself, were all those millions of people out there with *no* insurance, and probably even less money, doing? How many necessary medical treatments were being dangerously postponed because of financial problems? After talking with both experts and ordinary folks, I began to find out what happens to such people: They postpone going to the doctor until suddenly they *have* to or are delivered in an ambulance, at which point their illness has reached a bank-breaking crisis or led to an unnecessary death. In addition, I found out that when they finally do go to the hospital, they are often turned away!

This situation is never faced by people in Canada, Great Britain, Germany, or Sweden. In fact, in every industrialized nation except the United States and South Africa, health care is considered a fundamental right. Instead of leaving the health of the citizenry to the vagaries of the marketplace, and allowing the ancillary sectors of the health-care industry to profit from the illnesses of the general public, these nations make certain that health care, like public sewers, waterworks, and transportation networks, is available to all at only nominal out-of-pocket costs. As I thought about my own situation, and the fortune I was paying each year for a grossly inadequate health insurance plan, it made me angry.

Medicine, like teaching, fire fighting, the ministry, or journalism, has always seemed to me to be one of those professions where one *ought* to be motivated by a desire to serve society. But the six-figure incomes earned by many doctors, not to mention the fancy cars I often see in the reserved spaces of private physicians' parking lots, have made me skeptical about the motivations of some doctors.

I remember back in 1968, only a few years after the creation of the federal Medicaid program (which was supposed to pay for health care for the poor), seeing a sign on the door of my family doctor's office which said No Medicaid Patients. What shocked me even more than the coldness of the message was the sign itself, which was made of laminated plastic and had obviously been mass-produced for a large number of private physicians. My doctor was no lone violator of the Hippocratic oath!

But health care was not my favorite topic as a journalist. Rather, I was fascinated by politics and economics. By 1979, after six years as a staff reporter at a variety of newspapers and on television, I was writing on a freelance basis for magazines, primarily about business, economics, and political affairs.

One of those magazines was *Venture*, a slick new publication for and about entrepreneurs and their companies. In 1983 *Venture* assigned me to research and write a story, modeled on the annual *Fortune Magazine* story about the five hundred largest American industrial firms, but targeting instead the one hundred largest and fastest-growing *entrepreneurial* firms—those companies that are still being run by their founders.

It was the dawn of the computer revolution, and the assumption at the time my editor and I discussed the piece was that the computer industry would dominate the list. To our surprise, however, we discovered that the fastest-growing sector was for-profit hospitals, an industry neither of us had even heard of before. The three hospital companies on our list, Hospital Corporation of America, Humana, and National Medical Enterprises, had rung up average sales gains of 31 percent in 1982, while earnings rose by an average of 47 percent (1982 was a recession year, too!). In contrast, the computer companies, which included such well-known firms as Apple, Wang, and DEC, had seen aggregate sales rise by only 21 percent, and earnings by only 11 percent. [2]

At the time, I knew I was witnessing an important phenomenon. But it was not until I started thinking about the implications of such startling growth by companies who bought existing hospitals and turned them into "profit centers" that I contemplated investigating the industry and writing about it.

What really jarred me into action was Humana's decision in 1983 to pioneer a series of implants of Jarvik artificial hearts. As will be explained later in the book, this decision was motivated not simply by scientific curiosity, but also by the potential for profits and, even more immediately, for public relations benefits. Suddenly, at least one of the hospital companies had leapt from total obscurity into national prominence. For weeks, Humana was on the front page of the nation's newspapers and on the evening news, as the drama unfolded of patients living without their hearts, tethered by tubes to a machine. Riding on Humana's publicity coattails, the other big for-profit hospital chains also had their day in the sun, as reporters—at least for the limited time that American journalism accords celebrity to an issue—profiled them, their owners, and managers.

Right about that time, during 1984 and 1985, many of the approximately seven thousand hospitals in America were being bought up or—in the face of corporate competition—closed down. My gut feeling was that putting dozens, or hundreds, of far-flung community hospitals into the hands of executives at some remote corporate headquarters could not be a step forward for health care, any more than it has been for restaurant cuisine.

In the course of researching this book, I have had my initial suspicions about health care for profit largely confirmed. The bottom line is that when profit considerations enter the arena of medicine, health care suffers, especially for those who are most vulnerable and least able to take advantage of any choices made available by the new marketplace. Marketplace medicine may mean that the well-heeled Yuppie couple, who can shop around before choosing a doctor or hospital, can have their next baby in a cozy homelike birthing room. But it doesn't do much for the family of a worker whose employer provides an HMO-style health plan mandating use of a specific doctor and a specific hospital. Nor does it do much for the ghetto mother and her most likely premature delivery of an underweight baby.

In looking at the big hospital companies featured in this book, I have come to know some of their leading executives. Nearly all were generous with their time and answered every question I put to them. I have not found them to be villains. Indeed, most of them are extremely charming people—well educated, urbane, interesting to talk with, and generally well informed about the issues involving health care in the United States. That is to say, they are typical of the executives of most large U.S. companies.

They are *not* medical philanthropists, however. Both David Jones and his partner, Humana co-founder Wendell Cherry, have given enormous sums to the arts in Louisville, to Louisville University, and to other charitable and cultural organizations. But their company, Humana, has not been particularly charitable when it comes to taking care of the medically needy. The same can be said of the other big chains: Hospital Corporation of America (HCA), American Medical International (AMI), and National Medical Enterprises (NME).

All the major hospital companies have well-developed media and marketing operations, not to mention the slick public relations office of their Washington trade association, the Federation of American Health Systems. All are quick to tell an inquiring journalist about their caring, concerned approach to health care. But to find out what these companies are actually doing when it comes to providing care for those who need it most, I had to look elsewhere. A prime source was the legal aid offices across the country, where poorly paid poverty lawyers have had to battle to get their clients or their clients' relations into (and in one case even out of) hospitals where the first medical test for any patient was a "wallet biopsy."

For Gordon Bonnyman, a lanky homespun poverty lawyer in

HCA's hometown of Nashville, marketplace medicine has been a source of endless legal battles. Patients have been denied access to good hospitals, and sometimes even to medical treatments that were unavailable elsewhere. In colorful language (he told me local Tennessee politicians of both parties take to hospital industry campaign funds "like pigs to a mudhole"), Bonnyman regaled me with stories of patients turned away by HCA and other Nashville hospitals. He also referred me to colleagues in cities across the country with similar hospital experiences to relate involving other firms. He was the first person to explain to me how the bottom-line approach of the for-profit industry was also altering the behavior of the not-for-profit hospital sector.

Another eye-opening source of information about this new industry was Wall Street. There, I found that the public relations veneer was neatly stripped away. Health-care industry analysts didn't want to hear public relations stories about kind-hearted hospital executives. They wanted to hear about how the hospital companies were tightening financial controls, getting tough about billing patients, and controlling the "patient mix" to maximize their return on each admission (a euphemism for keeping indigents out of the hospital). Wall Street had developed its own jargon for the health-care industry. Patients have become "revenue bodies," free-standing clinics and company-owned health insurance subsidiaries are now "patient feeder systems," and each hospital is now a "profit center." Here were people who defined the "right" and "wrong" kinds of patients as, respectively, those who meant a profit for the hospital (usually those who weren't very sick and who had insurance) and those who meant a loss (the poor or the very frail and sick and those with inadequate coverage).

Of course, physicians were also a major source of information about the hospital industry, but they posed a peculiar and disconcerting problem. With rare exceptions, those doctors who had the most familiarity with the for-profit hospital sector—those doctors, in other words, who practiced in for-profit hospitals— were unwilling to say anything critical on the record. Whether legitimately or not, nearly every such physician I spoke with, or who contacted me after I ran ads requesting information in several medical journals, feared reprisals from the hospital companies if they spoke critically and were identified. Many wanted to talk, as did nurses and other hospital employees, but they were afraid to have their names used.

This attitude contrasted sharply with the physicians in the not-for-profit hospital sector, who nearly always spoke freely about shortcomings at their own institutions. Most disconcerting to me was finding this same perceived lack of freedom of speech at academic hospitals owned or run by the for-profit hospital industry—places where academic freedom is supposed to be respected! One medical school dean was so afraid of repercussions when he mailed me a critical document about the for-profit firm that ran his school's teaching hospital that he said he was sending it in a plain brown wrapper with no return address.

I came away from all the years of research which went into this book with a sense of alarm and with hope. I'm alarmed that while policymakers have been turning to the idea of a "free market" as a way of grappling with the twin issues of rising health costs and diminishing access to medical care, they and the American public have been missing an underlying movement toward corporatization of the health-care industry. Given the history of industrialization of other sectors of the economy, such a trend—paced by the hospital corporations—should have been anticipated. At the same time, I am confident that experiments with deregulation and encouragement of market solutions will demonstrate the failure of for-profit hospitals to either limit costs or guarantee access. Hopefully, there will still be time then to explore the one avenue American health planners and government policymakers have never really tried: a government-run, government-financed health system.

Today, as this book appears, Congress and the Bush administration are both, for the first time in over a decade, taking a cautious look at the first timid step toward nationalized medicine: a program of national health insurance. If such a plan were to succeed, it would eventually have to involve the government in price-setting, or it would simply become an endless drain on the Treasury and the taxpayers. That, in turn, would mean taking on the whole corporate health-care industry, not something the American government does lightly, or very often.

The question is: Can such a thing happen, in light of the growth of multibillion-dollar hospital companies and an even larger health insurance industry? The next few years will be critical.

My critique in this preface has been of the American medical system in its entirety—the hospitals, the doctors, the drug companies, the insurance industry, and the government. This book, however, looks more narrowly at the hospital industry. The reason is that for decades, hospitals—the focal point of most health-care activity—resisted any efforts at corporatization. Atomized into thousands of community-based institutions, and run by the physicians who practiced in them, they were an obstacle to any wholesale industrialization of health care. The rise of the for-profit hospital chains has changed all that. The hospital companies may now become the leading players in the industrialization of American health care, or simply big subsidiary operations of other elements of the medical-industrial complex. In either case, through their own efforts in acquiring chains of acute-care institutions, they have paved the way for corporatization to occur.

1

Acute Questions About Hospitals for Profit

The industrialization of episodic medicine was not the original intent of the market idealists of the early 1970s who favored health maintenance organizations. Many of them regard chain hospitals and emergicenters as the antithesis of what they had in mind. They wanted corporate involvement to change the nature of health care; it seems likely, in the foreseeable future, to reproduce the defects of the traditional system on a grander scale.

—Paul Starr
in *The Social Transformation of American Medicine*

America is facing a crisis in health care, a crisis of both cost and availability, but in the end a crisis of quality as well.

As recently as 1980, the United States could accurately boast that it had the best medical care in the world. It can no longer honestly make such a claim. For one thing, far from being a leader in reducing the rate of infant mortality, a basic measure of the health of a society, America has fallen behind in recent years. According to UNICEF, the United States ranked twenty-first in

1990—behind such countries as East Germany, Singapore, and Hong Kong—thanks to the drug epidemic, widespread poverty, and, in no small measure, inadequate or unavailable medical care. But infant mortality only tells part of the story. More broadly, medical care here is neither universally available nor is it available in anywhere near equal measure, even to members of the same community. While those with pricey insurance plans or endless personal resources can, like the president or the late shah of Iran, have their ailments treated at what are unquestionably still among the best hospitals in the world, millions of others are left almost without any care at all. In the parlance of the age, the latter group has "fallen through the safety net" of the welfare system. This metaphor, however, hardly seems adequate: 37 million Americans—15 percent of the population—have no health insurance coverage, thanks to a combination of soaring insurance premiums, a trend toward part-time employment, and twelve years of cutbacks in the eligibility standards for Medicaid, the government program of health coverage for the poor.[1] A circus with so shredded a net under its high-wire acts would be shut down as a safety hazard.

To add insult to injury, the health-care system in the United States *does* rank first in the world in one category: cost. After rising steadily for decades, [following the Second World War,] the federal Health Care Finance Administration (HCFA) reports that by 1990 medical-care expenditures accounted for a staggering 12.2 percent of the nation's $5.5-trillion gross national product (GNP), or $647.3 billion. This high cost of getting care makes health care the second largest American industry after defense.[2] Its cost is a matter of no small concern even to the insured middle class, which still must shoulder 20 percent of major medical bills and a good deal of the cost of initial office visits to physicians. By contrast, the British spend only six percent of their GNP on health care, and the Swedes, with their gold-plated system that pays for everything, five percent. Even in neighboring Canada, which boasts the second costliest system in the world, health care accounts for only 9.5 percent of GNP.

Blaming the Wrong Villain

For years, as the costs of medical care have soared, patients and taxpayers have taken an iatrogenic view of the disease of medical cost inflation, railing against doctors as the most visible symbol of the problem. While physicians as a group have grown fabulously rich since the institution of the Medicare program for the elderly and disabled in 1965, they are hardly the major recipients of America's health-care dollars. That distinction belongs instead to another sector of the industry: hospitals.

That Americans have tended to blame the doctor for their soaring medical bills should not elicit much surprise. Since most insurance plans have deductibles (the base amount a covered individual must pay in a year before any reimbursement is possible) and "copays" (an amount a patient must pay for any treatment), the cost of an average doctor's office visit is paid by the patient. As a result nearly everyone—even those who are basically healthy—has felt the sting of physician charges.

On the other hand, people don't get a bill from a hospital until they've had to spend some time in one. Then the bill's a whopper; the total amount due is not only more than the initial deductible amount the patient must pay, but is also into the "major medical" portion of the insurance plan, which covers 100 percent of the bill. As a result, even if the patient has to pay a few hundred dollars for the initial deductible and the typical 20 percent of the first $1000 or so, the remainder of the bill is payed by the insurance company. This naturally tends to salve most of the pain and make the hospital appear a much less vexing target.

More importantly, however, the hospital has always occupied a peculiar position in American life. Few institutions are as critical to our well-being, yet as little understood by the average person. We stand in awe of them, are afraid when we have to use one, and yet all want to have one in our community. People who might instinctively fight for their rights in other situations will passively accept the worst indignities at the hands of hospital personnel because of the medical mystique surrounding the institution—that sense that "they" know how to cure us, and we don't know how they do it but don't want to get in the way.

Despite its astronomical bills for treatment, most of us in fact probably still think of the local hospital as a philanthropy. Though most Americans have long accepted the idea that doctors, at least as a group, are just professionals out to make a living, and judge them accordingly, people think differently about hospitals. Our most public-spirited retirees still volunteer to assist in the lobby, community leaders raise funds for special hospital projects, local newspapers write human interest stories about them.

Such beliefs are rooted in tradition, for the early history of hospitals in America *was* philanthropic. They were founded to care for the poor. It's hard to accept the idea that today hospitals are becoming just another business. But they are. As we will see in Chapters 8 and 9, not only is this industry no stranger to the rough-and-tumble of business-related politics, from city council to Washington, D. C., but it is also at home with big sums of money. Each year, according to the Health Care Finance Administration, hospitals take the lion's share (about 44 percent) of the nation's health-care expenditures, with doctors getting 20 percent, and the remaining 36 percent going to pharmacies, drug companies, hospital equipment makers, etc.[3] In 1989, that meant about $250 billion of the total health bill of $647 billion, as estimated by HCFA, went to hospitals. A largely recession-proof industry, hospitals have earned profits that would make the average businessperson green with envy—14 percent in 1984,[4] 17.6 percent in 1985, and 15.7 percent in 1986.[5] They are active players in the Wall Street takeover game. Their executives earn anywhere from a paltry $150,000 (the typical salary of a small hospital's chief executive) to a whopping $18 million, which was earned in 1984 by Humana Chairman David Jones. While Jones's salary and stock option bonuses weren't as high in subsequent years, his annual compensation has consistently been measured in millions of dollars. In 1988 the top executives of the nation's four largest hospital chains earned a combined $14 million in salaries and bonuses.

As the American health-care crisis has grown, hospitals have come to assume even greater importance, for they are major contributors—if not the major contributor—to health cost inflation. Moreover, efforts to contain these soaring hospital costs, such as the introduction of cost controls by the Medicare program and, earlier, the establishment of a regulatory program to limit the expansion of hospitals and hospital equipment, have often backfired. Despite several years of tough efforts by federal and state governments, third-party insurance companies, and employers to limit hospital costs, hospital room charges in 1987 were up 16 percent over 1986, and the average cost of a hospital stay was up 19 percent, according to a study by Equicor Equitable HCA Corp.[6] (Until it was bought by Cigna in 1990, Equicor was a joint venture of the Equitable Life Assurance Company and Hospital Corporation of America, one of the largest of the hospital chains.) This giant leap in costs came at a time when the overall Consumer Price Index rose only 1.9 percent (with hospital costs factored out, the balance of the index would have risen by even less, about 1.8

percent, according to the Bureau of Labor Statistics). The year before, hospital costs had already risen 7.5 percent. In 1988, hospital costs overall rose by another 9.3 percent, while the CPI rose only 5 percent. Rather than abating, the hospital inflation rate seems to be increasing, even as the Consumer Price Index inflation rate has slowed. According to the Labor Department, in 1989, when overall inflation was running at 4.8 percent, hospital costs rose 11.5 percent, a rate that was significantly higher than even the already high overall health-care inflation rate of 7.7 percent. For the June 1989 to June 1990 period, the story was similar: While the overall health-care inflation rate was 9 percent, hospital costs rose by 10.7 percent. During that twelve-month period, overall inflation was running at just 4.7 percent.

Hospitals have also become central to the debate over the health insurance crisis. Since they account for almost two thirds of the typical medical bill, hospitals are a key reason for rising health insurance premiums. This means that any effort by insurance companies to cut costs tends to involve trying to limit use of hospitals. Yet what has concerned many about the growing insurance crisis in the first place is precisely that it tends to reduce hospital access for the poor and even the middle class.

The rising cost of medical care has been most dramatically reflected in mounting premiums for private health insurance and ever higher outlays for government insurance for the elderly, disabled, and poor. In January 1988, not surprisingly, insurance companies nationwide, citing rising hospital costs, raised premiums for health insurance by between 10 and 70 percent, with the average running about 12 to 15 percent.[7] At the same time, Americans covered by Medicare faced premium increases of 38.5 percent. This increase was followed by a 16 percent increase over the next two years, so that in 1990, the nation's elderly, who were supposed to have been having their medical care fully covered, were facing monthly per-person health-care premiums of $28.50—a total of $10.8 billion that year alone.

With hospitals clearly the single largest factor in the average medical bill, and 55 percent of the average Medicare bill, private insurers and government alike have tried to cut those costs by limiting hospital usage. These efforts have taken many forms, ranging from increasing the "deductible" paid by the insured individual for each hospitalization, to the "gatekeeper" approach used by many HMOs (health maintenance organizations), where a designated physician—often one with a direct financial incentive to limit hospital referrals—must order a patient's hospitalization in order for the stay to be covered. The actions of government and the private sector have conspired to limit hospital access another way, as well. Over the past decade, states which individually set eligibility standards for Medicaid, the joint federal/state insurance program for the poor, have almost universally acted to narrow coverage by lowering income ceilings. At the same time, private insurers have raised rates beyond the reach of low-income workers and small employers. A trend among employers, particularly in the service sector, toward part-time and temporary positions with no insurance coverage at all, has added to the crisis. Today, if these people, the so-called medically indigent, are lucky enough to live in a major city, they can usually get treated at a publicly owned hospital in an emergency. If not, they may have to rely on the charity of private physicians and private hospital administrators for their care. And charity is a commodity that is in increasingly short supply in the new bottom-line-oriented health-care industry.

Pay As You Go Health Care

Everything about hospitals is changing, but only when we have to deal with one do we realize how profound that change is. Then, the discovery can be a terrible shock. Consider what happened to Cathie Ann Kirby, whose case illustrates just how close many unsuspecting Americans can be to medical indigency.

Kirby, a twenty-six-year-old nurse, was working on the floor of Hendersonville Hospital, a small facility just outside Nashville and at the time owned by the Hospital Corporation of America, the nation's largest hospital corporation. (Hendersonville was later sold along with over one hundred other small HCA facilities to a new firm, HealthTrust, in 1988.) The young licensed practical nurse had just started at the hospital, where the nurse registry—essentially a temporary agency for nurses—she worked for had sent her. She knew the routines well, as until a few months before she had been on the staff at Donelson Hospital, another HCA institution, for seven years.

Nursing was hard work, but she enjoyed it. This particular day though, everything seemed more difficult for her than usual. She was sweating profusely and feeling wobbly. Gradually she realized that something was wrong. By then her pulse had soared above 150. She was getting dizzy.

When she collapsed, she was rushed on a stretcher to the emergency room, where she was found to have a pulse rate of 240 beats per minute. She was suffering what was diagnosed as ventricular tachycardia, a severe form of heart arrhythmia that can lead to death.

Hendersonville wasn't equipped to handle this kind of case, and in any event the doctors there were having no success in getting her heart under control. So the hospital transferred Kirby to the familiar surroundings of Donelson, a larger HCA facility with a staff cardiologist. She immediately felt relieved. Her own doctor practiced there, and she knew everyone on the staff. Over the next few hours, the doctors managed to find a combination of drugs that restored her heart's normal rhythm. But that's when her real problems began.

It had come to HCA's attention that Kirby, now diagnosed as having a serious heart problem, wasn't fully insured. She had had Blue Cross coverage as an HCA employee, but when she left Donelson, the policy had lapsed, and she had not worked long enough to get coverage through the nurse registry. Her husband, Danny, a security and fire safety employee of the Nashville Metropolitan Airport Authority, had insurance that covered both of them up to 80 percent of hospital costs. But their funds were scarce when it came to paying the other 20 percent, an amount that, in an intensive care setting, could be high.

HCA then decided it wanted Kirby transferred to neighboring Vanderbilt University Hospital, which it claimed was better able to diagnose and treat her problem. Her doctor concurred, though Donelson was equipped to treat heart patients and had an intensive care floor. Danny called Vanderbilt to arrange to have her admitted, but was told that it would take a while—several weeks it turned out—to get her admitted as part of a special research program. "No matter," he recalls thinking. "She's in good hands for now at Donelson." Yet incredibly, four hours after Kirby claims her doctor had told her she could "drop dead any minute," she found herself being unhooked from the equipment that until then had been monitoring her at all times, and discharged to go home. Her husband was called at work and told to come and pick her up.

"I was given some new medicine to try for the arrhythmia, but I would have to start taking it in my house," she recalls. "My current doctor says it's dangerous to try a new heart medicine at home. It *can* turn out making the condition worse, which in my condition could be fatal. He won't change my medicine unless I'm in a hospital on a monitor for several days."

Money wasn't mentioned to the Kirbys, they say, but much later, when Cathie obtained her medical records from the hospital, she saw that under the careful cross-hatching on the line labeled Comments on her discharge paper were the unmistakable words *did not have Blue Cross* (another remark was blotted out more effectively). And in his written report to her family physician following her sudden discharge, Donelson cardiologist Robert C. Ripley's first words were:

> Mrs. Kirby was discharged from Donelson Hospital yesterday when Vanderbilt was unable to accept her in transfer. She had problems with insurance, and the clinical research program at Vanderbilt did not have an opening for two weeks.

After describing her treatment, he concluded:

> This complex type of arrhythmia I thought would best be handled at Vanderbilt Hospital. . . . For one reason or another we were not able to transfer her to Vanderbilt, therefore I elected to treat her with 40 mg of Inderal three times daily as an outpatient and observe the therapeutic response. Ultimately, she will see Dr. (Ray) Woolsey at Vanderbilt as an outpatient, and if necessary as an inpatient. I do not know what the risk of sudden death with her ventricular tachycardia is, but certainly do feel that because she is symptomatic with her ventricular tachycardia she best have this arrhythmia suppressed.

NBC News, which did a story on Kirby's case, sent her hospital records to Dr. Jack Ferlinz, chairman of adult cardiology at Chicago's Cook County Hospital. After reviewing them, Ferlinz provided NBC with an analysis of her treatment saying, "It is totally inappropriate to send a patient who is a candidate for sudden death out of a hospital on oral medication, the efficacy of which has never been established." He added, "It is exceedingly disturbing to see that the question of her medical insurance keeps surfacing throughout her hospital stay."

The importance of the bottom line in decision-making about medical care was highlighted in a January 1987 *Newsweek* magazine story.[8] The lead in this twenty-five-page article, "The Revolution in Medicine" by writer Gregg Easterbrook, proved to be the poignant tale of a hospital administrator who was faced with an agonizing decision. The family of an eighty-year-old stroke victim had instructed him not to have his hospital make any effort to resuscitate their only "moderately coherent" father, should he suffer a heart attack. In his article, Easterbrook quoted the administrator as saying that the family

> talked about his life, a full life in which he had never depended on anybody for anything, and whether in his final moments he would want to be webbed up in thoughtless machines. And they talked about money. . . . If he clung to life, family members would have to watch helplessly as his hard-earned legacy to his children was wiped out.

Easterbrook reported that the administrator told the family:

> When we provide a service it's got to be paid for by somebody. If not by the patient himself, then by the taxpayer or by the next patient down the line. You can't shirk this reality no matter how much you want to, even in tragic circumstances.

Administrator Ed Stainback turns out to be the stroke victim's son. The hospital was HCA's Donelson—the very place that sent Kirby home. In the NBC documentary, Stainback argues that Kirby was treated properly, saying, "The physician [at Donelson], I believe, discharged her according to what he felt was necessary, after consultation with the physician at Vanderbilt and according to the chart."

Cathie Kirby was lucky. Nothing life-threatening happened during the two weeks it took to get her admitted as a research patient at Vanderbilt. Her heart problems now under control, she works as a nurse on the staff of St. Thomas Hospital, a Catholic institution in Nashville. But her experience with HCA is a chilling reminder to all of us—even those who assume they have adequate insurance—that medical care in America is undergoing a dramatic change, one which increasingly pushes monetary concerns to the fore. For, while HCA may be one of the largest for-profit corporate hospital chains, it is by no means alone in assigning primary concern to the bottom line.

Spearheaded by a group of aggressive hospital chains like HCA, the entire hospital industry is becoming profit-conscious, even hospitals that are technically called not-for-profit corporations. This means charging every penny that can be charged for patient care, and avoiding as much as possible the treatment of patients unable to pay. It also means marketing, or offering paying patients what they *think* they need, while eliminating services a community might *really* need but which aren't profitable. At HCA, we thus see valet parking for patients and their visitors. At Humana, another large corporate hospital chain, it's birthing rooms to provide a homelike environment for expecting parents. In and of themselves, these new amenities are fine. But naturally there are tradeoffs. HCA's Parkview hospital, now known as Centennial Medical Center, with its valet parking doesn't provide much indigent care, and Humana's Women's Hospital in Tampa may attract young middle-class parents with the promise of luxurious birthing rooms, yet the number of deliveries of indigent babies, even of government-reimbursed Medicaid babies, was so small in a 1990 survey done by the State Department of Health as to be almost immeasurable.[9]

Making Hospitals into an Industry

The emphasis on making money off sickness is hardly new. For at least two generations, a medical degree has been and continues to be a ticket to financial security, if not to a life of ease (average physician pretax net income in 1990, according to the American Medical Association, was $144,300). Indeed for years now banks have been soliciting medical school students with offers of credit cards and credit lines. What's new is that the power over life-and-death decisions—both for individuals and more importantly in broad policy matters—is shifting away from physicians and community leaders into the hands of corporate bureaucrats and medical industry entrepreneurs—most of whom have never seen the inside of a medical school.

This shift has led to some remarkable developments, some good, some not so good, and some truly awful. The profit-driven investor-owned chains are forcing the not-for-profit hospitals to become more "businesslike" in everything from management style to admissions policy, a long-overdue challenge to wasteful practices of the past. But this trend toward a corporate style of behavior is at the same time a phenomenon that has led to an increase in "dumping" of poor patients onto publicly owned hospitals and, in turn, has created a budget crisis at the nation's public hospitals. As the public hospitals then face bankruptcy, the corporate chains often step in either to manage them for a fee (with mixed results) or to buy them at fire-sale prices, at which point they cease to be hospitals for the poor. In the one notable exception to this pattern, Gateway Medical, a small for-profit hospital chain, tried to carve out as its industry "niche" precisely such troubled urban public institutions. By obtaining them at low prices, the company claimed it could run them as poor people's hospitals at a profit. But by 1989, only five years after it had set out, the company was dissolved, according to its founder James Cheek, and its six remaining hospitals were being reorganized in bankruptcy. The lesson: It's hard to turn a profit on poor patients alone.

Humana, a tightly run corporate chain with a reputation for keeping indigent patients out, is still best known as the company that put artificial hearts into several dying heart patients at no cost to them or their families. Even after the Food and Drug Administration revoked its permission for further human experiments with a permanent artificial heart in January 1990, the company continues to hark back to its artificial heart program as an example of its involvement in medical research. However, it was clear from the start that the millions of dollars the company committed to the project over several years were actually perceived by management as an investment in public relations. And Humana Chairman David Jones stated candidly in 1984 that the company hoped its much-publicized artificial heart program would go a long way toward the "modest goal of becoming a national brand of health care."[10]

Hospital administrators, the people who actually run individual hospitals, and the executives of hospital chains are setting new standards for medical care. They put pressure on doctors not to overadmit, and not to admit at all when a patient's ability to pay is in question. The corporate executives of these vast far-flung health-care systems decide where hospitals will be located, whether and when they will be shut down, and even how many nurses will work on each shift. What has traditionally been a cottage industry, with the local hospital being the focus of community health policy and practice, is rapidly becoming a national industry. In the process health care has become a commodity, with standards being set not so much in a Washington still enamored with deregulation, but rather in the executive offices of a few Fortune 500 "health services" corporations. Such corporations are run for the most part by nonmedical people whose motivation is profit and whose expertise is in finance or real estate, not health.

In one sense, it is a process long overdue. While other industries in America consolidated decades ago, the health-care industry remained curiously fragmented. There were insurance companies, independent hospitals, drug companies, laboratories, independent physicians and physician groups, and independent hospitals. Even within the health-care industry itself, it was the hospital sector where the hierarchical management style characteristic of American industry was slowest to develop. There lingered in hospitals a curious system of dual authority involving hospital administrators and the so-called medical staff, or physicians who had the "privilege" to practice at the hospital but who were not employees of the hospital.

Now, this anachronistic situation is being revolutionized. The sectors within the field of health care are merging, with insurance companies linking up with hospitals, hospitals combining with each other and with other health-care industries, or "joint-venturing" with physician groups who may jointly own testing equipment, office buildings, or even a hospital. And the hospital sector itself is being "industrialized," i.e., made to resemble structurally and organizationally the rest of corporate America. Between 1987 and 1990, we read in the business pages stories about unfriendly takeover attempts against American Medical International, the nation's fourth-largest hospital chain. We read about the Humana board of directors' actions to make the company harder to acquire. Or we read about HCA's creation of HealthTrust, a giant, management-owned holding company. This move was designed to allow HCA to unload its stock of relatively poorly performing hospitals and improve its own balance sheet and share price (steps the company admitted were also defensive moves to guard against unfriendly takeover efforts).

These changes made in corporate suites are not readily visible to health-care consumers, or even to many physicians and health professionals. The brick and mortar of the local hospital still looks the same, whatever the ownership, and most of the daily procedures still might appear traditional. But such appearances of stability can be deceptive. Dramatic changes are underway both inside and outside those walls, and what happens to the hospital industry is bound to have a profound effect on overall medical care in America.

This is true not only where patient care is concerned; costs too will inevitably be affected. Consider a few statistics. According to the Health Care Finance Administration, in 1987, the last year for which the agency had complete data (its budget was severely cut during the Reagan years, and many statistical studies, including this one, were axed), personal health-care expenses in the U.S. totaled $442.6 billion. Hospitals collected 40 percent of that money, or about $170 billion. With hospital costs rising at a 9.3 percent clip in 1988, and 11.5 percent in 1989, according to the Bureau of Labor Statistics, that figure had risen to well over $200 billion by 1990.

Public Money, Private Gain

The American hospital as we know it today got its start back in the mid-nineteenth century, when a number of privately owned charity hospitals were founded to provide care for the poor. As physicians grew in power and stature, they began, around the turn of the century, to build and operate their own hospitals and to take over the operational control of the charity facilities, too. With the addition of the concept of public—usually municipal or county—ownership of some hospitals, the basic structure of the industry was established early in the twentieth century. The cost of medical care, until after World War II, was never great; indeed, medical insurance was a rarity because people generally were able to pay for whatever care was needed. Families might be bankrupted when a breadwinner was incapacitated by illness, but rarely did they go under as a direct result of the medical bills themselves.

Even after World War II, and through the 1950s, health-care costs remained so modest that by a process of cost-shifting, doctors and hospitals were able to provide care to poor patients by simply charging more to paying patients. But by 1960, it was clear that this situation could not last. Increasingly hospitals were unable to handle the growing expense of caring for the poor and elderly, and doctors were beginning to avoid treating those with no financial resources. Medical care was moving out of reach for the nation's urban and rural poor.

The first winds of major structural change in American medical care came in the mid-1960s with the advent of the Johnson administration's War on Poverty. As part of that campaign, Medicare and Medicaid, health insurance programs for the aged and the poor, respectively, were instituted. Initially resisted by the American Medical Association (AMA) and the American Hospital Association (AHA), these two programs—and especially Medicare—quickly became medical El Dorados: fabulous sources of seemingly endless enrichment for doctor and hospital alike.

By the mid-1980s, most hospitals in the country were essentially dependent upon Medicare for their very existence, with many hospitals deriving more than half their revenues from the program. Likewise, physicians grew fat on government insurance; by 1985, Medicare was *the* major source of physicians' earnings. Medicaid was a different story. With its generally much lower reimbursement rates and with eligibility standards and reimbursement levels set state by state, it has served the poor inadequately. Still, while it hasn't been the goldmine for the medical field that Medicare has, Medicaid has nonetheless helped to enrich the health-care industry by providing supplemental coverage for low-income *Medicare* patients.

It is no coincidence that the big hospital corporations like HCA, Humana, American Medical International, National Medical Enterprises, and many other smaller firms were all founded within a few years of each other following the advent of Medicare. With reimbursement in those days set, like military procurement programs, essentially on a "cost-plus" basis, it was almost impossible for a hospital to fail. It was equally impossible that some astute entrepreneurs would not realize this opportunity and seize it.

These new hospital companies benefited from tax policies that favored expansion for expansion's sake. Rapid depreciation allowances for purchases of plant and equipment, investment tax credits of up to 10 percent, and full deductibility of interest on debt payments, all meant that the taxpayers subsidized much of the cost of corporate hospital expansion; Medicare even included in its reimbursements a "return-on-equity" bonus for for-profit hospitals. Such companies also benefited from a narrow investor focus on revenue growth instead of actual profitability. From 1965 to about 1985, all a hospital company had to do to quicken the pulse of analysts and financiers on Wall Street was buy more hospitals and add the newly captured patient revenues to the top line of its consolidated financial statement.

For the hospital industry, as indeed for the rest of the health services field, this two-decade period was a golden age. Hospitals borrowed money wildly to expand, knowing that all their costs, *including debt service*, could be passed on in higher patient billings, and that depreciation of acquired facilities could absolve them of taxes on any profits. If a hospital added a wing and then couldn't fill the beds, no matter. Just raise the rates for the patients you had. The same was true for new equipment. So what if a community already had an underutilized CAT-scanner at one hospital? Every hospital could afford one by factoring the price into patient billings, even if it only got used occasionally. The government didn't care, and neither did the big private insurers like Blue Cross. They just raised their premiums to employers.

Everybody grew fat in this period, but it was the investor-owned for-profit hospital chains that really prospered. For years, they were among the nation's fastest growing entrepreneurial firms, outstripping even the presumed growth industry: computers. While the not-for-profit hospitals, still essentially local or regional in their perspective, were content simply to expand what they had, the corporate chains used this time of easy money to expand geographically and geometrically. Buying existing hospitals and constructing new ones, the corporate for-profits created first regional and eventually national networks of hospitals before anyone outside Wall Street even realized what was happening.*

By the end of the 1970s, however, there were signs that this golden age was drawing to a close. The nation was suffering from

---

*According to the American Hospital Association, there was a total of 5,455 acute-care hospitals in the U.S. at the start of 1990. These fall into four basic categories: research/teaching institutions, public hospitals (owned usually by local governments and subsidized by tax revenues), not-for-profit, and for-profit hospitals. The term for *not-for-profit institutions* varies widely. In the Northeast, they are *voluntaries*, in the Southeast, *charity hospitals*, in the West, simply *not-for-profits*. Ownership varies, too, from community-based foundations to church organizations. For-profits, often referred to as proprietaries, also vary in type of ownership. Many single for-profits are owned by groups of doctors. Others, especially those in chains, are investor-owned, either by a relatively small group of private investors, or by a large number of holders of publicly traded stock. The primary differences between the for-profit and not-for-profit institutions are that the former pays taxes while the latter does not, and the former distributes a portion of its profits to investors, while the latter must retain any surpluses within the organization.

inflation the likes of which people had not seen in generations, and this was particularly true where medical costs were concerned. In the late seventies, health costs increased 13 percent a year and hit a peak of 15.1 percent in 1981 (a year when the overall inflation rate was only 8.9 percent). Federal, state, and local taxes were a growing topic of concern, and medical costs were seen as a major contributing factor. The Medicare program, once foreseen as a relatively minor budget item, was ballooning, with costs rising at 20 percent per year by 1980. In 1982, health-care spending passed a milepost, for the first time exceeding 10 percent of gross national product. It has since risen to over 12 percent of GNP in 1990 and, according to HCFA, could reach 15 percent by the year 2000, when it will top $1.5 trillion.[11]

Inevitably, there came a backlash to the policy of cost-is-no-object health care. When concern about rising health costs first surfaced in the mid-seventies, the presumed solution was price controls and some kind of national health insurance system. Indeed, in 1976 Jimmy Carter campaigned successfully for the presidency on such a platform. But resistance from the health-care industry, for which the idea of socialized medicine is of course anathema, and a sense of crisis that seemed to demand more immediate action, stalled such far-reaching reform, and by the 1980 election year, Carter had dropped such ideas from his campaign rhetoric. With the advent of the Reagan administration a year later, national health care simply vanished from polite political discourse, to be replaced by the reigning ideology of free enterprise.

In this new environment, the for-profit chains thrived. Under the Carter administration, the Federal Trade Commission had brought a number of successful antitrust cases against the various corporate chains, charging monopolistic practices. But the Reagan administration pushed the idea of competition as a solution to health-care costs, pulling back on antitrust enforcement where hospital purchases were involved and generally reducing health-care regulation.

Then came the reform of Medicare: a radical shift from cost-plus reimbursement to "prospective payment," popularly known as DRGs, for diagnosis-related groups. Under the new system, passed by Congress with the blessing of and, as we shall see, with thanks to the lobbying efforts of the for-profit hospital industry, prospective payment meant reimbursement at a rate set by the government for each of the 477 ailments listed in its catalog.

Designed to create an incentive to keep costs down, the system meant that if a hospital could treat a patient for less than the DRG figure, it could pocket the difference. If not, the hospital had to take a loss on the case.

The for-profit chains generally had greater control over patient access then the not-for-profits, both by deliberate choice over siting of the hospital and often by their lack of a public emergency room (where just anyone could come in the door, with or without a doctor's referral). With their greater ability to select patients with more "profitable" medical problems, the chains hoped they could profit on DRGs, and at the same time, use them to increase the financial pressures on the not-for-profit competition.

The Revolution in Health Care

It didn't work out quite so neatly. DRGs proved to be hard on the entire industry, and simultaneously, the patient census at all hospitals was declining for a variety of reasons. This hurt for-profits and not-for-profits alike. Still, the prospect of DRGs so intimidated many not-for-profit and public institutions that the period 1981–85 saw record numbers of hospitals offered to or acquired by the chains. In 1983, for instance, according to the Federation of American Health Systems, the chains added 103 new facilities to their rosters. Only 14 of these were independently owned, proprietary facilities that sold out. Some were newly constructed facilities, but most had been public or not-for-profit hospitals the year before. In 1985, the picture was similar. That year the chains added 138 new hospitals, 14 of them formerly private for-profit entities, and most of the rest formerly public or not-for-profit. This frenzied period of corporate expansion also saw the remaining not-for-profit hospitals across the nation react to the growth of the corporate chains by imitating them further and establishing their own networks.

Experimentation also began with the idea of vertical integration, or the assembling, within one corporation and under one management, of all the various components of a health-care system, from doctors' offices to hospitals, to insurance operations and nursing homes. Since the key to success in the hospital business is filling the beds with paying patients, the corporate hospital chains, followed by the not-for-profit competition, began dreaming up ways to corral these lucrative patients, or "revenue bodies," as they came to be called in the industry, into a particular health-care system, and especially into a particular hospital or group of hospitals. One way to accomplish this was by establishing out-patient clinics, free-standing "emergency rooms," and other "patient-feeder" systems. Another way, pioneered by Humana, was to create a captive health insurance plan that would in effect require use of a company hospital.

Health care in America today is indeed in the midst of a revolution, the result of which, as in any revolution, is hard to predict. The picture is made all the more cloudy by the proliferation of an alphabet soup of new insurance arrangements—HMOs, PPOs, IPAs, PCNs—and by the shifting alliances between the different sectors within what has quite properly been called, borrowing from President Dwight Eisenhower's phrase, a medical-industrial complex.[12]

What is clear amid all the struggling for position is that hospitals remain central to the entire medical system. The parallels are not perfect, but if an analogy is made with the military-industrial complex, a hospital, because of its massive capital base of plant and equipment and its huge employee population, would be the "prime contractor," the medical equivalent of Boeing, Lockheed, or LTV Corporation.

Because new technologies and procedures make certain treatments possible in a doctor's office or even at home, some observers have boldly predicted the demise of the hospital (much as some predicted the demise of the private practitioner in the early part of the century). Such prophets, however, fail to consider the latest advances in complex medical therapies—transplant technology or neonatology, for example—which *increase* hospital use. Moreover, the much noted "graying" of America—the growing percentage of older persons in the population—ensures an expanding supply of acute-care patients, particularly as the postwar baby boomers enter middle age. According to the U.S. Department of Aging, in 1989 there were 31 million Americans over 65, about 12.5 percent of the population. By 1995 that figure will rise to 34 million, or 13 percent. Baby boomers, those 36.5 million people who at 35–44 were on the cusp of middle age, already represented 15.5 percent of the population in 1990.

The differences between for-profit and not-for-profit hospitals are becoming harder and harder to discern. This is true not so much because the two types of operations are merging, but because the for-profits, unfettered by tradition and charter, centrally run, and able to make decisions more rapidly, are writing the new rules of competition and setting the pace of change. Consider that important innovation of the for-profits: advertising. According to statistics compiled by the Steiber Research Group of Chicago, in 1989 hospitals spent a record $687 million on advertising, and another record $853 million on other marketing, up 15 percent from 1988. This new phenomenon has been most pronounced in those regions where the corporate chains are most prevalent—the South and Southwest. Steiber Research found advertising expenditures per hospital there to be between 26 and 29 percent higher than the national average. In 1986, Humana alone, though owning only 1.5 percent of the hospitals in the country, spent 4 percent, or $20 million, of the total national hospital ad budget that year of $500 million.[13]

The corporate hospital chains are steadily expanding their share of the total hospital inventory. By 1991, one in four nonfederal acute-care hospitals was investor-owned.[14] Almost all projections for the future state that the investor-owned share of the industry will grow dramatically, even if the chains accomplish this by standing still while not-for-profit and public hospitals are closed. Large corporate entities—life insurance firms, major employers like General Motors or AT&T, or chemical/pharmaceutical giants—may buy up the hospital companies at some point. The late 1980s, which saw hospital use decline, may then be looked back upon as a kind of desert the industry had to cross before the baby boom population started to develop the infirmities that come with advancing age. Before that happens, however, current vacancy rates as high as 50 percent at many hospitals have made the industry temporarily vulnerable to takeover. In any event, whether the chains remain independent or become subsidiaries of larger firms, they will continue to push medical care further in the direction not just of privatization, but of concentration in ownership and centralization in management.

The Issues That Lie Ahead

Such amalgamation raises a number of important issues: medical, social, and political.

• At least until very recently, the growth and consolidation of the for-profit hospital industry has been largely an unintended by-product of government health policy. When Medicare was being developed in the mid-sixties, for instance, no one was thinking about how that program would engender a new industry. The whole intent at the time was to "mainstream" segments of the population—the elderly and the poor—that were correctly seen as being excluded from the medical system. How then, over the last two decades, did the for-profit hospital system develop to its present position? And where is it headed now, particularly as government policies are actually *encouraging* its dominance of the market?

• The new medical marketplace, following the lead of the for-profit chains, is wooing the health consumer just as Detroit learned to woo the traveling public. The "See the USA in your Chevrolet" ad of the fifties has become the ad for a new nose or larger breasts courtesy of one of Republic Healthcare's hospitals. And the buyer of health services is probably even less able to judge the product than the paradigmatic auto consumer who is reduced to kicking a tire when evaluating a particular vehicle. What kind of health care are we getting in this new medical market? Is it a change for the better, the worse, or a little of both? And how are we to know or decide, when there isn't even a tire to kick?

• The centrally run hospital chains seek to reduce the power of physicians over patient care in the name of cost control. At what point does aligning the doctor's interests with those of the hospital instead of the patient become a threat to health?

• The for-profit chains claim that they have the answer to the nation's problem of rising health-care costs: the free market. Yet most studies to date either challenge this assertion, or offer ambiguous results. And recent experience should encourage skepticism: In 1990, after six full years of the kind of efficiency incentives that investor-owned chain executives promised would let them "show their stuff," the Bureau of Labor Statistics found hospital costs to be rising at twice the rate of overall inflation. It is possible that consumer knowledge and choice—a key element to the successful working of market forces—may not exist in the field of medicine. If this is true, is the headlong drive to free-enterprise medicine justified?

• Increasingly, the new investor-owned chains are moving into the teaching hospital arena, either buying such institutions outright, leasing the facilities on a long-term basis, or establishing some kind of affiliation. This is happening at the same time as the federal government, once the primary funding source for medical research, is pulling back. Given American businesses' well-known tendency to seek short-term returns on investment, what will be the impact of having hospital companies in charge of major research centers?

• For-profit investor-owned hospitals in the same demographic location as not-for-profits *may* be charitable in a particular patient's case, but they rarely are located in the settings that present them with many poor patients in the first place. Chains have demonstrated a propensity to choose sites convenient to their moneyed patients—particularly since many states have eliminated construction permit requirements. Will the expansion of investor-owned hospital chains mean a growing disparity in the care of the poor and the middle class? With the growing number of medically indigent patients resulting from the AIDS epidemic, this issue becomes increasingly urgent.

• Given the history of other industrial sectors—automobiles, steel, airlines, railroads, pharmaceuticals, communications, power companies—where concentrated industries used their financial and political clout to gain control over the government regulatory apparatus, what will be the political impact of having health care, once a local, community-based industry, fall into the hands of a few large corporate entities?

• Finally, if corporate medicine is *not* the panacea some in political, economic, medical, and financial circles claim it to be, what can be done to direct the industry's development so that it can become the affordable and democratically controlled health-care system that nearly everyone wants for the nation?

These are all issues that need thorough discussion before we as a nation commit ourselves fully to the concept of marketplace medicine. There is an added urgency to the need for debate, because by all accounts the nation is at present woefully "over-bedded," a condition that cannot long endure. According to the American Hospital Association's records, between January 1980 and January 1990, over 550 community hospitals failed. The pace of closures rose through the latter half of the decade: 49 in 1985, 72 in 1986, 79 in 1987, 83 in 1988, 65 in 1989, and 50 in 1990. These figures do not include mergers, which often result in one hospital in a community ceasing to function. In coming years, hundreds more can be expected either to close or to be turned into something else—nursing homes, detox centers, and the like. This "weeding out" process can be done in a planned way, as some states, notably New York and New Jersey, are attempting. Alternatively, the determination as to which hospitals will survive and which shall disappear can be left to market forces and the decisions of socially and politically unaccountable corporate boards, a more common method.

The growth of for-profit, investor-owned hospital corporations has advanced already to the point where they are certain to be major factors in the future of medical care in America, regardless of the outcome of any debate on their merit. Billion-dollar companies and a multibillion-dollar industry don't just disappear. It is essential, therefore, for us to know what these companies are, how they developed, how they operate, and what they envision for the future of American health care.

2

A Giant Industry Is Born

It is certain that there is something in the nature of the corporate beast that requires it to grow in order to remain viable on its own terms.

> —Stanley Wohl, M.D.,
> in *The Medical-Industrial Complex*

A highway. A long string of cars. Inside the cars, of course, there were people. . . . All of them were driving because they owned a car. They weren't driving, the cars were driving, and the cars were driving because they were cars.

> —Ilya Ehrenburg
> in *The Life of the Automobile*

As America's once atomized hospital industry is being transformed into another branch of big business, the companies in the vanguard of this process are following the bumbling path of the early American automobile industry. Like a caricature of the new drivers of early horseless carriages, the hospital entrepreneurs find themselves breathlessly racing at full throttle into a future of almost endless financial promise, but at the wheel of a powerful machine they are still only learning to drive. It has already taken some entrepreneurs careening down wrong turns and winding paths, often with disastrous consequences, but it should eventually get many of them where they want to go.

The early parallels between the two industries, autos and hospitals, are intriguing. Just as Ford grew by acquiring Lincoln, and General Motors by merging Buick, Cadillac, Oldsmobile, and Oakland (eventually Pontiac), today's biggest hospital firms grew by acquisition, with AMI acquiring Chanco Medical and Lifemark, Humana acquiring American Medicorp, and HCA taking over Hospital Affiliates. Just as the early car makers tried the idea of vertical and horizontal integration, hoping to establish market dominance and, particularly in the case of General Motors in 1910, nearly foundering in the process, the hospital companies have tried, with mixed results, to enter related fields. Where the young car makers dabbled injudiciously in everything from parts suppliers and lantern makers to steel mills, the hospital companies have diversified by buying or setting up hospital supply houses, free-standing "urgi-centers," nursing homes, and health insurance companies. For the most part, the results have been similarly dismal. Like the auto industry in the 1920s, the hospital companies expanded at a feverish pace through hospital acquisitions in the early days of the Reagan administration, expecting that reforms (partially of their own design) in the reimbursement system for Medicare would give them an edge in virtually every market area. Instead, they discovered that their reach had exceeded their grasp. Their various failures of strategy, management, or simply timing have led some observers of the health-care industry to write it off several times, but each time the industry has recovered handily. Meanwhile, the corporatization of hospitals and health care in general has continued unabated and largely unremarked.

There's a lesson in the tale of the auto industry. Though Henry Ford built his first car in 1896, the first production automobile was by most accounts made by the Pope Manufacturing Company, a bicycle maker based in Hartford, Connecticut. The now little-remembered Colonel Albert A. Pope made two mistakes: He got caught up in an ill-conceived acquisition fever around the turn of the century, and he ignored internal combustion engines in favor of electric cars until it was too late to recover from his strategic error. His company went belly up in 1907. The General Motors Corporation, born in 1908, expanded rapidly through acquisitions, only to almost collapse in 1910. In the early part of the century, the auto industry was still a gamble; even in the twenties many car companies remained risky investments at best. Yet despite many wrong turns and the effects of the Great Depression, which sank many well-established car makers, the auto industry as a whole, faced with the almost endless demand in America for personal transportation, triumphed. So too, the hospital industry, through all its travails, has its future virtually assured by the sheer size of the demand for health services, a demand which according to the U.S. Health Care Finance Administration will surpass $1.5 trillion annually by the year 2000.

The Early Days

The histories of the individual companies are widely different, but the for-profit hospital chains large and small are all the product of a sudden change in the political-economic environment in the mid-1960s—the creation of a government insurance system for the elderly (who in 1990 accounted for about 60 percent of hospital admissions) and the poor. In a sense these for-profit chains are a peculiar and unintended side effect of that change (much as the auto industry has been said to be the unintended result of pressure by an American bicycling public for paved roads: the Good Roads movement of the 1890s). Medicare and Medicaid advocates intended to push American health care toward the European concept of the government assuming a major responsibility for the health of all citizens. The last thing on anyone's mind at the time was the promotion of a vast corporate system of profit-making health-care enterprises. Yet, in retrospect, what would be more likely to happen in an environment where profits were virtually guaranteed by the federal and state governments?

Simply put, under Medicare and to a lesser extent Medicaid, hospitals were reimbursed for care of the elderly and poor on a cost-plus basis, their stated costs for a patient's care plus a predetermined rate of profit which even took into account return on investment. Almost like utilities, with their guaranteed rates of return, the more the parent company spent on a hospital, the more it could charge the government for treatment of government-insured patients in that hospital. And private insurance plans operated much the same way, paying hospitals whatever they said their charges were, and passing those costs on in the form of higher premiums. Moreover, because of generous depreciation rules in the tax law, the acquiring companies were and still are able, like any other business, to write off the cost of capital investment—in this case the purchase of medical facilities—against earnings. This amounts to a government subsidy for their expansion programs, whether beneficial to society or not. Hospital companies that grew fast enough could have write-offs each year that totally wiped out their annual tax bill.

"In a sense, we set up these companies," says Luanne Kennedy, an analyst of the industry who teaches hospital administration at Baruch College of the City University of New York. "People on the left, like myself and liberals and others, kept pushing to 'mainstream' people, to get them into the health-care system, and with the reimbursement system that was created, we encouraged higher [health-care] costs."

Furthermore, because the advent of Medicare and Medicaid coincided with a perceived need for more hospital beds in the sixties, the reimbursement system was actually designed to encourage expansion. If a hospital company bought or built a new hospital, it was able to recover its investment through its patient charges, so that the faster a chain grew, the more money it made. And the return-on-equity provisions in the Medicare program (of no use to not-for-profit hospitals), by making for-profit hospitals virtually a sure bet, guaranteed investor interest. As one industry analyst put it, "Under cost-plus reimbursement, you could make money at a hospital even with only one Medicare patient: the cost of the patient's treatment would be the cost of running the hospital, plus a return on equity." This situation, in turn, provided almost unlimited access to capital. As Professor Kennedy explains, referring to the rapid expansion of the hospital industry and the escalation of costs for health care during the late sixties and seventies, "From a purely financial point of view, these companies have behaved rationally."

The entrepreneurial response to the introduction of Medicare, like the auto industry's earlier response to creation of the gasoline engine and a system of paved roads, is almost legendary. Indeed, while economists and stock market analysts were crowing over the torrid pace of expansion of the computer industry, in the late seventies and early eighties it was really the hospital companies that deserved the plaudits. Over the last two decades, this small group of aggressive corporations took what has traditionally resembled a kind of "cottage industry" of thousands of local, independently owned and managed hospitals, and turned it into networks of dozens, even hundreds, of centrally run facilities. In the process, they established themselves as a significant factor in the delivery of acute-care medical services, not just in America, but in the rest of the non-Communist world where the American chains build and still own scores of facilities and run many more on a management basis.

There's nothing new about hospitals being run on a profit basis. For over half a century there have been a large number of usually relatively small for-profit facilities owned and run by the doctors practicing in them. Much of the early rapid growth of the big hospital chains actually came through the acquisition of these small so-called proprietary properties. In fact, this phenomenon partially obscured the growth of the chains for some time, since the total number of investor-owned hospitals and their percentage of the total hospital universe changed very little during that early phase of the companies' expansion. It was just a shift to more concentrated ownership within that one sector. For instance, as the number of corporate hospitals grew between 1978 and 1979 by 37, the number of independently owned proprietaries fell by almost the same amount, 29, suggesting that all but eight, or roughly a fifth of the growth, came from a shifting of ownership *within* the for-profit sector of the industry. By 1986, however, the situation had changed. While the number of chain-owned corporate hospitals increased during 1985 by 93, the number of independent proprietaries had fallen by just 21. As the list of attractive proprietary investments thus shrank—from 268 in 1986 to 233 in 1991[1]—the big corporate chains and small growing chains alike had shifted their sights to the field of community not-for-profit and public hospitals, and even to the giant teaching hospitals.

Of course, back in the mid-1960s, when corporate-owned hospitals first appeared, few people, even hospital entrepreneurs, imagined where the industry was headed, just as the early mechanical tinkerers in Detroit didn't realize what they had wrought with their much-derided horseless carriages.

AMI and the "Golden" Appel

In the early days of the automobile, it was all very simple. If you had some mechanical know-how, a decent-sized garage, and enough capital to buy a few carriage frames and internal combustion engines, you had yourself a car company. Hospitals weren't quite so simple or inexpensive a business to start, but, in the early days of the for-profit hospital industry, it wasn't all that hard either. And if anyone made it look easy, it was Uranus J. "Bob" Appel, founder of American Medical International, the first major hospital company. A man of many talents and great ambition, Appel, with his undergraduate degree in bacteriology from the University of Pittsburgh, might not have seemed destined to build a hospital empire. But he did have the characteristics of the classic entrepreneur: versatility, ambition, and a willingness to take risks.

During World War II, Appel served as lab officer for a European theater military hospital, which gave him an important introduction to the inner workings of the hospital industry. The experience would later serve him well, but he didn't initially choose that field. Returning from the war after the armistice, he instead sought his fortune in several speculative business ventures unrelated to medicine, including record distribution, liquor importation, and goldmining. He proved to have something of a Midas touch, amassing a tidy personal nest egg over a period of eight years.

"At that point," he recalled to me in a 1988 interview, "I decided I wanted to get back into the medical area, so I went back to school." This time it was graduate studies in bacteriology at the University of Southern California in Los Angeles. At the same time, to support himself, Appel went to work at Medical Diagnostics, a small medical laboratory that served a number of local hospitals. "I was getting paid two hundred fifty dollars a month," Appel says. "Then, the company started having problems, and so I bought it." He promptly renamed the company American Laboratories and gave himself a raise to $750 a month. "I've always kept my pay low," he explains. "That way I could keep *all* my labor costs down, since nobody can get paid more than the president!" (Of course, when you *own* a growing company, you don't really need much of a salary. Your share value is what will make you rich, as Appel well knew.)

During the next several years, he set up new branches of American Laboratories, whose primary business was contract work for area hospitals. In the course of that business, he began to notice that many of his customers—for the most part hospitals set up by physician groups to meet the needs of a rapidly growing suburban population in Southern California—while doing fine work medically, were in a woeful financial state. Doctors had underestimated the work involved in managing a hospital and, he discovered, were letting the business slide in favor of practicing medicine. "Doctors don't generally know how to run a business," he says.

Appel, who had worked in the hotel and restaurant field while in college, was confident that he could handle the business end of things more effectively than did his physician/manager customers. He thus decided to try his hand at the hospital business when an opportunity came in 1960 to lease a small twenty-six-bed facility in central Los Angeles called Westlake Hospital. Things began to fall into place. Westlake was in foreclosure, but it was on land that a local bank, World Savings and Loan, dearly wanted for a building site. Appel struck his first hospital deal: The bank got the lease on the land, and he got a loan of $180,000—enough to get the hospital out of foreclosure and to buy an option to purchase the facility.

Appel immediately replaced hospital management and claims, "We had the place making a profit in six months." Shortly after that, he brought American Laboratories public with an initial stock offering, underwritten by a local investment bank, California Investors. At a time when the company boasted sales of $640,000, and a net income of $40,000, the offering raised $200,000—a paltry sum by today's standards, and small even then, but enough to permit American Laboratories to buy another hospital, Westside.

According to American Medical International, the direct corporate descendent of those initial purchases, at that point Appel had created the first for-profit investor-owned hospital chain in America—at least the initial two links of one. It was several years later, in 1965, that the name was changed to American Medical Enterprises and later to AMI, to reflect the shift in emphasis from laboratories to hospitals. By 1968, the company owned seven hospitals in Southern California, was listed on the American Stock Exchange, and was ready to expand to other parts of the country. Today, even after some radical "downsizing" in 1988, which included spinning off a group of less desirable hospital properties into an independent company called EPIC Healthcare Group, Inc., and a not terribly friendly takeover in 1989 by IMA Holdings, an investor group led by the Pritzger family of Hyatt Hotels fame, AMI is still the fourth-largest hospital company with 38 acute-care hospitals in the U.S., 34,000 employees, and 1990 revenues of $2.5 billion.

Says Appel, now retired and living in Playa del Rey, California, "When I got that second hospital, I realized that I could grow forever that way. I saw that I could solve the problems doctor/owners couldn't solve themselves. You know, a hospital is really just like a hotel—you just have to understand the medical side, and I knew that already."

Appel's initial goal, he says, once he realized how easy it was to expand his chain, was "to grow in California, and maybe to get sales up to a hundred million dollars." But, he says, "When we spread into Texas, I suddenly realized that the same situation existed elsewhere. Maybe you couldn't do this kind of thing in Pittsburgh or in New York or New Jersey, but in the Southwest, where distances were greater, the idea of a chain of hospitals worked."

From such humble beginnings, a giant industry of corporate hospital chains was born, one that by 1991 accounted for 21 percent of all hospitals in the country, where an estimated one in seven of all physicians now practice. (If the 332 not-for-profit hospitals are factored in that are managed under contract, but not owned by corporate chains, the chained for-profit sector in 1989 could be said to own or run 27 percent of the nation's hospitals, according to the Federation of American Health Systems, the industry's trade group. Adding the other 233 independently owned for-profit hospitals, fully 31 percent of all U.S. hospitals—almost one in three—are now run on a for-profit basis.)[2] Appel won't disclose his health-care wealth except to say modestly, "I'm a multimillionaire." But AMI and its five largest competitors—Humana; Hospital Corporation of America; National Medical Enterprises; and HealthTrust and EPIC Healthcare, the HCA and AMI spin-off companies—together boasted annual sales of over $18.5 billion, and profits of over $1.5 billion in 1990. If Quorum Health Resources, the HCA spin-off that manages 188 hospitals under contract and which remains 10 percent owned by HCA, is included in the total, the revenue figure approaches $20 billion.

The Federation of American Health Systems reported that in 1991, there were 96 investor-owned hospital companies, including 72 which owned or managed at least three hospital facilities. In 1988, those companies collectively earned $6.35 billion in pretax profits. While the FAHS no longer reports total industry profits, it stated that in 1989, the top eight firms earned over $1 billion in profits just from their acute-care hospital operations.

HCA: Just What the Doctors Ordered

At about the same time that Appel was putting together the first pieces of his hospital empire, Thomas Frist, a cardiologist in Nashville, Tennessee, was taking the first tentative steps that would lead to the creation of an even larger corporate hospital chain, the Hospital Corporation of America. In 1965, however, Frist simply wanted an adequate place to work. Despairing of having to practice cardiology in what he considered to be Nashville's poorly run and even more poorly equipped hospitals, Dr. Frist set up his own fifty-bed acute-care facility, which he called Parkview Memorial Hospital.

Faced with the same need to set up a quality care medical facility, community leaders across America had traditionally turned to local sources of charity and philanthropy, and to the federal government's Hill-Burton guaranteed loan program for hospital construction for the funds needed to modernize and enlarge a local hospital or to build one from scratch. The result was usually a community hospital, owned either by the public or by a not-for-profit corporation. But Frist, dissatisfied with the results of similar philanthropic efforts in Nashville, took another approach.

His path—to build his own small acute-care facility, a hospital run on a for-profit basis which would depend not on the charitable instincts of the Nashville community, but rather on his managerial, marketing, and medical skills—was nothing original. Doctors all over America had for decades set up their own hospitals. Indeed, around the turn of the century, most of the new hospitals being established were so-called proprietary institutions (to distinguish them from charity or "voluntary" hospitals or public facilities), and several hundred exist today, still owned and run by the doctors who practice in them.

Had Dr. Frist stopped there, with Parkview Memorial Hospital, he would have been a creditable success, providing the capital of country music with a first-rate facility for cardiac care, and becoming in the process a man of means as well as social importance. But spurred on by an ambitious son, Air Force surgeon Thomas, Jr., the elder Frist developed grander ideas. In 1968, unable to raise money from local investors to expand his new medical facility, Frist teamed up with his son and Jack Massey, a patient of the elder Frist, who was famous for developing the Kentucky Fried Chicken restaurant chain. Their idea: a chain of hospitals modeled, if not on Colonel Sanders, then on motel chains like Holiday Inn and Marriott.

A chain, they realized, would have two big advantages: It would save them heaps of money by enabling them to buy equipment, supplies, and services in bulk, and as a national corporation with high visibility, it would be able to attract investor funds from the public stock market. The idea had worked for most other industries in America, but for health care, it was a novel approach. It was also one almost guaranteed to succeed, thanks to Medicare and Medicaid.

For Massey, the creation of HCA meant a kind of return to his roots. Originally a successful surgical supplies wholesaler, Massey had sold that enterprise and invested his fortune in a group of little fried chicken outlets in neighboring Kentucky owned by a colorful fellow named "Colonel" Harlan Sanders. In the words of an admiring younger executive at HCA, "Massey is the kind of guy that, whatever you say to him, you know he's thinking, 'How can I make some money out of this?'"

When the younger Frist approached Massey, an old family friend, with his father's idea, Massey's acquisitive mind clicked into gear, and he bankrolled the new company. It was arguably the best business decision of his life. Long since retired, Massey made so much money on HCA that he set up his own personal venture capital firm, Massey Investment Company, with eight full-time investment bankers, to manage his estimated $100 million in assets. (Until 1988, his office was in HCA's Nashville corporate headquarters complex, where he remained a familiar figure.)

For Tommy, Jr. (as HCA employees refer to their still boyish-looking boss), HCA was a way to do something more exciting than surgery. "Tommy never wanted to be just a surgeon," recalls one associate. In fact, the usually soft-spoken Frist bristles when he recalls how in earlier days potential investors and health-care industry analysts, upon learning of his training, reflexively questioned his business acumen. "The medical degree was like an albatross around my neck," he says. "Nobody believed that a doctor could be a good businessman."

The younger Frist, whose calm demeanor conceals a dynamo, went far to prove the skeptics wrong. He was an avid long-distance runner with a reputation for stamina (until 1987, he sometimes ran the fifteen miles from Nashville airport to HCA headquarters after returning from a business trip). When HCA was founded, he spent much of his time flying a small plane across rural Tennessee and the rest of the South, landing in cornfields so he could confront rural hospital boards and convince them to sell out to the new chain. "A lot of times, if I arrived at night in those days, I would have to rely on car headlights to show me where the runway was," Frist recalls with a smile.

This was a typically aggressive approach his father, a classic Southern gentleman, could never have taken. It also (he confided to me during an interview decades later in his plush panelled office) put him in lively confrontations with "county officials who didn't want to lose some power in the community, and do-gooders who'd claim we were some kind of black sheep because we wanted to run their hospital for profit."

Massey and the Frists boldly gambled that a hospital chain would be just as able as a short-order fried chicken franchise to reap the benefits of scale and to interest public investors. As Tommy Frist, Jr., puts it today, "The secret of our success was the idea of bigness itself. In the early days, we didn't have anyone in the health field to copy. This was still a cottage industry of seven thousand hospitals. Holiday Inn was really our model."

They were right on both counts. Within six months, their Hospital Corporation of America already owned 11 hospitals and was beginning to save money by buying supplies in bulk and by centralizing management. By 1987, at its peak of expansion, 22 years after Frist opened his first hospital, HCA, with 70,000 employees, had become the largest of the nation's for-profit hospital chains, owning almost 200 acute-care facilities in 28 states of the U.S., plus 45 in eight foreign countries, including Australia, Great Britain, Brazil, and the Middle East. At that time the company managed another 210 hospitals on a fee basis, which placed it in a total of 44 states. HCA also owned 50 psychiatric hospitals and was building another 11. With patient revenues of $4.7 billion, had it been an industrial company instead of a service organization, it would have ranked eighty-eighth on the *Fortune* 500 list, alongside Amerada Hess, Bethlehem Steel, Deere and Company, and Campbell Soup. Even a year later, after it spun off 104 of its less profitable, mostly rural hospitals, HCA remained the largest of the hospital companies, with 85 hospitals in the U.S., 34 overseas, several hundred under management, and 50,000 employees. Company revenues even after divesting the 104 hospitals to HealthTrust were still $4.2 billion in 1989. And operating income that year was a record $853 million, which represents a net operating profit margin of 20.3 percent.

In Tennessee, where the Frists got their start, HCA was one of the state's largest private employers by 1988. As such, according to state campaign disclosure records, it contributed regularly to the campaigns of most of the state's legislators; had a former Republican governor, Winfield Dunn, as a vice president for governmental relations (Dunn ran again in 1986 for governor, losing to another HCA friend, then statehouse speaker and later Governor Ned McWherter); and owned or leased 10 percent of the state's 150 hospitals.

Hospital Corporation's founders were clearly correct about the advantages of emulating the cost-saving aspects of Kentucky Fried Chicken (some critics persist in referring to HCA as "Kentucky Fried Hospitals"): Between 1982 and 1985, HCA claims to have saved $85 million on supplies alone by buying on a large scale. Frist's comparison of the company to Holiday Inn is also on the mark. As he notes, "Holiday Inn changed the way people traveled in the South, by eliminating the boarding house." HCA and its competitors are changing the face of American medicine at least as dramatically.

Humana: What's in a Name

A third major player in the health-care-for-profit sweepstakes, Humana, Inc., like AMI, didn't begin as a hospital company. Rather, Humana got its start when two Louisville, Kentucky, realtors invited two eager young law partners out to a friendly game of golf at the Harmony Landing Golf Course. As the story goes,[3] David Jones, a ruddy-faced, tough-talking young lawyer and former amateur boxer from Louisville's West End, was reportedly teamed up with realtor Charles Weisberg. Jones's law partner, Wendell Cherry, a grocer's son from Horse Cave, Kentucky, was teamed with realtor Lewis Bass.

On about the sixth hole, in the midst of a conversation about how to increase the incomes of all present, Weisberg remembers Jones asking him casually, "Charles, what do you know about nursing homes?" The answer was "nothing," but Weisberg allowed that he *did* know something about real estate, and within a year, in 1962, he had arranged for the four amateur golfers to go into partnership on a new nursing home, to be owned by a company called Extendicare. The home, called with some sense of grandeur, Heritage House of America, was two-thirds owned by the four men, and one-third by its builders.

On the inaugural day, the head nurse suffered a medical emergency and had to be rushed to a hospital for surgery, leaving the new owners and their wives to do all the routine chores, like serving meals and changing bedpans. The experience didn't discourage these eager new entrepreneurs, though. And surely the problems on opening day were hardly an omen of the future, for the little company proceeded to grow beyond anyone's wildest imagination. In 1963, the company added another nursing home in Lexington, and in 1964, a third in Virginia. When the partners took the enterprise public with a stock offering in early 1968, Wall Street paid attention: The stock jumped from an initial offering price of $8 a share to $18 a share on the first day of trading. By week's end it was still trading at $16.50 a share.

Extendicare didn't stay in the nursing home field for long. Jones and Cherry, the active managers of the fledgling firm, working out of a 10-by-15-foot office rented from Weisberg for $30 a month, dabbled in other areas, including mobile homes, before finally deciding to try hospitals in 1968. At that point, flush with cash from its public stock issue, the company bought the Medical Center Hospital in Huntsville, Alabama. The hospital side of the enterprise quickly took over, and by 1972, the company owned forty-five of them. That was the year Jones and Cherry decided to unload their nursing homes and get out of the firm's initial line of business altogether.

Hospitals it was, but even then the two men didn't want to preclude future options, and after deciding that it was time for a new company name, they hired a corporate identity consultant in New York City. From some five hundred new names submitted, they chose Humana, explaining to shareholders in the company's 1973 annual report that the intention was "to more truly project the philosophy of the company, to stand out distinctively *and to provide an identity with non-limiting connotations*" (author's emphasis). If the company someday decided to dump hospitals and move into something else more profitable, the reasoning went, why get saddled with a corporate name that included the word *hospital*, and would only have to be changed again? Here was an early example of Humana as trendsetter. One and two decades later, companies like Standard Oil, U.S. Steel and International

Harvester, anxious to diversify, would also change their names to such nonlimiting appellations as Exxon, USX, and Navistar.

But there hasn't been much call for Humana to get out of hospitals; in fact the company quickly started playing the acquisitions game with a vengeance. Some, in fact, would say ruthlessness. On Wall Street, where investment analysts report that the company often dumped existing management at hospitals and hospital companies when it made an acquisition, the word was "Humana takes no prisoners." In 1978, in a bitterly fought hostile takeover, Humana bought American Medicorp for $304.5 million. This Pennsylvania-based competitor was at one time the nation's largest hospital company.

The takeover battle was widely watched in the financial community. For one thing, it was unusual in September 1977 for a smaller company to approach a larger one with an "unfriendly" tender offer; Humana sought 75 percent of American Medicorp's shares. At the time of the bid, many expected a protracted battle, with lawsuits, injunctions, and antitrust investigations lasting a year or more, all to the detriment of both companies' performance. American Medicorp had rejected the tender offer and had immediately sued Humana, alleging antitrust violations. There were also charges—as often happens in takeover battles—that Continental Illinois Bank of Chicago, which was helping Humana finance the takeover, was playing both sides of the fence. Continental was one of American Medicorp's major lenders.[4]

Humana also found itself competing for American Medicorp with a much larger "white knight": Trans World Airlines and its subsidiary, Hilton International. Humana's bid, initially $10 a share but later sweetened to $15 a share plus $0.05 for a new $2.50 share of Humana preferred stock for each share of American Medicorp, was lower than TWA's $20-a-share cash bid for 65 percent of the company. But Humana called the larger firm's bluff. It stood firm with its lower bid, in effect calling its rival. On January 10, 1978, citing a "review of the financial implications," TWA withdrew its offer, and American Medicorp's board threw in the towel, accepting Humana's bid. At the time, a surprised executive of the acquired firm, saying American Medicorp had been outfoxed by Humana, called the merger a case of "Jonah swallowing the whale."

At that point, Humana became something of a "whale" within the hospital industry. Jumping almost overnight from 59 to 114 hospitals, and with combined patient revenues from the two firms totalling over $1 billion, Humana was for a short while the largest of the hospital firms, and the first to join the ranks of America's largest 500 companies.

It was a brief moment of being number one in the industry, however. The tightly managed company immediately began selling off poorly performing hospitals until it was back down to a lean and manageable 87 facilities. HCA, meanwhile, with new acquisitions, continued to expand.

NME: Thinking Big

National Medical Enterprises, the fourth competitor among the giants of the hospital industry, founded by three Los Angeles lawyers, Richard Eamer, Leonard Cohen, and John Bedrosian, was a later and consequently much more deliberate creation than the others. Indeed, as AMI's Appel tells the story, the whole thing was more or less his doing. "When I was starting out in this business, Dick Eamer was an attorney for seventeen of the hospitals in the area. One time back in the late sixties—after Medicare—we were eating together, and he said to me, 'Bob, you've got the best ball game in town. I think I'll try it too.'"

Like AMI and Humana, National Medical Enterprises was founded not by doctors, but by businessmen aware of the profit and growth potential of the field. But unlike Humana, AMI, and HCA, NME was established at the outset as a health-care conglomerate, revolving around the ownership of a large number of acute-care hospitals but including a much wider array of health-care-related assets and operations.

Instead of starting small, the way the other three big competitors in this field did, NME's founders kicked off their hospital venture on May 8, 1969, with a $25.5 million stock offering. It was a time, much like the mid-1980s, when the financial markets were booming, and new issues by start-up companies were quite common. Still, asking investors to ante up $25.5 million for a company that existed only on the pages of an offering prospectus, in an industry that was largely unheard of, was unusual. It's an indication of Wall Street's confidence in the prospects of what was still a relatively new industry that the issue was underwritten by E. F. Hutton, then one of the Street's major brokerage houses. The offering was in fact not the wild success that many new issues were at that time. Where many new company issues were oversubscribed with prospective buyers even before their offering dates, it took some time for the NME offering to sell out. Still, Wall Street judges the success or failure of any enterprise by the bottom line results, and the bottom line of the NME initial offering was that the company sold 844,000 shares at $30 a share.

Investors in initial offerings of new start-up companies are by definition risk takers. Putting money into a company that has no track record and that essentially is nothing but a rented office, a typewriter, an official letterhead, and the dream of a few would-be managers can be the same thing as pouring it down the drain. It can also be a way of multiplying one's initial investment many-fold, of becoming a major holder of a large company, or of cashing in a large holding if the venture is a success. The NME offering, at first glance, might seem to have been the classic case of a high-risk investment. On closer examination, it is apparent why E. F. Hutton was willing to underwrite the offering, promising to make good on the investment if it was not fully sold to the public. In 1969 Medicare was in full swing: The government was guarantee-ing hospital owners reimbursement for their treatment of the elderly and disabled on a cost-plus basis, with a return on equity factored into the calculation. This meant that barring gross man-agerial incompetence, it was almost impossible for a hospital—or an investment in a hospital—to fail. And NME investors made out quite well. Someone who put $10,000 into NME at the beginning and held on to it, would by August 1990 have been holding $1.2 million worth of stock, not counting a string of hefty dividend payments.

Needless to say, the founders of the company, like those of the other three major hospital chains, are today very rich men. In 1983, for instance, Richard Eamer earned $1.1 million in salary and bonus alone. HCA's Tom Frist, Jr., that year pulled down even more: $1.4 million. Two years later, AMI then chairman Royce Diener earned just under $1 million in salary, bonus, and stock options. The big star that year, though, was Humana's Jones, who made headlines by becoming the nation's second-highest-paid chief executive, receiving a total of $18 million in pay and stock options.

The new capital from that first NME foray into the stock market was immediately used by the new company's founder-managers to purchase four California hospitals—Doctors Hospital of Modesto, Los Altos Hospital, Garfield Hospital, and Dominguez Valley Hospital—and three nursing homes.

Where Humana began as a nursing home company and evolved into a hospital chain, eventually selling off all its nursing homes, NME from the outset was perceived by its founders as a more diversified enterprise, one that would deliberately encompass both hospitals and nursing homes, as well as a host of related activities. As one company source observes, "Senior management saw health care as a single commodity of many interrelated medical services. By diversifying into related areas of medical care, NME's founders reasoned that their 'total health-care company' concept could realize the economic advantages of providing a full range of cost-effective medical services to its patients. For if a patient recuperated sufficiently to leave an acute-care hospital operated by the company yet was not quite ready to go home, he could complete his recovery in an NME long-term facility, a more appropriate, less costly level of care."

From $25 million in early 1969, NME grew rapidly. By the end of its first fiscal year of operations, the company owned five hospitals and three convalescent homes. It also owned two medical office buildings, another area of diversification that other companies eventually entered. NME further possessed three sites for new hospitals, was in the process of buying and building two others, and had purchased the Livingston Oxygen Company, a hospital equipment supplier that provided the parent firm with a solid cash flow for further acquisitions.

Five years later, NME joined AMI and HCA in going international, managing some hospitals overseas. And in 1979, the company became a significant national presence in both hospital and nursing care with the purchase of Medfield, a smaller southeastern hospital chain, and the Hillhaven Corporation, a convalescent hospital chain with nursing homes in thirty-three states. The 1982 acquisition of Psychiatric Institutes of America added another dimension to NME, positioning the company as one of the country's major providers of psychiatric care, an area viewed at the time as highly profitable by the hospital industry because of the relatively low level of capital equipment required compared to acute-care hospitals, and the relatively high reimbursements available.

Charting the Health of an Industry

Since its inception in the 1960s, the for-profit hospital industry has gone through several cycles of expansion and crisis. After heady growth in the early years thanks to Medicare, the industry survived two recessions virtually unscathed. (Health care has traditionally been viewed, and in fact historically has been, counter cyclical, meaning it is relatively immune to economic downturns.) Then it was hit by the Nixon administration's price controls. Even after initial price controls were lifted in January 1973 and the much more lenient phase of the government's antiinflationary program was introduced, strict controls were left on hospitals. They had to struggle for profits. Not surprisingly, in this environment, the investor-owned chains suffered.

The "hospital stock crash of '73" was actually precipitated by the leaking in late 1972 of the early draft of an adverse analyst's report from the Oppenheimer brokerage firm.[5] That report claimed the hospital industry was facing increased price regulation, a cooling of the "acquisition fever" that had been underway for almost a decade (for the presumed reason that all the good hospitals had already been acquired), and a decline in earnings that would make it difficult for companies to finance new construction. It also noted that occupancy rates in hospitals were not increasing. Within a week of the report's release (which resulted in the firing of the research analyst who allegedly leaked a preliminary draft to an employee of an investment counseling service, Scudder, Stevens and Clark[6]), AMI shares had fallen 20 percent in value, and HCA shares by 22 percent. Other companies were also battered. Even AMI founder/chairman Appel's angry denunciation of Oppenheimer—he called the report "amateurish" and warned of lawsuits—failed to restore investor confidence, and hospital stocks languished for most of the year, with price/earnings ratios falling 60 to 70 percent industry-wide.

The hospital industry recovered briefly and enjoyed an active period of growth and acquisition from 1975 to 1977, but then a new crisis hit. This time, it was investor fears that the new Carter administration was serious about campaign plans to set about nationalizing the health-care system. Again hospital stocks suffered a loss of some 20 percent, but it became increasingly clear that the specter of nationalization was wildly overblown. By late 1977, faced with rising overall inflation rates less than a year after taking office, the Carter administration was already backing off the idea of introducing any kind of comprehensive reform of the system. Economists were predicting that the administration's health insurance schemes would cost as much as $30 billion a year at a time when the federal budget deficit was ballooning. Carter tabled his health insurance idea, suggesting instead only controls on hospital revenues. But even this modest idea never made it past the American Hospital Association lobby and through Congress. By 1981, when he left office, his administration had essentially given up on the idea of controlling health-care prices.

Acquisitions, meanwhile, had picked up again quickly as hospital stocks rebounded. Indeed, far from being out of hospital markets to acquire, as the Oppenheimer industry report (and conventional wisdom) had predicted, the period 1978–85 proved to be the heyday of hospital acquisition and consolidation. Humana's takeover of American Medicorp kicked off a period when hospital chains were among the fastest-growing companies in America. In 1978, there were 445 corporate-owned hospitals in the country. By 1980, the number was 561, an increase of 26 percent. By 1982, there were 708 investor-owned corporate hospitals, another increase of 26 percent. In 1984 the number of corporate-owned hospitals had jumped to 955, up 35 percent (thanks to the early effect of Medicare reform, which scared a large number of independent hospitals into the corporate fold, often at reduced prices). The pace of acquisitions slowed over the next two years, to 24 percent and a total of 1,186 hospitals in corporate hands, in part a reflection of tougher times for the biggest companies, and in part just the natural result of the prior two years' rapid acquisition pace. By 1991, there were 1,382 for-profit hospitals in the U.S. (and another 75 overseas).[7] That represented 25 percent of all nonfederally owned hospitals in the U.S., according to the AHA.

HCA, temporarily displaced from the number-one rank in the hospital industry, had by 1980 regained prime position by acquiring Hospital Affiliates for $650 million. Then in 1983 AMI, the fourth-ranked hospital company, propelled itself briefly into the number-two industry spot, at the same time lifting the whole hospital industry into the merger big leagues, by acquiring fifth-ranked Lifemark Corporation, a Houston-based hospital firm, for a record $1 billion.

The early 1980s, then, found the hospital business finally in the position of being a major industry. It was still young, and there have been plenty of new entries in the field each year since, but the four key players had by then established themselves as seemingly unassailable industry leaders.

Four Firms, Four Approaches

Although they shared this position of leadership, the four companies varied widely in operating style and corporate culture. Indeed, they are as different now in their modus operandi as they were in their origins.

Humana's 27-story headquarters is a bustling center. Completed in 1986 and, at a cost of some $60 million, extremely gaudy and pretentious, it nonetheless has an electric feeling to it. Jones himself and lower-level executives are energetic and casual in addressing each other. The contrast between Humana's and HCA's operations is as great as that between their respective board chairmen. At Humana, there's the working-class ex-boxer Jones, whose bear-paw-sized hands still have an impressive grip, while HCA is headed by tall, slender, distance runner Frist, who hails from Nashville's gentry. Where Humana is brash and its towering gilt-edged post-modernist headquarters monolith showy, HCA, in contrast, more closely resembles a staid defense industry firm. The side entrance to the latter company's prosaic concrete bunker-shaped headquarters even boasts a fancy security system that recognizes fingerprints, and in executive suites, there's a calm, hushed feeling, especially when a top officer like Tommy Frist glides past over the plush carpet.

At NME central offices, the feeling is more akin to Humana, though without the latter's nouveau riche architectural pretention (executive offices are scattered across several parts of the West Los Angeles and Santa Monica area, and the low-slung glass-and-steel buildings are uninspired and unobtrusive, inside and out). There's a feeling of entrepreneurial energy, but lightened by a laid-back hint of Southern California that gives it less of an edge. There was less looking at watches during my interviews with top executives at NME, for example, than there was at Humana.

If NME is closer in style to Humana, AMI, at least for its first twenty-five years, resembled HCA. But again, the California (in this case on Wilshire Boulevard, Beverly Hills) address and the views of palm trees waving in the sun out most office windows make its management seem less straight-laced. When AMI's then chairman, Royce Diener, stepped onto an elevator during a visit I made to executive headquarters, the joking of two junior executives didn't let up a bit, and Diener, a patrician-looking fellow with a shock of white hair, even added a rejoinder as he departed. With the takeover of the company in 1989 by the Pritzkers and their investor/partners, the casual tone at headquarters is changing fast. The moving of corporate headquarters from downtown Beverly Hills to Dallas, Texas, is an indication of this. And AMI's new chairman, Harry Gray, the crusty former chairman of United Technologies, has a reputation as a no-nonsense, hard-nosed businessman.

Humana has always put its stamp on every facility it owns. Humana's co-founder, the late Wendell Cherry (he died of lung cancer in 1991), reportedly once stated that he wanted his firm's properties to be as uniform as franchise hamburgers and, in a way, they are. HCA, on the other hand, always much less centralized, tends to leave local management more to its own devices (as long as earnings meet corporate goals). At least until 1987, for instance, HCA hospitals never mentioned HCA in the name (that year, in a strategy change, the company moved to adopt a "brand name" approach akin to Humana's). In late 1983, Humana began very consciously and deliberately to parlay implants of the Jarvik mechanical heart into publicity that almost overnight made its name a household word. It capitalized on its fame by listing "Humana" first in every hospital title.

The various companies exhibit vastly different corporate cultures, and, while they work as a team with often stunning effectiveness in lobbying for their group interests in Washington, they are intensely competitive. Humana's David Jones, for instance, was openly contemptuous in a 1986 interview of HCA's continued drive as late as 1985 to acquire hospitals when most industry analysts were already saying the market for hospitals was overpriced and bound to come down. "That's their business," he said with a smirk. "We're not doing that." Humana, for its part, stopped buying and building new facilities in the early 1980s, and has been concentrating since on setting up its own captive health insurance program—known in industry circles as a "patient feeder system"—for steering patients into company hospitals, thereby boosting occupancy rates.

On the other hand, when asked about Jones's statement that "We don't think taking care of the indigent is our problem—it's society's problem and it needs a government solution," HCA's Tommy Frist, Jr., screwed up his face. He countered that he thought the "proprietary" industry (most of the hospital company tycoons dislike the term for-profit) had an "obligation to do its part, along with business and government, to find solutions to this problem."

In terms of both revenues and number of acute-care hospitals in 1991, Humana is the largest of the hospital companies, with 82 hospitals, 1990 sales of $4.85 billion, and earnings of $309 million. Humana's sales through the first three quarters of 1991 were $4.3 billion, leading most analysts to predict by midsummer that the company's 1991 revenues would handily top $6 billion.

In second place as of 1991 was HCA, with 1990 revenues of $4.6 billion (up 10 percent from $4.2 billion in 1989), and with earnings before depreciation, interest, and taxes of $957 million on assets of $6.3 billion. The privately-held company owned 75 acute-care hospitals, in addition to 53 psychiatric hospitals. HCA's reach is considerably wider than it might at first appear, however, as it retained as of 1991 a huge 34-percent stake in HealthTrust, the ESOP trust spin-off it created in 1987, which owns another 95 hospitals. (HCA's stake in HealthTrust was slated to drop to 10 percent under a plan the latter company announced in June 1991 to go public and repay $600 million in debt to HCA.) Hospital Corporation of America is also a 10-percent holder of Quorum Health Resources, another company divestiture which in 1991 was managing 187 not-for-profit hospitals.

Third place in 1991 belonged to National Medical Enterprises, with its 38 hospitals (three overseas) and 1990 earnings of $242 million on revenues of $3.94 billion. American Medical International, following its takeover and retrenchment, stood in fourth place in 1991 with 38 hospitals. AMI's revenues for the fiscal year ending August 31, 1990, were $2.5 billion. Some analysts rank NME below AMI as a *hospital* company on the grounds that only 42 percent of NME's 1990 revenues were generated by the diversified firm's acute-care hospitals. As a result of NME's long-held official strategy of becoming a kind of "cradle-to-grave" health-care system, the rest of its revenues came from its other 116 psychiatric, physical rehabilitation, specialty, and drug/alcohol dependency treatment hospitals, as well as from other operations.

It should come as no surprise that the hospital companies have been so varied in both strategies and style. The entire health-care industry is in upheaval, and no one has yet determined how best to compete in an area where competition is still a relatively new idea, and where the concept of a national market, and of health care as a commodity, is unprecedented. Hospitals in the middle to late 1980s were battered by declining patient admissions and shorter stays, the results of new medical techniques, treatment philosophies, and pressure from insurers, government, and employers who pay for most private insurance coverage. Only after 1988 did average occupancy rates and patient admissions start to edge back up again, and, according to the AHA, by 1990 the average occupancy rate for acute-care hospitals was still only about 65 percent. To some extent, this upheaval has worked to the chains' advantage. This is because the not-for-profit sector, hampered by tradition, bureaucracy, unionized workers, and sometimes simply a desire or need to adhere to a charter that makes charity care a priority, has had an even tougher time adapting to the new environment. And those that don't adapt are either sold to the for-profit companies at fire-sale prices or are shut down, often leaving the local health-care market to a surviving for-profit institution. But making money has gotten harder for the for-profit firms too. They worked actively to push the idea of set reimbursement schedules for Medicare in 1983, in the Machiavellian hope that even if it made life harder, they would fare better under such a system than the not-for-profit competition. The reduced revenue for acute care under DRG reimbursements, however, has hurt both for-profit and not-for-profit hospitals more than they anticipated, as has a trend toward ambulatory out-of-hospital care.

The once torrid pace of acquisitions among the largest hospital companies has slowed a bit since 1985, and indeed most of the larger companies deliberately reduced their size in the late 1980s by selling off weaker holdings. But few people expect the big firms to stop growing indefinitely, or for the overall trend in the hospital field toward concentration to halt. As editor of the *New England Journal of Medicine*, Arnold Relman, a prominent critic of the industry, once predicted that by the mid-1990s the chains would own 30 percent of the hospitals in America. In 1984, before the industry's latest bout of bad times, the American College of Hospital Administrators predicted even more concentration, projecting that the big firms would have 60 percent of market share by 1995.

Some such predictions may prove to have been overblown, though Relman's seems quite likely to be correct, or even too conservative (counting managed facilities and independent for-profit hospitals, it's been reached already). But even for the bolder forecasts, it is probably only the timing that is off. By 1988, HCA was already larger than all but 158 American corporations, and Tommy Frist, Jr., has still not renounced a long-held ambition to see his creation eventually become one of the nation's twenty largest businesses, joining the company of such corporate fixtures as ITT, Chrysler, and USX. Apparently, he has only deferred it.

Frist tried in 1985 to leap into the ranks of the nation's largest corporations almost overnight with the acquisition of the country's largest hospital supply company, $3.6-billion-a-year American Hospital Supply. The merger proposal, announced jointly by Frist and American Hospital Chairman Carl Bays to a packed hotel suite of health industry analysts, was almost concluded but then foundered. There was stockholder opposition at American Hospital, and a hospital-supply industry competitor, Baxter-Travenol, weighed in with a higher bid. Baxter-Travenol executives reportedly feared, with some justification, that a merger of the largest hospital company with the largest hospital supply firm would create a dangerous situation of market dominance through vertical integration. They were able to block Frist because hospital stocks were just weakening, and American Hospital shareholders proved receptive to the argument that their shares might be dragged down, at least in the short run, by the proposed linkage. In a proxy vote that year, they turned down the merger and voted to be absorbed instead by Baxter-Travenol.

Still, Frist's dream is not an idle one. Many leading Wall Street health-industry analysts say HCA and its competitors—while clearly having suffered a short-term setback in earnings because of a general oversupply of hospitals and problems in dealing with fixed-price DRG Medicare reimbursements—are a good long-term investment. "Ten years from now," said William LeConey of Liberty Street Capital in a 1987 interview, "they'll be seen as three of the ten or twenty great growth stocks of the eighties. Over time, they could be bigger than General Motors." Indeed, GM, which reportedly spends about $2 billion a year on employee health benefits, was at one point in 1986 rumored to have been briefly interested in entering the health-care field through acquisition. With General Motors saying health-care expenditures for its employees add over $600 to the cost of producing each GM car, such a move was reportedly being seen as one possible way for the company to gain some control over this aspect of its labor costs.

The Smaller Players in the Hospital Game

In the meantime, while the largest hospital chains were suffering from lower earnings (even as revenues continued to grow), other segments of the for-profit hospital industry were picking up the slack. Specifically, some of the smaller for-profit hospital corporate chains, ranging in size from a few to as many as twenty or thirty usually smaller hospitals, were buying and building new facilities from 1985 to 1988 at the kind of pace the big four firms displayed in the heady days of the late 1970s and early 1980s. These lesser firms actually often doubled or tripled their annual revenues in a year's time, and then repeated this performance two years in a row. Many of the properties these bush-league players were snatching up were hospitals that the bigger companies were divesting. Many of the new firms, for that matter, were being founded by former executives of the larger companies, suggesting in some cases continuing informal ties with the "parent" firm.

E. Thomas Chaney, for example, was controller of Hospital Affiliates before that firm was gobbled up by HCA. He then served as chief financial officer of ARA Services' nursing home division before stepping out on his own in 1986 with the creation of Community Health Systems, a company that grew from one hospital to eight in one year with the addition of six divested NME facilities.

In early 1986 L. Stanton Tuttle, senior vice president of HCA and head of that company's psychiatric care division, hired on as the new president of National Healthcare, an ironically named and curiously run small hospital chain with a fast-track growth record founded in 1981 by Stephen Phelps. (Phelps was another Hospital Affiliates veteran. In fact, so many hospital entrepreneurs got their start working at Hospital Affiliates that at least one veteran of the company says it was a kind of "school for hospital managers" before its absorption by HCA.)

In a chaotic environment reminiscent of the early days of the personal computer business, many of the smaller hospital companies have been stunning successes, only to run aground suddenly. Their almost frenzied attitude toward growth usually led either to their acquiring hospitals that they couldn't operate profitably, or to their simply growing too large for existing management to handle.

National Healthcare provides an object lesson in both the potential for riches and the potential for excess in the hospital industry. As late as 1986, a time when the overall hospital industry was being viewed skeptically by many Wall Street investors and analysts, the New York investment firm Bear Stearns wrote of the company:

While major chains have been hurt by declining occupancy and intensified competition from alternate delivery systems, NHCI [National Healthcare's NAS-DAQ abbreviation] has rapidly built a franchise in rural market areas, solely through acquisition. Since year-end fiscal 1985 (ended June), the company has acquired eight hospitals (bringing the total of owned/leased/managed hospitals to 22) and has agreements to purchase thirteen additional hospitals. Longer term, the company plans to acquire eight hospitals per year, while improving utilization and adding ancillary health care services in its existing markets. For fiscal 1986, we project a 150 percent earnings gain, followed by a 73 percent increase in fiscal 1987. Our single cautionary note is that NHCI's management systems and controls must keep pace with its growth to avoid problems down the road.[8]

Like most of the emerging new smaller chains, National Healthcare tried to focus on a niche—in this case small rural hospitals, exactly the place HCA got its start. As the Bear Stearns analyst pointed out optimistically in her report on the company, there were at the time over 2,000 unaffiliated rural hospitals available for potential acquisition (and another 250 owned by the chains). The potential for growth of this company obviously impressed investors. In November 1985, only two months after the stocks of the big hospital companies started to plummet on reports of reduced earnings, they snapped up 2.3 million shares of an initial public offering, providing the company with $17.8 million. At the same time, $30 million worth of twelve-year subordinated debentures were sold. The firm followed this with a second stock offering in April 1986, which raised another $25.5 million. It also secured a $100-million line of credit from a bank syndicate led by Citicorp, funds to be used for acquisitions.

Phelps, the exuberant founder and chairman of National Healthcare, saw big things ahead. As he put it in a 1986 interview, "I grew up in the construction business, and back in the 1970s, I saw this [the hospital field] as an industry that wasn't very cyclical, and a place where fortunes were being made."

He promptly set out to make one of his own. "I watched people getting together to form three hospitals and sell them off to HCA, and walk away millionaires. That was my interest. I went with Hospital Affiliates when they had thirty hospitals. They increased that to one hundred fifty hospitals and sold it to HCA, so I was there during some very exciting times."

Phelps's approach with National Healthcare was simple and fairly typical of the smaller hospital entrepreneur. "We're very aggressive," he reported in 1986. "We want each hospital we buy to make an operating profit in the first thirty days, and we do it." The key to the company's success? "We are monopolistic. We only buy hospitals that are the one hospital in an area, or if there are two, it's the primary one. Or a Protestant community where the only other hospital is Catholic. Of thirty-six hospitals, thirty are the sole community health providers."

When Phelps called his company aggressive, he meant it. The for-profit hospital industry has earned a reputation for cutting back on staffing when it takes over a hospital from the not-for-profit sector, but Phelps, like many of the smaller hospital company managers, has given the term *cut back* new meaning. "We bought three HCA hospitals in June [1986]," he recalled. "We eliminated one hundred fifty-three employees the day we took over. We cut $2.5 million in costs right away and earned $650,000 in the first thirty days."

Phelps had no illusions about what has been going on at the low end of the hospital industry, however, though he wouldn't say whether he hoped to follow in the footsteps of his early mentors and sell the new company for a profit someday. "We expect to be a $1 billion company by 1990," he boasted in 1986, "but we'll have to keep from becoming an HCA." He explained, "The reason the big companies are in trouble is that they've grown very fat. They never had to have tough management. HCA and AMI are really just collectors of real estate. They just don't have the killer instinct. To manage, you have to be a nice guy, easy to know . . . and mean as hell at running your company! It's extremely hard to screw up in management at HCA."

But mean guys don't always finish first in big business, where it is generally more important to know how to manage a bureaucracy than how to strip one down, and Phelps never said anything about going into big-league competition with the top companies in the industry. "The new small firms are being started by operators, not company builders. Where we're going to screw up is in growing companies. I believe that a lot of these companies are going to end up being acquired," he predicted.

This scenario would be consistent with the experience of venture capitalists, who have learned the hard way that it is the rare entrepreneur who is good at both creating new companies and running large enterprises. Frist, Cherry, Jones, and NME's three founders have demonstrated that they have both capabilities. But Appel, and his urbane successor Royce Diener, were both successively promoted out of an active role in AMI, reportedly by executives and key investors who felt the two weren't effective at running a big mature operation.

In the end, Phelps never got to demonstrate what his ultimate goals were. The company, which he once proudly described to me as "the Mary Kay of health care," with monthly "celebrations" where upper and middle management could "shout and holler, dress up, wear funny hats, and talk about our success," found itself in trouble. Heavily in debt, its books in disarray, National Healthcare was also the target of a $600 million shareholder suit that alleged, among other things, fraud and stock manipulation. (Shareholders also charged that the company had fraudulently inflated its hospitals' Medicare volume, for which rural hospitals can earn a bonus, by having company employees wear hospital patient gowns on census days.[9]) Without admitting wrongdoing, the company and its top officers eventually settled the suit out of court in 1987 for $9 million. As part of the settlement, Phelps and other top executives in the firm were forced out. The company also had to take a $9.1 million write-down of assets on its balance sheet to cover uncollectable debts in 1987.[10]

After flirting in 1987/88 with bankruptcy and with its headquarters relocated from Dothan, Alabama, to Atlanta, the company today is under new management and back down to a more modest nineteen hospitals, having sold off its most troubled holdings, according to a company spokesperson.

Most of the other new smaller for-profit hospital firms may be more prosaic than National Healthcare, and may be aiming at establishing different niches, but their patterns of rapid growth are similar. According to a special 1986 report on this sector of the industry published by the Federation of American Health Systems, new acquisitions by these small firms during the industry's tough period between 1985 and 1988 collectively rivaled the past acquisition record of the bigger firms, and kept intact the decade-long process of concentration in the industry despite a switch by the largest firms from a policy of acquisition to one of consolidation and divestment.

Community Health Systems started up in 1986 with two hospitals and by 1991 had ten acute-care facilities in five states.

AmeriHealth Incorporated went from one hospital in 1985 to three in 1986, and by 1991 was also managing another five hospitals (often a step toward eventual outright ownership). Comprehensive Care Corporation increased its holdings by 36 percent between 1986 and 1989, from 14 to 19.

And so it went.

As Phelps and most of the analysts on Wall Street concede, these are not corporate names that, like GM, Ford, IBM, or Standard Oil, will likely be etched into the corporate firmament. They are probably fated like the Willys, Packard, and Reo automobiles, to someday be acquired by or merged into larger corporate entities. What their successes *do* mean is that as an industry, the for-profit hospital business is still robust, a great place to put your bets if you're in it for the long haul. As one Wall Street health industry analyst put it in early 1988, "It's probably a terrific place to put your IRA investment, if you're under fifty!"

Hard Times for Hospitals: Relapse and Recovery

In September 1985, Wall Street was stunned at the disclosure by HCA, once a darling of investors, that it expected earnings to be flat through 1986. With that news out, the paper value of the stock of all the hospital companies plummeted almost overnight by a total of about $1.5 billion. Even Humana's subsequent report that its own profits were *up* 15 percent for the fourth quarter, and 12 percent for the year, to $216 million, on a sales increase of 10 percent, didn't prevent its stock from declining with that of the rest of the industry (the company's investors had grown accustomed to increases nearly double that amount).

Virtually a blue chip investment vehicle, able to tap easily even the Eurobond market for funds, HCA again shocked the financial community in 1987. After years of rapid expansion, it was suddenly going to eliminate 104 of its poorest performing hospitals. These it subsequently spun off as a unit in the form of an Employee Stock Ownership Trust (ESOP) with the company name of HealthTrust. HCA applied almost $600 million of the $1.6 billion it earned from the sale of these assets to buy back its own stock, with the balance of the proceeds going to pay off debt. A measure of the benefits to HCA's bottom line of selling off its weakest holdings came with word that 1988 revenues were $4.1 billion, a scant $600 million lower than in 1987 despite the loss of more than half the company's hospitals. By 1990, the company was posting record revenues and record profits. Meanwhile, the decision to sell more than half its hospital inventory by a company that until 1987 had seemed obsessed with the notion of bigness and market share, may not be all it appears.

As of mid-1991, HCA still retained a one-third ownership stake in HealthTrust, making it the new company's largest single shareholder. R. Clayton McWorter, HCA's former chief operating officer, was now HealthTrust's chairman and CEO, and some critics suggested all HCA might have done is shift the job (and the blame) to HealthTrust for shutting down the company's worst-performing, mostly rural hospitals, and cutting out unprofitable but perhaps locally needed or popular services. But while Health-Trust, awash in floating-rate debt, had some tough times as interest rates rose in the late 1980s, in mid-1991 the company announced that it planned to repay its debt to HCA by going public and raising money in the stock market. By then, Health-Trust, which had used the proceeds from the sale of 19 hospitals to pay off almost two-thirds of its bank debt, was boasting revenues of $1.9 billion and a profit margin of about 20 percent. By mid-1991, the company said it was ready to begin "selective acquisitions" of new rural and suburban hospitals.[11]

The hospital industry's lackluster performance in 1986–87, following HCA's merger debacle and sudden report of flat earnings in 1985, temporarily discouraged investors who were looking for a quick return (though by early 1988 hospital company shares had recovered substantially). Some analysts even apocalyptically predicted the industry was done for. But the 1986 downturn for the industry leaders actually masked a longer term reality: Hospitals are now, and will remain, central to the delivery of health care in America. As the industry's Washington-based trade association, the Federation of American Health Systems, regularly points out, hospitals will play increasingly important roles as the baby-boom generation enters middle age, with all its accompanying aches and pains. And increasingly, a few big companies—certainly several of the giant for-profit enterprises, but perhaps also a few not-for-profit entities—will control that center.

Then too, most of the biggest hospital companies didn't really do all *that* badly even during the worst of times. Todd Richter, an industry analyst with Morgan Stanley, recalls a dinner in the dark days of early 1986 at which an investor leaned over to Humana's Jones and said, "David, don't you wish you weren't in hospitals now? It's such a shitty business." Jones, recounts Richter, turned calmly and said, "What? Are you kidding? I make an eight-percent return on assets and a twenty-six percent return on equity. You show me where that's a bad business!" In 1989, Humana's return on equity was still an enviable 20.6 percent, and in 1990 during a major bear market, it was one of the stocks most money managers were recommending while the overall stock market lost 20 percent of its value and seemed to have no bottom.

Beyond that, for all the difficulties being experienced by the corporate chains, things have been much harder for the nation's public and not-for-profit hospitals, which have been in crisis and closing down in record numbers. The result is that though the number of for-profit hospitals didn't change between 1987 and 1988, that sector's share of the total hospital universe rose by one percent, thanks to closings in the other two sectors.

To date, the big area of competition in the health-care delivery field has been acquisitions. While the companies have frequently bid against each other for specific hospital facilities, there has been almost no head-to-head competition for *patients* among the bigger hospital firms, because there were plenty of markets to choose from, and by nature all the hospital chains have preferred to buy into locales where they would have a monopoly, or built-in market dominance. There *has* been such competition between individual for-profit and not-for-profit hospitals, but even this has never been large-scale, since hospitals almost by definition are regional, or even local, entities serving relatively small geographic areas. Now, with their national ambitions and centralized administrations setting overall policy for growth, marketing strategy, and health standards, as corporate hospitals seek to transform health care into a commodity, the competition is destined to become national in scope. And not just because of a battle for markets between the for-profit and not-for-profit chains. A national or even large regional arena of competition will pit the corporate chains against one another, and against other large entities, like established HMOs and the giant insurance industry, which though slow to act has indicated its willingness to compete by teaming up with hospital chains or consortiums.

Lawrence Selwitz, one-time member of NME management and now a health industry analyst with the investment firm of Bateman Eichler Hill Richards in Los Angeles, explained in a 1987 interview, "There is a very significant transition occurring right now in the hospital industry. The trend is towards 'managed care.'" The term, widely used in the industry, refers to the determination and subsequent provision, by one corporate entity, of the entire health care needs of a patient or a group of patients. Humana has led the way in this new managed-care direction by its establishment of a captive health insurance plan. Essentially a preferred provider system, this scheme carries no deductible like an HMO but allows patients to use any physician as long as the doctor in question makes use of a Humana hospital.

Jones admits that the company got off to a bad start with its insurance operation by at first failing to require physicians to use Humana facilities. Too many simply absorbed the patient's deductible and sent them to non-Humana hospitals, a practice which amounted to 40 percent of covered admissions during the first two years. In such a situation, Humana wound up making insurance reimbursement payments to competing hospitals! The company also initially failed to tell doctors what they could charge for a medical procedure, which simply compounded the damage.

But now, having made use of company hospitals a requirement for reimbursement, and having told doctors that if fees are too high they'll be dropped from the plan, Humana's insurance venture is on track and paying its way. In 1989, the insurance operation entered the black, while accounting for nearly one quarter of Humana's $4.1 billion in revenues. On $1 billion in sales, it earned its first profit of $1 million and was expected to become a significant contributor to overall company profits in the years ahead. At the same time, it is also helping to steer patients to Humana's empty hospital beds, a key goal of the whole "managed care" concept. By the third quarter of 1990, with the health plan operating in regions served by thirty-two of Humana's hospitals, it was accounting for 20 percent of all Humana's inpatient admissions. In 1990, Humana's insurance operation accounted for $1.5 billion of the firm's annual revenues of $4.85 billion, and even earned a healthy pre-tax profit of $49 million. As Jones put it, "We made some big initial mistakes but we're correcting it." Many on Wall Street agree with this assessment. Says one analyst, "Humana's betting the farm on this idea, and I think it's going to work."

Other hospital companies, including HCA, AMI, and NME, initially rushed in 1986 and 1987 to copy Humana's insurance scheme, but quickly (probably too quickly) bailed out when they saw Humana's early problems and losses. Now, most health industry analysts say it may be too late for them to copy the idea.

As analyst Seth Shaw explains, Humana has too big a lead in the market at this point.

There have been booms and busts in the hospital industry, as in any type of enterprise, and as the American public tries to confront the issue of ever higher health-care costs, it will surely have more of each. After all, the hospital business is almost as dependent upon the whims of government policy as is the armaments industry, where stocks slump every time a super-power peace conference is announced, and soar each time a Middle East war starts.

What seems to be clear at this point is that the hospital industry has attained a critical mass where it is probably bound to succeed in some fashion. That is, even if in the end the hospital companies were to become subsidiary operations of larger health conglomerates—a fate all the biggest firms have resisted vigor-ously to date—the goal to which their managers aspire of a corporate system of health care in America will likely be met.

3

The Hard Sell: A Brave New World of For-Profit Medicine

We are a young and aggressive company with facilities in California, Florida and Georgia. Our management philosophy is based upon . . . adherence to our credo . . . *to care, to serve, to heal* . . . We are seeking acquisitions, mergers, joint ventures, leases and management agreements.
—Advertisement for Jupiter Hospital in *FAHS Review*

Instant Impact. Create it with Career Apparel from Angelica. That all-important "first impression" will give you a competitive edge! Coordinated career apparel makes all the difference in projecting a professional appearance in Admissions, Medical Records, Patient Services and on all your "up-front" personnel. Choose an exciting Image Apparel program from the largest in-stock line in the industry.
—Advertisement by Angelica in *FAHS Review*

Brogan Kabot Advertising has sent a lot of people to the hospital. To Detroit's biggest, most prestigious hospital. . . . In just one year we helped create a major increase in clinic visits with our national award-winning broadcast, print, outdoor and direct mail advertising.
—Advertisement by the Brogan Kabot agency in *Advertising Age* magazine

Not too long ago, the place where you read about hospitals, if you read about them at all, was the metropolitan or society section of your local newspaper. On the metro page, you might find an article about the opening of a new wing of the community hospital (usually named after some local philanthropist or the deceased relative of same) or, in a larger city, a human interest piece about a heart transplant patient waiting for a donor. In the society pages would be a story about a charity ball being held to raise funds for the local health-care institution of choice.

Today though, one is more likely to find hospital stories in the business pages, where a typical article instead concerns an acquisition by one chain of another smaller rival, or a hospital company's new strategy to gain investor confidence. (Not surprisingly, many of the stories about Humana's artificial heart program ran in the *Wall Street Journal*, or in the business pages of the *New York Times*.) But the likeliest place to read about hospitals today is in the advertisements. Indeed, hospital ads are also common to radio and television.

With the burgeoning of giant acute-care enterprises across the nation—enterprises that are directly in contact with and in competition for patients—has come a sharp change in what was once a subdued, low-key industry. Now, like insurance, like cold medicine, like fast food, it's hard sell. In the March 1987 issue of *Healthcare Advertising Review*, Kerry Feuerman, associate creative director of Ford and Westbrook, a Richmond, Virginia, ad firm, explained why he wanted to see more daring ad campaigns by health-care companies:

> I think if I see one more doctor kneeling down to a kid with his stethoscope and the kid smiling and the mother there holding his hand, I'm going to . . . I'm just going to say that not only is it boring; it doesn't provide people with anything unique or interesting. *No reason to buy* [Feuerman's italics].[1]

Advertising is surely the most visible and—except for those comfortable with used-car sales pitches—the most unnerving sign of change. Wherever in the country you may live, you are now likely to run across hospital ads and more importantly to be the target of at least one hospital's marketing effort. SRI-Gallup, a business research company in Chicago, reports that in 1987 hospitals in the U.S. spent $1.2 billion, or about $25 per household, on advertising and marketing their wares to consumers, up 7 percent from the previous year. (Of course since the ads aren't even aimed at the third of the country that has no insurance or depends upon the government's Medicaid program to pay for hospital care, the cost is really probably closer to $50 per family.) SRI-Gallup also says the average advertising bill per hospital for 1987 was $146,000, with the for-profit sector accounting for a much greater share of the ad budget than the public and not-for-profit sectors: The average for-profit hospital in 1987 spent $179,000 on advertising, 25 percent above the average for all hospitals, and almost 50 percent more than the not-for-profit hospital average of $121,000.[2]

What did all this promotional spending buy? In Dallas, for example, health-care consumers saw Humana advertisements claim the company's hospital was the cheapest place to go to have a baby, though this is true only because the company waives the patient's insurance deductible (you don't have to pay it to them); its actual charges to the insurer were *higher* than at some other area institutions. HCA meanwhile chose the upper-crust publication *Smithsonian* magazine to boast about its provision of care to some poor child in rural Texas, prompting one poverty lawyer to observe wryly, "The *Smithsonian* magazine is the one place no poor people will read about the service, and get the idea of taking advantage of it." And in San Francisco, young, upwardly mobile professionals worried about the attractiveness of their body image could read in that city's glossy, upscale *San Francisco* magazine about a program offered by Republic Health called New Beginnings: The ad, featuring a well-endowed (or enhanced) woman staring dreamily out a window in a sheer nightgown, urges those readers unhappy with their bodies to sign up at a company hospital for cosmetic surgery.

For-profit hospitals are not the only ones that have tried advertising. In part to boost occupancy rates, but most often in response to competitive pressures from aggressively advertised for-profit hospitals situated in the same market, even some public hospitals have taken to advertising their services. At the 1987 national convention of the American Public Health Association, a well-attended panel on hospital marketing saw experts explaining to public hospital administrators how well-targeted advertisements could bring in patients and help to fend off competition. And according to Linda Miller, president of the Volunteer Trustees of Not-for-Profit Hospitals, a trade and lobbying organization for the voluntary hospital sector, these latter institutions started hiring public relations directors and mounting ad campaigns with a vengeance in about 1985, with budgets doubling in 1986 and again in 1987. But, says Miller, speaking in 1988, "Many of our members are now dropping the whole idea, saying they just can't afford it."

Advertising to consumers, while the most visible marketing strategy of the hospital industry, is only the tip of the iceberg. Other, less obvious, marketing campaigns are directed at employers and especially at physicians, who are, after all, the main groups that determine where a patient will go for hospitalization.

Consumer Confusion

One particularly clever, if somewhat cynical, marketing strategy many of the for-profit hospital companies have adopted is bound to contribute to consumer confusion about the whole concept of the for-profit hospital industry. When naming a new acquisition, the chains will either deliberately retain the old name, including the words *community, memorial,* or even *Saint,* or will actually give such a name to a new facility at the outset, as AMI did in its Kenner, Louisiana, institution, called St. Jude Medical Center.

The fact is, even with more than one in five U.S. hospitals now in corporate hands, most people remain blissfully unaware of the change that has taken place in their local hospital—public or not-for-profit—when it is absorbed by a for-profit chain. The best evidence of this is the way people continue to perform volunteer service at such institutions, though they have become corporately owned and clearly profitable ventures. We would be surprised to see people *volunteering* to make buyers at a car dealership or travelers at an airline terminal more comfortable. Yet there they are, the volunteer ladies in pink, at hospitals owned by HCA or AMI. Yet if volunteers weren't available and these firms thought such services were required to attract patients, the corporations would *pay* for those services. How the volunteer activities got there in the first place matters little; some activities may be holdovers from before a not-for-profit hospital was purchased by a corporate chain, some may have been organized by a community, and others at the initiative of local hospital administrators. The point is that because of what hospitals used to represent, people apparently will still volunteer to work without compensation for the benefit of what is in fact a profit-making venture.

One of the smaller hospital chains, National Healthcare, demonstrated how this confusion of identity can lead to an exploitative situation in which volunteers do work to improve a hospital's ambience and community image—work that otherwise the company would have to pay to have done. Over the years, National Healthcare's selfless elderly volunteers have done everything from staffing a hospital's information desk to raising funds to recarpet halls or to landscape hospital grounds—all for free. At one point, the company boasted in *Caring* (a slick monthly public relations tabloid it printed and distributed to every household in each community where there was a National Healthcare hospital) that its so-called "Community Hospital Auxiliary" was the most active of its size in the state. As the article put it, "When someone enters our hospital the first person they usually see is an Auxiliary member who greets them with a smiling face and cheery 'Hello.' The Pink Ladies are available to provide assistance in finding certain departments for patients and locating patient rooms for visitors." From 8 a.m. to 8 p.m., they write, those "dedicated ladies" were everywhere throughout the hospital running errands for patients and their families, while "standing ready" to help the professional staff "in any way possible."

The article in *Caring* continued:

> Right here at our own facility we see evidence of their hard work demonstrated by a landscaping project. One area of the hospital grounds which was completely bare now has new shrubbery including azaleas, flowering peach and some beautiful bedding plants. In the future they intend to sow grass to complete the project. . . .

Among the "Pink Ladies" projects described in the story was a yard sale which raised over $1,000, which would be used "to replace carpet in several areas of the hospital as needed."[3]

In every instance, including this marketing of a community's charitable instincts, the hospital chains are promoting their wares. This is the case whether it's an advertisement announcing the availability of a specific type of procedure, as in the Humana or Republic ads mentioned above, or just the projection of an image of caring and quality care, as in HCA's *Smithsonian* magazine campaign, or National Healthcare's volunteer program. As for any industry's marketing, the question is: Does the industry really offer what it says it's offering? And even if it does, does the consumer need it?

Healthy Competition

Free market theory argues that competition in an industry should lead to a maximum level of consumer satisfaction and to the most efficient distribution and pricing of goods and services. Now the reality of free markets can fly in the face of academic theory (as anyone who has traveled on an American airline or who made a long-distance phone call since the deregulation of those industries knows). Nonetheless, it is on the basis of this theoretical premise of the virtue of free markets that the federal government has over the past decade tried to promote the idea of competition by enacting, for example, prospective payment for Medicare. Likewise, citing the presumed advantages of competition, many state governments have acted to end their certificate-of-need permit requirements for construction of new hospitals or improvements to old ones. The result of this deregulating of acute health care has been a free-for-all, first with new hospitals springing up during the late seventies and early eighties, even in heavily served areas, and then in the late eighties with others closing down, often leaving some regions with no acute-care facility within an hour's drive. Through the course of the 1980s, when all the experts agreed that the nation was seriously over-bedded, the hospital industry spent billions of dollars adding new beds and replacing old ones. The reasons were sometimes sound, sometimes cosmetic—a phenomenon Volunteer Trustees' Miller dubs "reactive renovation."

Let me give one illustration of the sheer waste involved in this "beautification" process. An uncle of mine, a retired physician, now is an active investor in a company that goes around buying up warehouses full of what he says is "perfectly good" equipment, ranging from X-ray machines to adjustable beds, which companies like Humana have replaced with shinier, newer models. His company is able to turn around and sell this equipment to hospitals in other countries or even in poorer communities in the U.S. That's great for the buyers, but why did perfectly good equipment have to be replaced in the first place? And who pays for that in the end?

Competition in the field of acute health care takes many forms

beyond the simple rivalry between hospitals for patients' affec-
tions and afflictions. There is competition among hospital chains
for purchase of existing hospitals. Then there is competition for
physicians, competition for contracts with employers, and even
competition for investors' confidence. For instance, in 1988 the big
hospital chains collectively spent over $1 billion buying back their
own stock to raise share values. This was at a time when none was
in a particularly enviable financial position in the first place.

In many ways, this new competitiveness has been a boon for
the middle-class health-care consumer. In sleepy little communities and even larger towns where aging hospitals were falling
behind the times in terms of medical equipment and treatment,
and where physicians were leaving to practice in the more
professionally satisfying—and more lucrative—environment of a
larger urban hospital, the chains have come in with the capital to
renovate or even to build all-new facilities. They have also brought
in up-to-date medical care and even new doctors. In urban
centers, the introduction of aggressive for-profit hospitals into
once cozy relationships among existing public and not-for-profit
hospitals has shaken up those facilities, forcing them to address
long-ignored consumer concerns like the need for palatable food,
attractive delivery rooms, et cetera.

Indeed, especially in the area of style and ambience, corporate
hospitals are setting new standards. Visiting a hospital owned by
one of the for-profit chains is a remarkable experience for someone
accustomed to the typical dingy, or at best drab, not-for-profit or
public hospital, most of which are decades old. For example, at
Century City Hospital, a major facility owned by Los Angeles–
based NME, the halls are carpeted, creating a feeling of calm and
quiet more akin to a library than a hospital, and walls are painted
in pastel hues that further strengthen the urge to communicate in
whispers. Signs saying "Quiet—Hospital" are hardly necessary
here. This 195-bed institution that caters to the well-to-do residents of Westwood, Beverly Hills, and Bel Air employs magazine
ads, which are aimed directly at potential patients. These stress
gourmet cuisine (one sample ad I was shown featured a tray with
lobster, salad, and a vase of flowers and the headline "Technically,
you'll be our patient. Emotionally, you'll be our guest"), and
privacy (another, showing a patient chart emblazoned with the word
confidential, says that at Century City Hospital, ". . . you won't have
to worry about confidentiality"). The hospital offers VIP rooms for
treatment of drug and alcohol dependency, which may explain the

privacy ad, which goes on to say that if the patient had wanted everyone "to know," he or she "would have held a press conference."

But there's another side to this hospital, which at the southern end of the Century City office-tower complex on the edge of Beverly Hills abuts a large middle- and lower-middle-class residential community. Like many proprietary hospitals these days, it has no public emergency room. In response to my anxious inquiry as we gingerly dodged oncoming traffic while jaywalking from lunch to the hospital, NME public relations representative Anthony Pace told me that someone injured in a car accident right outside the hospital doors would probably not be brought to that facility. "The ambulance services know to take them to another hospital with an emergency room," he explained matter-of-factly. You could be dying in the street on Santa Monica Boulevard, and unless you had a doctor in the adjacent NME doctors' office complex who looked out the window, saw you, and arranged for your admission, you would have to be taken by ambulance (whenever that arrived) to the UCLA Medical Center miles away.

I was relieved to reach the curb intact!

Not all for-profits dispense with emergency rooms. This is only done at facilities like Century City Hospital, where it makes good business sense. At Century City, the target market for the facility is not the local neighborhood to the south. Rather, it's the wealthier suburbs to the west and north. Encouraging walk-in patients and random ambulance drop-offs, as a nearby emergency room would inevitably do, would be to risk seeing significant numbers of Medicaid patients or, worse, patients with no insurance whatsoever.

Obviously much of what is happening in the growth of for-profit medicine is beneficial, particularly to the middle class that has the resources to pay for treatment, and that is the object of all this attention. Communities like Aransas Pass, Texas, that never before had access to hi-tech CAT-scanners or lithotriptors or liposuction devices, get them, thanks to the aggressive marketing strategies of companies like American Medical International or its spin-off EPIC Health Group.

At least until its record divestiture of 104 hospitals in 1987, some 60 percent of HCA's hospitals were the only facility in their area, and as HCA President Thomas Frist, Jr., hastens to point out, his company has poured hundreds of millions of dollars into communities where hospitals were woefully underfunded, undersized, and out-of-date. Other hospital chains have done the same, not only adding beds but also bringing in costly state-of-the-art diagnostic equipment. Such equipment is sometimes placed on semitrailer trucks and shuttled among a group of hospitals in one region owned by the same chain (certainly a positive and creative innovation).

But there is a downside to competition, too. Especially in its early stages, it can lead to enormous waste, not just in the unnecessary renovation of buildings, which may be justified as improving patients' spirits, but also the duplication of expensive equipment. Every community might arguably benefit from having a lithotriptor, magnetic resonance imager, CAT-scanner, et cetera, but do they need two, or three? Each hospital is going to amortize the costs of that equipment in higher charges, and worse still, there will be inevitable pressure on doctors to use them—and overuse them—to help cover the costs.

Playing Monopoly

Even more serious is the inevitable drive of competing companies to gain market share, even to gain a monopolistic grip on a particular health-care market. And just as competition is said to lead to better and cheaper service, monopoly tends to produce poor service and high prices. This is a lesson the community of San Luis Obispo, a college town on the craggy earthquake-prone coast of central California, learned during the mid-1980s.

Long accustomed to controversy, the people of San Luis Obispo for years had watched hordes of antinuclear activists, coming from as far away as San Francisco and Los Angeles, demonstrate and protest against the licensing and startup of the Diablo Canyon nuclear power plant. Although strong opinions on both sides of that issue were aired in town, the big concern at the time wasn't nuclear power, but health care, as the city's competing hospitals were gobbled up one by one by a giant for-profit hospital chain, American Medical International. At the outset plenty of people were happy to see a big hospital company ready to enlarge and modernize their health-care facilities, just as many people were eager for the jobs the nuclear power project would provide, and the taxes it would pay. But later, the tradeoffs became apparent in both cases.

In the end, the power company won its battle, and the

problem-plagued Diablo Canyon plant went online. But AMI lost. An administrative law judge of the Federal Trade Commission found that the company had "attempted to monopolize" the local health-care market by buying its main competitor, and the FTC later ordered the company to divest itself of French Hospital, probably the best known of its three local facilities.[4] In the process, San Luis Obispo residents learned that turning the health-care system over to the vagaries of the marketplace can spark a chain reaction of unpredictable consequences, not all of them desirable.

AMI, a new enterprise at the time, entered the local health-care market in 1968 by purchasing the 93-bed Sierra Vista Hospital. By 1972, the company had added 79 beds, making it the largest facility in San Luis Obispo, and putting pressure on the other hospitals in a community that was already awash in empty hospital beds. But AMI wasn't content with being just one of several players in the increasingly competitive local market. As part of its purchase of a smaller hospital company that same year, Chanco Medical Industries, the company acquired a second medical institution, Arroyo Grande Community Hospital, located about fifteen miles south of downtown San Luis Obispo.

Very quickly, the company found itself in a highly competitive situation. French Hospital, founded by a local doctor, Edison French, and by this point owned and run by a partnership of local doctors, began to sense that it was being threatened. French Hospital had an edge in terms of its long-standing reputation for quality medical care, and initially fought hard to attract more of the area's limited numbers of patients, through lower patient and operating room costs, lower ancillary charges, and inducements to local doctors.

Here, it must have seemed at the time, was competition in acute health-care delivery at its best. But it wasn't to last.

According to evidence obtained by the FTC, as the competition heated up, AMI's administrator at Sierra Vista began writing worried memos home to headquarters in Beverly Hills. He was overreacting to the challenge, it turns out, for in 1978, the doctors' partnership, weary of the struggle, decided to put French Hospital up for sale. AMI executives jumped at the chance to end any threat of competition. Company Vice President Norman Lofton promptly urged AMI to purchase French. In a memorandum to the firm's contract development committee, obtained by FTC lawyers,[5] he wrote, "With the French acquisition, AMI would become the prime, if not the only, provider of health-care services in the area." He added:

> While it is true that if we do not acquire French, our health-care centers in the San Luis Obispo County region will continue to operate on a viable basis; however, we face a choice of paying a premium price, thus controlling health care services, while meeting our earnings expectations, or continue (*sic*) to struggle to capture basically the same patient load with French, or another operator . . . who may purchase French.

The "other operator" that worried Lofton was apparently NME, which owned a hospital in the next community north of San Luis Obispo, and which was known to have already expressed an interest in purchasing French Hospital.

AMI did purchase French Hospital in July 1979 for $10.9 million, and competition in the San Luis Obispo hospital market halted abruptly. The takeover meant AMI had 75 percent of the region's beds, but as is often the case, its market power was even greater than that number might suggest. Its only competition was the local public hospital, San Luis Obispo General Hospital, an old, poorly equipped institution that primarily served the area's indigent population. AMI actually would have had no interest in running the public hospital out of business, since the company would then have to care for the poor of the community. Not surprisingly, where there once had been price competition between French and Sierra Vista hospitals, after the purchase of French Hospital, AMI management moved rapidly to "standardize," or in practice, according to the FTC, to raise fees at its three facilities. And doctors, who a year earlier could induce one hospital to buy new equipment by threatening to bring their patients to the competition, suddenly found their leverage gone, and their requests acted on more slowly, or rejected out of hand.

More seriously, despite relatively low occupancy rates at all three hospitals, AMI refused to negotiate a volume discount rate with the locally owned health maintenance organization, the Los Padres Group Health Plan, according to Gary Gannaway, then executive director of the plan. As he later recalled, the county hospital didn't have a full range of health services, and so, "With three of the four hospitals in the city owned by AMI, we had no negotiating room at all. With our seven thousand members, had French and Sierra Vista been owned by different companies, we would have had devastating power to negotiate lower rates. As it was, AMI just refused, even though they offer deep discounts elsewhere." In the end, the HMO proved unable to afford to pay prevailing AMI charges. It filed for bankruptcy in 1985, and San Luis Obispo residents lost an important local health insurance option.

Gannaway now claims one reason AMI may have played hardball with Los Padres Group Health was that the little HMO was "a thorn in their side: We kept raising issues about pricing, like when we pointed out that they were charging almost twice as much for open heart surgery as hospitals in Los Angeles—which is a high-cost area."

AMI executives scoff at the idea that they were out to monopolize health care in the San Luis Obispo region. They claim their monopoly situation was simply the inadvertent result of buying Chanco, though the French Hospital purchase came later. But while the FTC never proved monopolistic practices existed (under FTC regulations, only the *potential* for monopolistic practices has to be demonstrated), it nonetheless did turn up considerable evidence that monopoly *was* a goal.

In 1985, the FTC, intending to prove monopoly practices, arranged for Los Padres Group Health Plan President Dr. Robert Boyd to testify about the plan's experience with the company before the administrative law judge in Washington, D.C. After spending the whole plane ride from California to Washington rehearsing his testimony, Boyd was told he would not be called. AMI had suddenly agreed to settle—without admission of guilt. His testimony never got on the public record.

To comply with the FTC divestiture order, AMI sold French Hospital in March 1986 to Summit Health, a small for-profit hospital concern based in Los Angeles. The selling price was $22 million, twice what AMI had paid for the facility. Some competition in the area may eventually be restored—though as part of its purchase agreement with AMI, Summit won a five-year noncompetitive pledge for its cardiac care unit—but the local HMO was already gone for good. Gone too in that community is a once widely held belief that hospitals were service organizations that existed to provide health care. After the FTC case, with all the testimony about market share, eliminating competition, blocking possible acquisition of French Hospital by another hospital corporation, and the like, many people in San Luis Obispo began to view hospitals in a very different light.

"These for-profit corporations are businesses. The whole emphasis is changing. Now hospitals exist to make money," says

Amy Arsenio, a former subscriber of the erstwhile Los Padres Group Health HMO in San Luis Obispo.

Since taking over French Hospital, Summit Health has down-scaled considerably the operation of what was once the community's premier hospital. Says County Health Agency Director Dr. George Rowland, "For some reason, Summit decided to put in an alcohol dependency unit and a psychiatric treatment unit. They've reduced the number of med[ical]-surgery beds from one hundred thirty to eighty-nine, and I doubt if they even staff for that number. They still do cardiac care, but once the protective clause runs out, I don't know if they'll keep that either."

Out of Control: A Chain Reaction

Lack of community control over what services a community hospital will offer or over the continued existence of the hospital itself is another hallmark of the chaining of America's hospitals by investor-owned corporations. Even when it is part of a chain or an affiliation, it is the rare not-for-profit hospital that makes major decisions about resource allocation, capital spending, borrowing, and provision of local services without consulting community leaders. And while not-for-profit hospital boards are hardly par-agons of participatory democracy, they are much more sensitive to local concerns (or political pressure), even when these may involve money-losing operations like a burn or trauma center, than are the centralized corporate bureaucracies of the for-profit chains.

The corporate chains have attempted to mask this lack of community control by mimicking traditional forms of hospital boards, but the authority of these bodies is strictly limited. While hospital-chain executives cite the existence of such boards and speak warmly of their corporate mission, board and mission, at least in specific communities, can be dropped very quickly when times get hard. This is true of both "low cost providers" like Humana and complete providers like National Medical Enterprises.

Such was certainly the case when NME, strapped with declining admissions and forced to strengthen its financial position, suddenly announced in mid-1986 it was selling nine of its hospitals. Its emphasis then shifted from acute care to a broader mix of acute-care, psychiatric, and specialty hospitals. As Randal S. Huyser, an analyst at Montgomery Securities in San Francisco commented at the time, "They are trying to reposition the company toward what they see as high-growth areas and reduce exposure in the hospital area, which has not been doing so well in the last couple of years."

What such a "repositioning" means for the people in the communities those nine hospitals served remains to be seen. None of the nine was simply shut down, though as the industry upheaval continues, hospital closings will follow as surely as plant closings occurred in the steel and auto industries. (By most accounts, 30 to 50 percent of the hospitals in the U.S. are expected to be merged or to shut down over the next decade because of low profitability and low occupancy, even though it's clear that many of these will be needed when the baby boom population reaches retirement age. At some point, probably fairly soon, there will cease to be buyers for many of these facilities, or the amount that buyers of surplus hospitals will be willing to pay will become less than the tax writeoff available to the parent company if they are simply boarded up or demolished.) Instead NME's nine properties were sold to other hospital companies—one to a private not-for-profit institution, the other eight to smaller for-profit hospital chains—whose operational plans and "corporate missions" may well differ from NME's. Residents of some of the affected communities may notice no real difference, but one thing is certain: If they *do* find things have changed for the worse, there is little they can do about it. And if they were counting on NME to "provide for all their health-care needs" into the future, they can forget it. For their communities at least, that corporate mission changed as fast as NME's quarterly profits report.

Six of NME's hospitals—all operating in the black when NME unloaded them—were snapped up by a little Houston-based chain only a year old called Community Health Systems. Company founder and President E. Thomas Chaney explains how he expects to make his new holdings even more profitable than they were under NME's management: "We're making more money with a better mix of patients," he explains simply.

But how he plans to accomplish such a shift when each facility has traditionally been the sole provider of acute care in its outlying suburban community should give pause to local residents. Says Chaney, "We do it by telling the doctors we don't do certain things, like cataract surgery for instance." He adds, "We also have good controls so we know in advance which DRGs we make money on. When a patient comes in we identify at the front end which DRGs he has. Then we work with the doctor to make sure the patient is fully taken care of but gets out of there quickly. And we identify which physicians give us problems continually." Those physicians who do "give problems" and who have "problem" patients may leave the community to find a hospital to meet their needs in the future.

The rural communities where a smaller chain, Los Angeles–based Nu-Med, Incorporated, was the owner of the local hospitals also got a rude awakening as to how changing ownership can leave patients in the lurch. After acquiring seven new hospitals from a Florida holding company, Nu-Med decided it only wanted two. In a move that must have made local residents dizzy, Nu-Med spun off the other five to an untested hospital entrepreneur, David Vance of Batesville, Mississippi. Vance and a childhood friend, millionaire realtor Robert Gladney, moved quickly to initiate their draconian style of hospital administration after assuming ownership of their first facility. They fired and replaced every financial controller and tightened management controls, then cut back on unprofitable services. "We provide emergency room services, basic primary care and general surgery—gallbladders, appendixes, and things like that," says Vance. Each of the rural community hospitals purchased was the only one for miles around and had historically served as the basic community hospital providing all needed services. But Vance only wanted money-making operations, and to achieve this end, he says, "We've eliminated obstetrics and orthopedics at all our hospitals. Why? Because these two are the biggest areas for malpractice [lawsuits], and also obstetrics are where you get most of your Medicaid patients."

Vance's stated intent in eliminating obstetrics at his hospitals is to avoid having to treat poor people for whom reimbursement would be negligible or inadequate. If such women needed a cesarean section delivery, the hospital could wind up losing $1,500 to $2,000 even after Medicaid reimbursement. But this means even insured middle- and upper-class women will have to travel much farther when they go into labor. That's quite a loss to both the rich and poor of a community. What Vance's customers *will* get in return for enduring such cutbacks in service is probably a nice American, Caucasian doctor. In recruiting doctors to come to areas where he has hospitals, Vance explains, "I strictly avoid foreign doctors. They don't go over well in the South. You know, people want to have a warm fuzzy feeling for their doctor, and with a foreign doctor—some guy from Jamaica or India—it just doesn't happen. We're recruiting just Huckleberry Finn good-old-boy docs. They're accepted by the community." Left unaddressed are the needs of another part of the communities around Vance's five hospitals: blacks who just might be *less* comfortable with a "good old boy" doctor. And what about "good old *girls*"?

Hospital Operating Procedures: Cutting Where It Hurts

Particularly common where they are operating the only hospital in an area, service cutbacks may even be made in competitive environments, as the chains hold the managers of their individual hospital "profit centers" to strict financial performance goals. Where they can get away with it without sacrificing their image in a community, the for-profit chains also tend to cut overall services. One place this shows up often is in levels of nursing and housekeeping staffing.

Bill Hamrick, seventy, has spent most of a lifetime working in and running hospitals. A graduate of Northwestern University, where he earned a master's degree in hospital administration, he spent from 1954 to 1964 as the first administrator at Methodist Hospital in San Antonio, Texas, a classic example of the religious charity institution with a stated mission of serving poor and uninsured patients. Back in late 1985, he got a bird's-eye view of how nurse staffing is handled at one for-profit chain hospital, the local Humana facility in San Antonio, where he went to have a replacement hip operation.

"My hip surgery went beautifully, praise the Lord," says Hamrick, "and because of my background, I think I got VIP treatment at Humana, but I was still distressed at some of the things I saw there."

They weren't the kinds of things an average patient might understand, or even notice, but as a former hospital administrator, Hamrick could tell when things weren't right. Furthermore, because the nurses on the floor knew his background, several apparently felt they could unburden themselves to him. As a result, Hamrick got a quick lesson in the corporate way to run a hospital. "I had just come back to my room from surgery," he recalls. "It was just a few days before Christmas, and the patient census was way down, so the hospital typed the census figures into their computer terminal and, *whack!* just like that, they got an order back from Louisville [Kentucky, headquarters for the Humana chain], telling them to send a number of the nurses home early. It was pretty amazing, watching some computer in Kentucky determine nurse staffing in a Texas hospital, but what they did didn't make any sense at all: They let the most experienced nurses go, not the less experienced ones."

Hamrick says it was immediately clear that the remaining nurses were overworked. For one thing, because of short-staffing, the hospital was sending surgery patients directly to the floor instead of moving them first into a postoperative recovery room. Since these were people in need of a great deal of nursing attention, this staffing decision further stretched the abilities of the nurses on the floor. Hamrick soon got concrete evidence of the staffing shortage. "I had a thirteen-inch incision in my hip, and the cut muscles went into a spasm. It was terribly painful, so I called a nurse and said I needed a shot. It was 'Okay, Mr. Hamrick, I'll be right there.' Now, I'm a chronomaniac, and I looked at my watch right away. Two minutes went by without a nurse so I called again. 'Okay, I'll be there right away,' she said. After another two minutes I called again and it was the same thing. I was in terrible pain. It felt like I was going to die, so after another minute had passed I called a third time and said, 'I said come!'"

This time, the nurse's reply was, "Mr. Hamrick, I'm sorry but the keys [to the drug cabinet] aren't on the floor."

This was too much, Hamrick recalls, even for a man of considerable patience. "I'm afraid I lost my temper, which I shouldn't have done, but I was really suffering. I said, 'You know, and I know, that those keys don't leave the floor. Now are you going to get my shot, or do I call the administrator?'"

What had happened? "It turns out that the charge nurse—the one with responsibility for the drugs on the floor—had had to leave the hall to bring a patient down to be discharged. The surgery floor was so short-staffed that there was no one else to go! That should never have happened. It's either gross mismanagement or understaffing . . . probably C, all of the above."

Most patients and visitors probably would have attributed the long response time to a lazy nurse. Hamrick believed otherwise: "When you run a hospital like that," he says, "with a central office telling you to cut nursing staff by the numbers, what they're doing is skimming the profits off the top for the people in charge."

It may be that the staffing choices made that particular night at Humana were just badly handled at the local level, but with Louisville determining the gross numbers, local managers were obviously operating within tight constraints. (As at most of the big chains, local managers of Humana hospitals are held to standards of profitability that could easily lead them to let more experienced and not, incidentally, higher-paid staff off early.)

In general, when a corporate hospital chain takes over a hospital, it reduces the level of nursing staff, surely the primary ingredient in establishing the level of patient care. Such cuts are not readily discernable to patients, which may be one reason nurses are a particular target of corporate cost cutters.

Accentuating the Positive

At AMI, a reduced level of nursing staff is presented in a positive light. Jean Settlemyre, the group vice president for management development at AMI until 1988 and a former nurse and one-time director of nursing at an AMI hospital, explained how this works. "When hospitals were running at seventy-five percent occupancy, no modifications were made. But when occupancy dropped to sixty or fifty percent, the cost of doing business wasn't dropping."

The way the company eventually dealt with lower occupancy at many of its hospitals was to experiment with eliminating nurse's aides, turning all nursing duties over to registered nurses. This approach was sold to potential patients in local communities, who were told that all their in-hospital care would be provided by skilled professionals, which sounds good. The reality can be something else, though, even if having RNs change bedpans and give bed baths does reduce overall labor costs.

Says one former AMI nurse, "On paper the idea [of all primary nurses] sounds good, but remember, it means your only backup is another nurse, and when you're giving that thirty-minute bed bath, your other patients are having no one looking after them. It's an enormous amount of work." In fact, since nurses were being forced to do the work of nurse's aides, the cut in nurse's aides amounted to a cut in nurse staffing levels.

In the end, at her particular hospital, nurse's aides were hired again because overworked RNs were reportedly resigning in droves. (Apparently, the community outside the hospital also came to recognize what was really going on and started talking about "such short staffing at AMI that the nurses have to take out the garbage themselves.") But across the country, and even at AMI hospitals, experiments continue in trying to reduce nursing staff to keep labor costs at a minimum. A National Institutes of Health study of for-profit medicine reported a 1986 survey conducted by the AMA in which, though gross nursing staff levels varied little between for-profit and not-for-profit chains in the aggregate, only 48 percent of physicians whose primary hospital was part of an investor-owned chain thought their facility's nursing support was better than at other hospitals with which they were familiar. At hospitals owned by not-for-profit chains or consortiums, the figure was 60 percent.

At Humana hospitals, another cost-cutting approach is widely used: the hiring of registry nurses, people who, like temporary secretaries, work for an agency, not for the hospital itself. This has the advantage of flexibility as well as freedom from fixed labor costs in the form of fringe benefits, including health insurance. If the daily patient census drops at a hospital, fewer nurses are hired without there being any penalty in the form of unemployment compensation to those let go.

The trade-off is patient care. Not that registry nurses aren't good nurses, but every hospital is different, and doctors rely on nurses for reports on their patients' conditions—something that requires continuity. Even AMI's Settlemyre, acknowledging that some AMI hospitals, acting on their own local administrators' initiative, rely on registry nurses, says, "It is my theory that registry nurses are the single largest hazard to the safety of patients. I know that every nurse that goes to work for a registry has the highest level of concern for patients' care, but when you put these nurses in the stressful, high-pressure environment of a strange hospital, and have them seeing new patients every day, the potential for error is enormous. It's a misallocation of resources."

Former hospital administrator Hamrick has a particularly interesting theory about the corporate chains' emphasis on RN staffs, whether salaried or hired from registries. "It has nothing to do with providing a higher level of care to patients," he says. "It's just a way of cutting back on labor costs. A trained RN will never give patients bad care. They'll just work until they drop. You can't cut housekeeping staff or maintenance crews or even nurse's aides without getting poor results, but you can overwork the RNs. If you're going to abuse a group of workers without unduly affecting the care of patients, that's the one to do it to."

What Hamrick observed during his stay in a Humana hospital was a typical centralized corporate bureaucracy at work. No longer is the institutional imperative simply survival and growth, as it was in the traditional not-for-profit and even the independent, doctor-owned for-profit hospital. Stockholders aren't just interested in earning a dividend on their shares; they want the value of their shares to grow, which in turn drives each chain to expand its revenue base, as well as improve its earnings. The chain is hardly just a benign corporate overlay on an unchanging system of individual hospital units, as local corporate hospital managers have to worry about investor reaction to each quarterly report.

Humana Chairman David Jones stated clearly the view of his corporation on the matter of corporate versus local control in a 1985 address to the alumni association of the Hospital and Health Care Administration of the University of Minnesota School of Public Health. Referring to the company's operation of the University of Louisville Medical School teaching hospital, now called Humana Hospital-University, he said:

> These alliances don't have a prayer of being significant competitors unless there is the willingness to surrender enough sovereignty on all the participants' parts to create enough authority in one body, the governing body. If you don't approach it that way, all you do is create a federation. Why doesn't Blue Cross own the world of health-care insurance today? Because they are a federation with seventy-seven or seventy-nine different organizations.[6]

Having central authority is what Humana's hospital system is all about.

Other hospital companies have varying perspectives on the appropriate degree of centralization (and none of the larger chains are as tightly run by the home office as Humana, which by 1989 was reportedly trying to save money on registries by shuttling nurses from one hospital site to another by air). Still, it remains true that the corporate chains are all far more centrally directed than the not-for-profit hospitals, even those not-for-profits that have joined such federations as the Voluntary Hospitals of America (VHA) or Associated Health Systems (AHS). If the investor-owned chains' corporate headquarters don't all set employment levels on a daily basis, they do determine longer-range policy, particularly where financial matters are concerned. And even at such companies as Hospital Corporation of America or American Medical International, which tout their decentralized management systems, employees report that visits from home office staff and memos on operating procedure and staffing levels are frequent.

Gains and Losses: A Corporate Hospital Balance Sheet

Nor is this corporatization of hospitals just a matter of nurse-to-patient ratios. Whether it's a matter of copying the auto industry in laying off workers every time the assembly line slows, or copying the entertainment industry in acquiring the competition, hospitals are increasingly big business these days. And when a big business, with larger corporate interests paramount, moves into a community, it may solve one local problem but create many more, as when a big chemical company creates jobs but also toxic wastes.

Most of the critics of the trend toward investor-owned hospital chains have focused on the issue of health care for the poor, instead of looking at the whole picture. As Victor Sidel, past president of the American Public Health Association and chairman of the department of social medicine at Montefiore Medical Center in New York City, put it in an interview, "I suppose there are questions about whether the average insured middle-class patient will get equally good care at an investor-owned hospital, but really, it's hard to prove over the short run that these companies will hurt that group of people. What you *can* say is that if the average patient benefits from the shift to investor-owned, it will be purely by chance. The real argument against these companies has to be a societal one. They are moving us towards a two-tiered health system, in which the poor will get less good care. It's not just that society will pay more in the long run, which it will because poor people will increasingly put off treatment until they are much sicker. The real argument must be that we don't want to have an unjust society. And that's what you get if you have public medicine for the poor and private medicine for the rest."

Indeed, there are many, including fierce critics of the current direction of hospital care and ownership, who argue that the middle class stands to *benefit* from it all, after a fashion. Economist Uwe Reinhardt (a critic of America's lack of commitment to treatment of the poor, but usually a defender of the investor-owned, for-profit chains) in the February 27, 1985, issue of the *Princeton Alumni Weekly*, wrote, with ill-concealed cynicism:

> Before the decade is out, our nation will be dotted with veritable medical boutiques—hospitals and ambulatory-care centers—offering their (paying) customers not only high-quality care, but also amenities hitherto unheard of in health care. There will be hospitals with exquisite atriums, with gourmet food, with personalized services, and with all of the other good things America's well-to-do enjoy elsewhere in life. For otherwise healthy but slightly-less-than-perfect Yuppies there will be periodic "surgi-sales," in which surgical perfections will be crafted upon the Yuppies' bodies, all within the context of an otherwise fun-filled holiday for Yuppie and consort. And for business executives and investment bankers there will be sumptuous VIP suites in hospitals offering all imaginable fineries, including orchids with breakfast, personal secretaries, hairdressers and manicurists, a personal concierge at the patient's beck and call, and, last but not least, state-of-the-art medical care.

Most of Reinhardt's "future" has indeed come to pass, at least in sample form, as witness NME's Century City Hospital menus; the many VIP suites offered by for-profit hospitals; or AMI's much ballyhooed health services mall in Irvine, California, where paying patients can find not just a hospital and every conceivable ambulatory service, but health spas and shopping to boot. AMI calls it "the hospital of the future."

Is that good health care? That's another question. Republic Health, one of the midsized hospital chains, has its New Beginnings program for cosmetic, or what the company calls corrective, surgery. Another company offers a free hairstyling with a face-lift or nose job.

Traditionally, the view of the medical profession was that unnecessary surgery was to be avoided. Are these necessary services? And is advertising aimed at patients' personal insecurities really just providing information to educate the consumer, or is it manipulation?

Doctor Dependence

Reinhardt argues that as long as the physician remains independent of the hospital and is thus able to act as the advocate of the patient, there is no problem, but he says he is not sanguine about such a situation prevailing. "The real threat to health care is when the doctors' and the hospitals' interests become aligned against the interests of the patient. It's possible that the corporations could usurp the physicians' power," he says.

In fact, they are already doing so, and compelling all hospitals, even those that traditionally existed to serve doctors, to follow suit or risk losing the physicians upon whom they must depend for bringing patients in the door. While seemingly innocuous, the competitive deals developed by hospital firms in their efforts to lure the physician to practice at particular hospitals often tend to put the physicians in league with the hospital against the patient. That is surely the worst news of all for the American health consumer.

It's probably no news to anyone that under the fee-for-service system of health care, physicians have traditionally had a direct pecuniary interest in providing the most costly treatment possible. But the medical profession has worked hard at establishing itself as something more than just another group of businessmen, by adopting licensing procedures for schools and practitioners and by developing ethical standards. Patients have consequently come to assume, and indeed have demonstrated in court, that physicians have a personal and fiduciary responsibility to their patients that overrides monetary concerns. While examples abound of physician malpractice and outright corruption at the expense of patient health, that assumption still prevails.

Hospitals, at least so far, have the same legal responsibility to provide the best care possible to patients—at least to the ones that they agree to admit. But can one expect the relationship between a physician and a patient also to work in the case of an institution and a patient, especially if there is strong countervailing fiscal pressure working against the patient's interests? And do patients realize that third parties—the hospital and, if it is not part of the hospital company, the insurance company—are wooing and blackmailing the physician to stray from that once more or less monogamous physician-patient relationship?

That's not to say that making money and caring for those suffering from disease or injury cannot occur at the same time. The current level of physician income in a country where the quality of health care, at least for those who can get it, remains among the best in the world attests to that apparent compatibility. But the two objectives *can* and increasingly *do* clash. And where the institutional priority is making money and showing quarter-to-quarter earnings growth, as it must be in the case of shareholder-owned corporations, that imperative may interfere with the quality of the product being delivered. There is, in other words, little reason to assume that a hospital corporation will behave much differently from a car manufacturer, a building contractor, or a defense firm where the interests of the consumer are concerned.

One thing is clear: Despite all the talk about increased competition, the trend seems to be, ironically, *away* from freedom of choice for consumers. Doctors are becoming answerable to hospital managers and insurance companies, hospitals are becoming answerable to investors (often insurance companies!), and hospital chains are bidding for restrictive health-care contracts with employers to set up "managed care" systems.

Whether it's David Jones at Humana talking about the need for central authority, or Shamrock Investments' Charles Reilly, formerly of AMI, saying that health care needs to be made into a "seamless system," control over our health is rapidly passing from the local doctor and community hospital—and from government—into the hands of corporate executives. Instead of working out treatment strategies with their physicians, patients will increasingly—and usually unwittingly—be plugged into "systems" that will determine where and how much care they will have for a particular ailment, unless they have the independent resources to pay for whatever care they wish. Says Henry Werronen, former head of Humana's insurance division and now an independent health-care industry consultant in New York, "By the early 1990s, I think it's fair to say that most people will be in some kind of managed health-care plan."

Yet it is perhaps instructive, and ominous, that not one official in the White House or Congress, where policies are being made that encourage the establishment and expansion of for-profit medicine, has opted for a health plan, like an HMO or a PPO, that limits freedom of choice of doctor, hospital, or course of treatment, or places a cap on the amount reimbursed for a particular treatment.

For theoretical and ideological reasons, many experts have automatically accepted as a given that the application of market incentives and discipline to hospital care would mean improved service to consumers. In its landmark 1986 study of the issue, the National Institute of Medicine, while conceding that the available means for measuring quality of care are "rudimentary," concluded that the difference between for-profit and not-for-profit hospitals was negligible.[7] Still, the study, *For-Profit Enterprise in Health Care*, cautions in its chapter on quality of care that:

> Evidence now available does not support the fear that for-profit health care is incompatible with quality of care. . . . However, as with many other topics in this report, the past may not predict the future. . . . Although there are many differences from hospitals, evidence from nursing homes is not reassuring regarding how investor-owned institutions will behave if profits require that quality be traded off against cost.[8]

"What is developing is fundamentally a system of rationing health care," says Chicago internist Quentin Young, a professor of preventive medicine and community health at the University of Illinois College of Medicine and president of the Health and Medicine Policy Research Group. "Americans—patients and physicians—have been running frightened from a phantom of nationalized medicine, when they're going to be gobbled up instead by corporate medicine."

4

Physicians in Corporate Hospitals: Doctors Faust, Patients Last?

Now in order to succeed as health-care providers the corporations needed the cooperation, conscious or otherwise, of physicians, for hospitals and nursing homes become populated when physicians consign patients to them. The conquest (by gentle persuasion, of course) of the medical profession by corporations was therefore a vital step in the operation.
　　　　　　　—Stanley Wohl, M.D.,
　　　　　　　　in *The Medical Industrial Complex*

Conflicts of interest are commonplace in the professions. Nowhere are the consequences more serious than in medicine. Here conflicts lead directly to death and injury for which satisfactory accountability is usually nonexistent.
　　　　　　　—Morton Mintz and Jerry S. Cohen
　　　　　　　　in *Power Inc.*

The American Medical Association, with almost 300,000 physician members in 1990 (each of whom pays $400 a year in membership dues), is one of the most powerful lobbying organizations in America, with offices in every state capital, and a political staff of forty in Washington. It is one of the biggest spenders of PAC (political action committee) funds in national politics, and doesn't hesitate to take on the federal government when it feels doctors' incomes are at stake. In 1978 it successfully fought against President Carter's hospital cost containment bill, and in 1982 it beat back an effort by Reagan's Federal Trade Commission to assert jurisdiction over the medical profession in antitrust matters.

But on September 22, 1985, the giant trade association turned its guns on a much smaller target, the Paracelsus Healthcare Corporation, a German-owned chain of twenty U.S. (and thirty-eight foreign) hospitals headquartered in Pasadena, California. What aroused the ire of the AMA? It seems that the relatively small privately held for-profit hospital company was offering cash rewards to affiliated physicians who kept services to a minimum, including length of stay for elderly patients on Medicare. This, of course, boosted the company's own profits, thanks to the new DRG fixed-rate reimbursement system for Medicare payments to hospitals. Paracelsus was reportedly paying monthly bonuses as high as $825 to its staff physicians for, in effect, giving less care.[1]

Why did bonuses like that bother the AMA, an organization that has, among other things, traditionally acted to maintain and improve physicians' earning power? According to the AMA, the bonuses, which Paracelsus called a "physicians' sharing cost savings program," can prove to be a kind of Faustian bargain or, in the words of AMA Executive Vice President James Sammons, "an attempt to encourage physicians to act out of selfish economic interests rather than their primary concern for patient care."[2] In other words, using bonuses as a kind of carrot, a hospital firm could influence the way doctors practice. And whether by stick or carrot, the AMA doesn't want doctors' decision-making power over health care to be diluted.

In the view of the AMA, the payments to doctors by Paracelsus constituted a kind of "kickback," something the company vehemently denies. As company attorney Donald Goldman put it, "What they [the AMA] are concerned about is that the quality of care does not suffer, and it hasn't."[3]

At the urging of the AMA, Richard P. Kusserow, inspector general of the U.S. Department of Health and Human Services, began a probe of operations at Paracelsus in 1986. The company ultimately pleaded guilty to mail fraud and agreed to pay the government $4.5 million in fines, penalties, and restitution for improper billings to Medicare—billings for things like Dom Pérignon champagne and country club memberships for executives, expenses for domestic acquisitions, gifts to physicians, and the like. The issue of kickback payments to doctors was dropped as moot when Congress, reacting to publicity about the Paracelsus case, passed a law that same year making physician bonuses tied to care of *individual* patients illegal. Annual bonuses for all physicians, or bonuses tied to savings on overall care of patients, remain legal under the new law.

Hospitals Want Power over Medical Care

Looked at broadly, it seems that the AMA jumped on Paracelsus because of a growing awareness that hospitals are beginning to apply pressure on physicians to alter the way they practice medicine in order to enhance revenues and profits for the hospital. As Dr. James Todd, president of the AMA and the association's representative on both the National Institute of Medicine's Committee on Implications of For-Profit Enterprise in Health Care and the board of directors of the Federation of American Health Systems, observed at the time, "The game plan on the part of the hospitals is to get physicians locked in to a particular system. Ultimately that means employee status."

Such a servile future for physicians seems improbable only because their economic and social position is relatively high compared to the general patient population. But believe it or not, times are becoming increasingly hard for the nation's half million doctors, at least in a relative sense. As a result, it *is* possible to apply economic pressure on at least some of them. Although established physicians may be relatively wealthy with their six-figure incomes, no one likes to see his or her standard of living *decline*.* And a growing number of doctors find they can no longer routinely expect their earnings to rise annually, even though health-care costs continue to surge ahead (at a 10.7 percent annual clip between June 1989 and June 1990, according to the U.S. Bureau of Labor Statistics). As a Los Angeles orthopedist reports,

---

*The vigorous lobbying by special interests representing the wealthiest members of society during the writing of the 1986 Tax Reform Act, and subsequent lobbying for special new loopholes after its passage into law, clearly demonstrate that even the truly rich can be particularly sensitive to loss of income.

"Most doctors I know since at least five years ago have been advising their kids not to go into medicine. Why? Look at me. My income has remained constant over the last six years. With inflation though, that means I've lost thirty percent of my income because my costs have skyrocketed. And it's not just malpractice [insurance premiums]. Office rent has soared, employee costs are higher, and now my payments are going down. Look, don't pass the hat! I'm doing all right, but my disposable income has gone down. And that's common."

No doubt about it, doctors are feeling threatened. And efforts are underway, both within the health-care industry and in Washington, to reduce substantially their actual share of the health-care dollar from the twenty cents they currently get. Paracelsus is only a minor actor in the investor-owned hospital industry, which is playing one of the major roles in this campaign to remove money from physicians' pockets and shift it into hospital coffers.

As *Medical Economics*, a respected trade journal for physicians, reported in a November 1985 cover article on the growing economic power of hospital chains:

> In the worst-case scenario—and you don't have to be totally paranoid to conceive of it—one of the big [hospital] chains might acquire such a dominant position in a particular market area that it could lock doctors into its own delivery system, putting them on salary if it chose. Any doctors it didn't need would be locked out—and hungry.[4]

That's an extreme vision, and the article went on to say that it was "highly unlikely" that doctors would so thoroughly lose their bargaining power. It is nonetheless clear that a shift in power is occurring, hastened by the growing surplus of doctors in many specialties. Toward that end, hospitals are seeking to reduce the authority and autonomy of the physician. Even though at first glance the physician incentive plans being offered by hospitals might seem remote from issues like control over patient care, they must be seen in that light.

Charles Reilly, former executive vice president for corporate development at AMI and now a private health-industry investor in Los Angeles, explained the hospital industry's view of the evolving situation to me this way:

Look at the health-care system today. There is a pool of potential patients. The traditional pattern of referring patients to providers relied on random methods, usually starting with a physician, and *that* was the source of physician economic power. Now as concern about cost control increased, government, business, and the other providers of health care have become more interested in using *their* economic power to deal with it. That gave rise to the PPOs [preferred provider organizations), HMOs [health maintenance organizations], et cetera, all of which serve to reduce that pool of potential patients by routing one group or another through a [specific] system.

So what's happened between hospitals and physicians? The traditional role was that hospitals served not only patients, but also physicians, creating inducements for physicians to bring their patients to the hospital. As hospitals have begun to participate in organizations such as Humana Care Plus or an HMO, then, in a sense, the organizations with which they are affiliated are going out and getting the patients.

It reverses the roles. The hospital is now bringing patients to the doctors. Now, if it were a simple reversal, you would have a battle, and much of the concern expressed by physicians [about the hospital companies] is due to a perception that this is what's happened. But it hasn't. Actually, it's just an added dimension. Hospitals will continue to serve patients brought in by physicians. The roles need not conflict, but they will require more cooperation than the traditional role of customer and supplier.

"Our goal is not to hire doctors," asserted Robert A. Reeves, president of HCA Insurance Services, the medical insurance arm of the Hospital Corporation of America. "I consider doctors to be independent businessmen." Of course, that doesn't mean HCA doesn't want to influence the way doctors do their business, but as Reeves said, "I always say it's a lot easier to ride a horse in the direction he wants to go." His choice of metaphor subconsciously demonstrates how much times have changed: While doctors used to be in the saddle where health care was concerned, now hospitals are holding the reins. The doctor has become a vehicle of sorts in this construct.

Every hospital management pays homage to the central role of the physician in health care, and insists that it's not about to tell the doctor how to prescribe medicine. Yet my efforts to learn from doctors how they like practicing at investor-owned chain facilities elicited almost universally fearful responses or no responses at all, unless the physician was offered by the chain for the interview. Rightly or wrongly, doctors with staff privileges at for-profit chain hospitals—in dramatic contrast with their more voluble colleagues at public or not-for-profit private facilities—refuse to criticize "their" institutions on the record, claiming they fear reprisals. Many, indeed, are so fearful they refuse to talk at all. Others point out that a hospital company can ruin a physician by simply saying all beds are full or that the operating room is booked. A doctor who has built a practice in the vicinity of a particular hospital, and who may even be getting help with malpractice insurance premiums or office expenses from the company, is especially vulnerable.

Why are hospitals trying to gain control over physicians? It's not simply a turf battle. Rather, hospitals have realized that physicians are critical to their bottom-line results. On the one hand, the right physician can steer large numbers of paying patients into a hospital, hence the desire to lock physicians into specific facilities. An example of how this works *in extremis* is provided by a former corporate hospital chain employee who worked as a nurse in "utilization review," watchdogging the activities of staff doctors at a hospital in a very competitive region. She reports that one particular physician there almost single-handedly filled the institution's beds with lucrative Medicare patients. "They'd actually call him to tell him if they had a lot of empty beds, and he'd fill them," the source reports, "and I know for a fact that he admits one hundred fifty percent more then he should, on the basis of high blood-pressure readings and the like. We knew that, but if that one physician took his patients away, the hospital would close." (The utilization review procedure was originally designed to prevent unnecessary hospitalization and treatment.)

On the other hand, the wrong physician, or even a very busy physician with the "wrong" kind of patients—very sick and underinsured—can wind up costing a hospital a lot of money, hence the effort to gain control over which physicians can use a hospital and over how staff physicians do their job once there.

Historically, Doctors Were in Control

Traditionally, in the hospital-physician nexus, physicians wielded enormous power, particularly where patient-care issues and doctors' earning power were directly involved. Medical policy was set by staff committees that were elected by hospital staffs—physicians who, in the typical voluntary hospital, were self-employed doctors with admitting privileges at a particular facility. Who got admitted to a hospital staff was also determined by medical staff committees, making power self-perpetuating. Until recently, by most accounts, such hospitals (and even more clearly, the proprietary hospitals founded and owned by physicians) were run for the benefit and convenience of physicians. Even in public hospitals owned by government agencies, where significant numbers of doctors were actually on salary as government employees, the tradition of physician control prevailed.

As Paul Starr convincingly argues in his book *The Social Transformation of American Medicine*, doctors began running hospitals around the turn of the century, assuming control from the wealthy trustees who had founded them. Later, as hospitals grew in size and complexity, doctors began having to share power, or vie for it, with hospital administrators. Physicians initially achieved their central role for good reasons, says Starr. Sociologically they had developed professional authority where medical issues were concerned. Economically, their power stemmed from their ability to bring in the revenues of paying patients. As Starr puts it:

> Unlike [most] corporations [in the late nineteenth century] . . . hospitals saw authority devolve more upon outside professionals, the medical staff, rather than upon [their] own salaried management. This peculiarity of organization arose because of the special role that outside doctors came to play in the prosperity of the institution: They had replaced the trustees as the chief source of income. When hospitals relied on donations, the trustees were vital. But as hospitals came to rely on the receipts from patients, the doctors who brought in the patients inevitably became more important to the organization's success.[5]

Later, hospital administrators began to gain equivalent power because of the complexities of hospital management. Exclusively medical concerns, however, were left until recently to the staff committees, which were the strict preserve of the doctor. Writes Starr:

> The absence of integrated management [of the entire hospital system] made it incumbent upon individual hospitals to develop a more elaborate administration than hospitals in other countries where administrative functions are more centralized. . . . Each hospital had to raise its own funds for capital expenditures, set its own fees, do its own purchasing, recruit staff, determine patients' ability to pay, collect bills and conduct public relations efforts. All these activities required staff, money and space. At the same time, the American system of attending physicians (doctors who are "on staff" at a hospital, but are not employees of that hospital, and as such are free to set their own hours, fees, et cetera) also created demands for more administration. . . .
>
> So, paradoxically, as a result of the independence of both hospitals and doctors from higher bureaucratic authority, hospital administration became professionalized.[6]

Now, it might be argued, the for-profit hospital corporations have brought the system full circle. They have turned local hospital administrators into little more than paid managers of individual "profit centers," relegated physicians to the de facto role of employees, and given power to top management in the central corporate office and ultimately to shareholders (such as investment banks and pension funds)—the corporate analog of the nineteenth-century trustees.

The advent of corporate hospital chains has actually produced a fundamentally new system, while generally preserving the facade of traditional hospital management, something that has led many observers to conclude incorrectly that there is little difference in the way for-profit and not-for-profit hospitals are run. The essential difference between the two hospital types, however, is the creation of a new bureaucratic layer atop the old management chart at the corporate chains: the central, or home, corporate executive office. Even in the most decentralized corporate systems such as that at Hospital Corporation of America, it is there that most financial decisions are made, as are most other policy decisions regarding quality of care, staffing levels, hiring and firing of top management, and the like. (Even HCA said it presents local hospital administrators with weekly performance evaluations, showing managers how their operation is measuring up against corporate goals for the facility. The message for a local HCA administrator is unambiguous.)

The old medical staff committees still exist at the individual hospital level of most corporate chains. Where these once wielded (and reportedly in not-for-profit facilities for the most part still wield) serious power, however, their influence is now greatly reduced. Routine medical issues as well as larger issues such as institutional goals and financial operations are now largely removed from local control.

As evidence of the altered situation, Baruch College's Luanne Kennedy says, "One of the things I've observed just among my own graduate students is that the corporate chains are hiring people with an MBA or accounting degree and two to three years' experience to be the chief financial officer of a typical one-hundred-bed hospital, and paying them low to midrange salaries."

They can get away with hiring people with such little experience, maintains Kennedy, because "in a corporate chain the local CFO is just collecting data and filling in the blanks. Financial *policy* is being made centrally. The same situation exists when it comes to CEOs [chief executive officers, usually the top administrator position at a hospital]." The voluntary hospitals are a completely different story, she says. "In the not-for-profit hospitals—even the more centralized of the church-owned chains—there is not a financial policy being made centrally for each hospital. The central office role is more advisory, with targets being set locally. So the top positions at those hospitals can't be given to people with little or no experience."

What does all this mean where physician power over healthcare issues is concerned? "If the financial future and organizational structure of a hospital is being decided at corporate headquarters," explains Kennedy, "then the physicians or the medical committee can ask the CEO for something, but that CEO cannot say yes without asking headquarters. Decisions on physicians' needs certainly won't be made simply on the basis of medical need where that's the case. Instead, financial considerations will dominate."

There's another way to observe how the power relationship is changing. In the traditional (not-for-profit) hospital a foundation was first established, incorporated under nonprofit legal status, and run by an appointed board of community leaders, usually including several physicians. Doctors in the community formed a staff committee to set medical policy and control physician access to the facility. The board, usually with the concurrence of the medical staff, then hired an administrator to run the institution, and that was it. Since all business at the hospital came through the referrals of physicians with staff privileges there, the administrator and the hospital board could be expected to be solicitous of their concerns and needs. (As a matter of fact, the traditional deference of not-for-profit hospital boards to staff physicians has been the target of criticism by some advocates of marketplace medicine, like Professor Regina Herzlinger at the Harvard School of Business Administration and Professor Uwe Reinhardt at Princeton, who claim with some validity that this solicitude has led to higher-cost health care.)

In contrast, when a corporate chain builds a hospital, it approaches the physicians or physician groups it wants practicing there, considering both their competence and reputation on the one hand, and their potential impact on hospital revenues on the other. Where the chain purchases an existing institution, instead of building one from the ground up, it may start off working with the established physician staff, but should it feel the staff is incompetent or is unable to generate enough revenue, it doesn't hesitate to force people out and bring new doctors on board. As a top executive at AMI confided during a visit to corporate head-quarters, "Some of the hospitals we've purchased have been pretty awful. I wouldn't want to have gone to them. But we've replaced the incompetent physicians and brought in good people in most of them."

David Vance, founder and president of First Health, a three-hospital chain based in Alabama, gave a more detailed illustration of how this kind of recruiting and winnowing process works. After recounting how he had recruited a number of family practice physicians to the rural areas where his hospitals were located, providing them with office space and guaranteeing them first-year incomes of $60,000 to $75,000 (a bargain since, he claims, each physician is worth $250,000 in business to the hospital), Vance then described how he got rid of several physicians already practicing at several locations. "If you got a dud, you run into all kinds of problems if you just try to throw him out," he said. "But you can make his life hell and drive him away. You can give him scheduling problems. You can ride the hell out of him on medical records requirements. You can terrorize him with audits. Eventually he'll leave."

The point here is not that allegedly incompetent physicians are being ousted from medical staffs, which no one would complain about. But the other side of the coin is that corporate managers, who, like Vance, rarely have medical credentials, are able to make such determinations and to use their own criteria in determining who's a "dud." The medical profession has traditionally been self-regulating because government bureaucrats were considered unable to do so. Now, for better or worse, particularly in the for-profit hospital chains, that power is passing into the hands of corporate bureaucrats. Are they likely to be any more competent at regulating medical practice than their government counterparts? Probably not.

There have been calls for some time among health advocates for more patient control over health care, and to the extent that physicians' loss of power and authority reflects enhanced patient knowledge and control, it is probably a positive development. The passing of such power from physicians to corporate bureaucracies, however, is not necessarily in the patient's best interest. Indeed, while such a shift could conceivably lead to lower costs over the short run (a case that remains to be demonstrated), it may well prove in the final analysis to be a distinctly negative development for the patient/consumer.

Carrots and Sticks: The Recruiting of Physicians

Some fifty years ago, doctors were seen as essential to hospital profitability because of their role as patient "feeders." Now, however, although still important as generators of revenue, they are also part of the cost side of the equation. They affect profitability not directly as employees, perhaps, but indirectly in the type of patient they bring to the facility. Health-care analysts point out that a hospital makes most of its money during the early days of a patient's stay, when large numbers of tests are run and any surgery is performed. The postoperative recovery days are far less remunerative. Particularly after an operation, the patient usually requires more nursing care, further reducing net earnings on the bed. Accordingly it is generally better for a hospital's earnings if doctors bring in patients for short stays. This becomes even more important when, as with Medicare, the hospital is reimbursed for a set number of days per illness, and loses money on sicker patients who have to stay longer. (Because room charges cannot be camouflaged on a bill, hospitals typically keep these artificially low—a tendency that has further enhanced the relative profitability of short stays.)

In a period of low or declining patient admissions and government limits on reimbursements, all hospitals must be able to control costs wherever possible, especially if over and above operating costs and funds for needed replacement and modernization they must earn a profit for shareholders. As long as health-care costs could be passed on to consumers—whether individual patients, taxpayers, or employers—with impunity, the loose management structure, with its multiple lines of authority, typical of American public and not-for-profit hospitals, was acceptable. Even the for-profit chains could be relaxed in their relationship with staff physicians. Then beginning in the late 1970s, government, insurers, businesses, and patients themselves began to object to cost-is-no-object health care. As hospital costs began to rise annually at a double-digit pace, adding seriously to employers' labor costs, the traditional system of hospital management had to go. For many of the old not-for-profit hospitals, this was a wrenching transition. But for the corporate chains, where, as in the rest of corporate America, the management structure is unambiguously hierarchical, there was no question about what needed to be done: Doctors had to be put in a subservient role to hospital administrators.

Whether by carrot or by stick, hospital companies recognize that if they want to control costs, they must gain the upper hand in determining how—and how much—care is delivered to patients, and even which patients will be treated at all. Choosing which doctors will practice at the hospital is increasingly being determined by the corporate chains—through hospital medical committees to be sure, but committees that the company has a major role in selecting, and on which management often has representation.

As in most of the dramatic changes taking place in acute health care today, the for-profit hospital chains are leading the way in devising new ways to influence and control physician practice. "There's nothing that we have done that any voluntary hospital couldn't do. They just haven't done it," says David Jones of Humana.

Jones may exaggerate however, for some things are beyond the ability of even the largest not-for-profit institutions because of community resistance or lack of an adequately broad patient base. One example is the corporations' power to completely change the mission of a particular institution from providing full acute-care services to acting as an emergency and secondary-care center, or set up a company-owned medical insurance subsidiary. And, as Starr notes, "The corporate chains *are* able to move much more rapidly to take advantage of the changing political and economic environment."

Where physicians are concerned, the goal of the pioneering for-profit corporate hospital industry is to reverse the traditional relationship which had medical staffs running hospitals. In the new power relationship, doctors will be in the position of serving the needs of hospital management and ultimately of shareholders in the corporation. This will inevitably compel physicians to place the bottom-line financial considerations of the company above patient care, or even their own economic self-interest.

One physician who says he resigned as medical director of a Charter Medical hospital over the issue of physician control over patient treatment, and who also worked at an HCA facility in Georgia, says, "I left both places because I hated to see what was happening. Charter, which started out with a philosophy of wanting to make people well, as it became a shareholder-owned business, run by a bunch of people with management degrees, started putting making money first. It's okay for businesses to be businesses, but I always thought the way you did it was to provide quality service, and then the profits would follow. These companies aren't satisfied with that approach, though. They've got hospital administrators dictating treatment—admissions, discharge, and even treatment itself."

While the major hospital chains aren't all necessarily following Paracelsus's lead in making overt cash rewards to physicians who help bring treatment of elderly patients in under DRG reimbursement schedules, they *are* influencing the thinking and practice of affiliated physicians just as effectively in other ways.

One popular "carrot" being used by hospital companies is to offer physicians joint-venture business arrangements, which effectively align physicians' interests with those of the hospital. Particularly common is the joint ownership by a hospital and a physician, or physician group, of some expensive medical equipment, like a CAT scan device or a lithotriptor for sonic removal of kidney stones. NME has been a leader in applying this approach. More recently (during what many thought was an unsuccessful attempt to take over the company), a major holder of AMI stock, Florida financier M. Lee Pearce, began increasing his holdings and urging other major AMI shareholders to press the company to expand joint-venture operations with physicians.

A second approach has been the joint operation of free-standing outpatient emergency-care centers, such as Humana's Med-First operation. Typically, the hospital finances and owns the facility, and a doctors' group operates it, with referrals going to the hospital partner in the arrangement. In the early to middle 1980s, Humana aggressively installed patients directly into its hospitals, as a challenge to existing local physicians. It only stopped the project when it found that Med-First was a money loser, at which point the subsidiary was sold. In one case, in Greensboro, North Carolina, local health officials say Humana backed off after local doctors responded to the establishment of a Med-First facility by collectively boycotting Humana's local hospital.

A more recent approach being tried by many of the corporate chains has been the "purchase" (an industry term) of physician group practices. While not actually buying the physicians, the hospital company does pay a large sum to a doctors' group to induce it to move into the vicinity of the company hospital, often into a medical building owned and operated by the firm. Standard practice in such cases is for the company to help the group sell its old real estate, buying it up itself if necessary to facilitate the move. In return, the group is implicitly expected to bring all its business— that is, to send all its patients who require hospitalization—to the company hospital.

NME, HCA, and especially AMI have all been buying physicians' practices for some time. In New Orleans (a particularly competitive locale for the hospital industry because of the number of hospitals bought or built by the chains in their efforts to capitalize on the high-growth potential of the area), AMI long boasted that it was the most aggressive pursuer of physicians. The company claims to have spent $100,000 a month on what it calls "contractual agreements," even during a period in the late 1980s when it was suffering financial reverses. As *New Orleans City Business* reported in a cover story on March 3, 1986, the corporations have been offering doctors "management, financial, marketing and computer services," plus subsidized office space, all in the hope that the doctors will then bring their patients to company hospitals.[7] The chains deny that there are any strings attached to their deals that would require such admissions, but there is little other motivation for them to spend the money required to acquire physician practices.

Because Humana Chairman David Jones says he is against the concept—on ethical grounds—of purchasing medical practices, Humana instead recruits physicians from outside the area, helping them with relocation costs, start-up financing, reduced office rental rates, et cetera. This may be time-consuming and slow to show a return to the company, since such new physicians have to build their practices from scratch, but because their offices are adjacent to Humana's facility, and all their patients are familiar with Humana's hospital, these relocated doctors tend to remain loyal to the company. (In fact, it's hard to see how much ethical difference there is between buying an existing practice and subsidizing a new one, if the ethical problem is having doctors too closely allied to hospitals.)

Jones clearly expects the recruits will be loyal. As he told an interviewer from *Fortune Magazine*, if a doctor recruited by Humana later failed to bring in enough profitable patients, he could find himself out on the street. "I'm damn sure I'm not going to renegotiate their office leases. They can practice elsewhere," he said.[8]

Whatever their methods, the hospital chains recognize the importance to their bottom line of recruiting the right physicians to work in their facilities. As Jimmy Ledoux, administrator of Humana Women's Hospital East Orleans, explains it, "The quickest way to increase [patient] census is to recruit a physician," since each physician many bring in a hundred patients.[9]

The hospital chains are apparently just as willing to apply the stick as the carrot in their effort to control the practice of medicine in their facilities. In some locales, Humana has sent memos to staff physicians warning them that their staff positions are in jeopardy if they don't bring in more patients to a hospital. At Humana Hospital West Hills, in Los Angeles, for instance, a memorandum was circulated in 1986 and 1987 warning physicians that "those desiring reappointment to the Courtesy Staff must meet utilization minimums of at least five admissions . . . during the previous period of appointment." The memo goes on to say that failure to meet those minimums would result in a probationary reappointment, and, if repeated, to "removal from staff."[10]

A staff physician there who asked not to be identified for fear of reprisals comments, "That kind of thing would *never* have happened at a hospital, *never*, prior to the arrival of these corporate chains." This physician adds that the pressure can be intense to overadmit or to send patients to a less convenient or less appropriate institution. "Let's suppose you're a doctor who doesn't do a lot of hospital work . . . and many don't. Maybe you admit ten patients a year. You may practice at three hospitals. They'll all pressure to shift all patients to their hospitals, and once you do shift to one, you're a serf, or you just admit more patients to all the hospitals than you would have before."

The doctor adds, "But you can't admit just anybody. These companies have a doctor's profile on computer. It tells them how many patients you admitted, how long they stayed, whether they paid their bills, et cetera. What's going to happen is that the doctors who don't admit patients will lose their privileges, and the ones that have really sick elderly patients who might exceed DRG reimbursement rates won't get beds."

Why would a physician opt to practice at such hospitals? "I have no choice. I have nothing but corporate hospitals around me now."

Jones's hard-nosed approach to physicians is shared at the other hospital companies. At NME, doctors who too frequently exceed DRG reimbursement rates risk jeopardizing their relationship with the company. Nathan Kaufman, formerly of HCA and later senior vice president for marketing and physician relations at NME, explained it to me, "If a physician comes to us and requests a lot of tests, we're going to provide them for him, but we're going to ask questions like, 'Is this a line of care we want to be involved in given the level of reimbursement?' Over time, we might get into saying to a doctor, 'We don't want to be into that kind of care.'"

And woe to a doctor who starts treating low-income patients at an NME hospital who are only covered by MediCal (California's Medicaid program), which only reimburses hospitals at about 40–60 percent of what they claim their costs really are. Says Nora Ryan, assistant director of nursing at Century City Hospital, an NME "full-service" facility in Los Angeles, "We have very few MediCal patients here because of the kind of physicians we have."

Physicians interested in practicing at HCA hospitals, meanwhile, may find their profit-potential being examined. One Texas doctor who went through just such scrutiny after expressing some interest in staff privileges at the company's hospital in Village Oaks reports, "They weren't interested in my medical qualifications. What they wanted to know was what kind of patients was I treating and how profitable was my practice. What they wanted to see was my books."

Aside from the impact on physicians of this growing power of the hospital industry, there are also grounds for patients to be concerned. A major danger is that the doctor who feels pressure—or temptation—to admit might consciously or unconsciously recommend unnecessary hospitalization or might send a patient to a company hospital when another, neighboring facility might be better equipped to handle a specific problem. Another doctor, already chastised for bringing in too many indigents or Medicaid patients, might balk at admitting yet another patient whose insurance might not cover a major operation in full.

Corporate hospital executives tend to explain their recruitment of physicians in terms of quality of care and a desire to have only first-rate physicians at their facilities. In an interview with *New Orleans City Business,* however, Thomas P. Gore, marketing director for AMI's New Orleans region, bluntly gave the real reason for his company's recruiting efforts:

> It is without apology that we confirm the fact that we are seeking to reach as many agreements with physicians as we can. . . . If AMI could drive some hospitals into Chapter Eleven, it would willingly do so. We're not going to push them into Chapter Eleven; conditions are going to do so. And we're one of the conditions.[11]

Whatever the arrangement, the intent is to offer financial inducements to physicians to bring their lucrative patients to company facilities. The advantages to the physician of the offers are readily apparent: thousands of dollars a year in profits from joint ventures or profit-sharing revenues; reduced rent on company-owned offices, accounting and other back-office services; and in some cases even assistance with malpractice insurance premiums and guaranteed first-year incomes. According to the American Medical Association, which periodically surveys operating expenses for physicians, the average internist spent $100,000 in 1987 on office overhead, salaries, supplies, and insurance. Of course, this figure is much higher in the urban and suburban areas where many physicians practice, which makes the offers of the corporate hospital chains extremely attractive.

Says Dr. Calvin Fisher, president of the medical and dental

staff at Humana's hospital in Hoffman Estates, Illinois, "They give certain doctors that they think will be big admitters low-interest loans, reduced office rent, assistance in getting practices started . . . things like that. And I think that this does subtly affect patient care, though the patient may not ever know it."

Earlier in his career, Don Stern, a young pediatrician who later became regional director of the state Department of Health Services in western Virginia, declined a relocation recruitment offer from Humana. He discloses that the company offered him a guaranteed $5,500-per-month income in his first six months, and projected his first year's income in a Louisiana community at $150,000. The company threw in a promise of a rent-free office for one year, with paid nurse, secretary, office equipment, furniture, utilities; paid health, dental, life and most importantly malpractice insurance; a company car, moving expenses, a country club membership, and a free visit to look the area over. With start-up costs for setting up a solo practice running at about $50,000 (not counting living expenses until patients start coming in the door) according to the AMA, the offer must have been inviting. But in his reply, Dr. Stern indicated an awareness that things might not be so rosy the next year.

"Are the people in the community who will be supporting this pediatrician aware of your offer?" he asked in a letter of response, adding that he wonders "how many of them have insurance themselves?" While this doctor expressed outrage at the "impressive" benefits being offered on a one-year basis, he also worried about how long he could expect to be living on easy street in a small town where Humana runs the only hospital. "If most of my patients proved to be uninsured, they'd probably lose interest in subsidizing me pretty quickly," he speculates, adding that as a physician who likes to try to minimize patients' visits to the hospital, he worried about feeling pressured to start "rethinking" his philosophy with an eye to increasing hospital admissions.

New Relationships, New Conflicts

What does all this mean for the physician—and for patient care? In an address to Minnesota University health-care administration alumni, Humana Chairman David Jones said:

Our role is to integrate the financial system with the

delivery system in a way that is sensitive to the partici-
pants. Anyone who builds a system by hammering on
doctors is going to come up short. You can't have a
medical system in which doctors aren't at the center. The
system must be sensitive to the needs and values of
doctors.[12]

Some hospital companies, like Republic Health, a mid-sized
for-profit chain, have already pioneered in billing themselves as
the place to go for such elective operations as face-lifts and
"tummy tucks." Would physicians, under pressure to increase
patient admissions so as to retain their office subsidies, use their
inherent authority with patients to recommend such procedures?
Shouldn't the patients of doctors working under such arrangements know of their physicians' relationship with a hospital
company?

One development in this "new relationship" between physicians, hospitals, and other segments of the health-care industry is
the use of doctors as "gatekeepers" for insurance plans. The plans
themselves—whether Humana's captive PPO, an HMO like U.S.
Healthcare which contracts with hospitals—all offer some kind of
bonus to physicians for minimizing referrals to specialists and for
minimizing hospitalizations. And as growing numbers of states
and insurance companies adopt "all-payer" systems that mimic
Medicare's use of DRGs, the pressure on doctors to "undertreat"
increases.

Even a once-a-year bonus to physicians who keep hospital
stays short and referrals to a minimum would seem to differ little
from the Paracelsus plan that so incensed the AMA. Indeed at
least one doctor at an AMI hospital flatly referred to a utilization
review bonus offered by that company's erstwhile captive insurance plan, AmiCare, as a "kind of kickback."

Bob Brand, director of policy research at the National Hospital
Workers Union, says, "Anytime an insurance plan permits individual doctors to recoup funds for patient care, instead of returning savings to the pool of doctors participating in the plan, it's
clear that the company in question is trying to encourage under-
utilization."

Consider how such a bonus might distort a physician's
decision-making process: Say a doctor has two patients, A and B,
both suffering from a similar ailment. If patient A's general health,
age, and mental attitude suggest that a shortened stay would be
possible, the doctor would probably admit that individual to the

company hospital, in the process, getting the bonus for certification. Patient B, older and in poorer general health, would be another story. If the doctor has run afoul of the utilization review process a few times already, he or she might feel pressure from peer reviewers not to "abuse" the system—a term one doctor says is widely used to describe such cases. The doctor might decide to treat B as he or she did A, and send both home early, to patient B's detriment. Alternatively, the doctor might decide to avoid the issue altogether by admitting patient B to another, perhaps less desirable, hospital or by referring the patient to a specialist. Whatever choice is made, it's clear that simply keeping B in the hospital longer, and running extra tests, would involve, at least to some extent, going against the system and foregoing a cash bonus.

"Of course the in-house insurance plans are going to influence the way a doctor practices," says a physician familiar with Humana's paradigmatic PPO program. "Since patients get to choose their own physicians, they don't realize that the doctor has to answer to the company. In many ways, though, it's not much different from going to a doctor in a [clinic-type] HMO" —something many Americans have explicitly rejected.

The AMA has not specifically addressed the issue of bonuses in prepaid insurance plans, and when asked about the ethics of this and of joint ventures and other incentives, Michael Sugarman, program director for the association's Department of Practice Management, referred me to an AMA handbook on ethical issues. In the case of insurance plans, that handbook states only that "physicians should not be subjected to lay interference in professional medical matters and . . . their primary responsibility should be to the patients they serve."[13]

As for sharing in joint ventures or having a financial interest in for-profit hospital operations, the handbook, after affirming that such links are permissible, says:

> Under no circumstances may the physician place his own financial interest above the welfare of his patients. The prime objective of the medical profession is to render service to humanity; reward or financial gain is a subordinate consideration. For a physician to unnecessarily hospitalize a patient or prolong a patient's stay in the health facility for the physician's financial benefit would be unethical.

If a conflict develops between a physician's financial interests and the physician's responsibilities to the patient, the conflict must be resolved to the patient's benefit.

A physician who derives economic benefits from commercial ventures involving his or her patients has an interest that potentially may conflict with the physician's practice of medicine and service of the patient's medical interests. It is unethical for a physician to use his fiduciary relationship to abuse, exploit, or deceive the patient for the physician's personal gain, including profit from a commercial venture.

Significantly, the handbook adds:

Physician ownership interest in a commercial venture with the potential for abuse is not in itself unethical. Physicians are free to enter lawful contractual relationships, including the acquisition of ownership interests in health facilities or equipment or pharmaceuticals. However . . . the physician has an affirmative ethical obligation to disclose to the patient or referring colleagues his ownership interest in the facility or therapy prior to utilization.[14]

No state, however, requires doctors to post a list of their conflicts of interest on the waiting room wall—much as that would serve to enlighten patients—and it would be the rare physician indeed who would do so on his or her own. Indeed, given the low probability that an HIV-positive physician would inadvertently infect a patient, it is ironic that in 1991 the government would require that such doctors notify patients of their condition. Patients should be far more concerned about their doctors' commercial conflicts.

An indication of how conflicted such profit-sharing relationships can be came when I contacted one of my own doctors, an internist who practices at an NME hospital and rents office space from the company. He declined to comment on the company and its operations, saying, "I can't really discuss them because I have a financial relationship with them." Asked for details of the relationship, his slightly embarrassed reply was simply, "I'd rather not say." (Had I ever been hospitalized by that physician, which I fortunately never was, I'm sure I would now find myself wondering about the circumstances under which he admitted me!)

While some in the corporate hospital industry seek to characterize the shifting power relationship between hospitals and physicians in relatively benign terms, others put things more bluntly. Says one AMI executive who asked not to be identified, "In the past, doctors have played this enormous role, through the American Medical Association, with hospitals as witting or unwitting handmaidens, in creating the present inequities. People now see that the focus has to be health insurance and controlling patient flow. Doctors are going to be left out in the cold; they're going to become employees, actually or in effect, unless they are able to use their still enormous political clout to throw a wrench into the system that's developing."

Not everyone, least of all doctors themselves, would agree with such a confrontational view. There are all kinds of divisions in the profession, for one thing. To young doctors fresh out of medical school, facing the prospect of a long struggle to build a practice in the face of increasingly stiff competition, the hospital companies can offer a quick start: putting them on a referral list for subscribers to their insurance or HMO plans, or giving their names to prospective patients who might call the hospital for a recommendation. That's not to mention the help many companies offer in defraying start-up costs. (Since many hospitals have begun using physician referrals as a marketing device, consumers should be aware that other factors now enter into a hospital's screening process when it develops its list of recommended physicians than just the doctor's reputation as a medical practitioner, such as what economic class of patients she or he serves, how frequently hospitalization is recommended, or how likely the doctor is to accept hospital guidelines.)

Particularly if their specialties coincide with the profitability goals of a local chain hospital, established physicians or physician groups can still be in the position to bargain for good deals: services, joint ventures, special equipment. As Dr. Calvin Fisher of Humana Hoffman Estates comments, "For doctors willing to play the game, these companies are offering terrific opportunities. There are doctors who are making out real well."

The AMA has taken an ambiguous position, as its refusal to challenge all but the most blatant forms of "bonus payments" and its weak ethical guidelines on joint venturing with hospital companies indicate. Some of its members are part owners of the several hundred remaining old doctor-owned proprietary hospitals that still dot the nation. Besides defending the basic concept of hospitals for profit, these physicians might also view the chains as potential buyers of their property. Others are well established community physicians who are being actively courted by hospital chains eager to have them bring in their established patient base, and who, in any case, have loyal patient followings, which give them a measure of security and autonomy in dealing with large corporations. Still others may have followed an investment adviser's guidance and purchased hospital corporation stock, or gotten involved in joint ventures with hospital companies. Not surprisingly then, the AMA has taken no position on the whole subject of for-profit medicine, though its assertive action in the Paracelsus case indicates a certain uneasiness.

Hospital chain executives say they aren't interested in making life hard for doctors, and even argue that they go out of their way to attract doctors as a way of bringing in more patients. L. Stanton Tuttle, an HCA executive who later became president and chief operating officer of National Healthcare, says that each physician recruited by a hospital company can be worth as much as $500,000 a year in patient revenues.

And there are plenty of doctors who speak appreciatively of the corporate chains. "They've really turned things around here," said Dr. Gordon Ward, a physician with staff privileges at Coastal Bend Hospital in Aransas Pass, Texas. Serving a rural and small-town community faced with depression conditions because of the 1985 collapse in the oil industry, Coastal Bend Hospital was rescued from impending closure by an AMI takeover. (The foundering local community hospital had just been purchased by Lifemark when AMI closed a deal to take over the former hospital chain for $1 billion.) Ward cited the introduction of a mobile CAT-scanner, shared with other AMI hospitals in the region, and improved lab and X-ray services, as important improvements wrought by AMI. The hospital company, he said, also recruited physicians to provide services that in Aransas Pass were either nonexistent, like plastic surgery, or in short supply, like obstetrics. "Sure, the patient charges probably increased, but if AMI hadn't bought the hospital, it would probably have closed," he concluded.

Dr. Ward may eventually wind up singing a different tune. Not long after he was interviewed back in 1987, AMI decided in 1988 to spin off Coastal Bend Hospital and smaller hospitals to

EPIC Health Group. This debt-ridden corporate creation could easily founder if interest rates were to rise, dragging most or all of its hospitals down with it. In 1989, Lorraine Stehn, another physician on the staff at Coastal Bend, observed, "At this point, we don't know what will happen. We just want to get out of this big corporate mess." In 1991, she was still concerned about the future, but said the hospital was "still hanging in there." She reported that EPIC had left the old AMI management of the hospital in place, which she considered a plus, but added that the parent company was also "keeping capital expenditures pretty tight."

During a visit to corporate headquarters, I asked a group of AMI executives for a tour of one of the company's "typical" facilities. They immediately volunteered the Tarzana Regional Medical Center in Los Angeles County, and provided three top physicians with staff privileges at the facility for interviews, along with the hospital's local executive director. All three doctors expressed concern about the impact of broader national developments in health care on physician practice, but said their experiences with AMI had been positive. (They claimed the hospital does not threaten loss of staff privileges because of low utilization rates, as other companies have started doing.) Specifically, one doctor, a urologist, said that when he requested that the hospital purchase a lithotriptor, a costly device used to crush kidney stones nonsurgically, it was done. What this act of corporate largess proves is not all that clear, however. Lithotripsy is a profit-making procedure for the hospital and is one of the services the hospital advertises directly to the patient community. While the machine's purchase certainly made the doctor happy, it's really more a case of a commonality of interests.

A second physician, a neonatology specialist, was brought in to the hospital to oversee the creation of an advanced, state-of-the-art neonatology department, not involved in research but capable of dealing with premature infants born at twenty-four weeks. The doctor said that as part of his agreement with the hospital, it was determined that patient resources would not be a factor in determining admission to this department. This is clearly an example of a for-profit hospital taking on a significant losing operation, one that should be very lucrative, however, for the physicians involved. Why was it done? According to the executive director, Arnold Kimmel, it was a small-scale, local version of Humana's artificial heart program—in other words, a public relations move that "enhances the hospital's image as a top-quality facility" for anyone wanting to have a baby. On balance, then, despite almost guaranteed losses for the operation itself, it would prove to be a good investment if it attracted more deliveries overall. (As will be seen in a later chapter, this scenario is also typical of the clinical "research" activities of the for-profit hospital sector in being essentially a marketing ploy.)

At Tarzana, Kimmel added, four of the nine members of the local hospital board of directors are physicians. This apparent bow to physicians may actually reflect the fact that, as he explained, "For us, the majority of our beds are filled by patients brought in by the docs," a situation that ensures physician power in the relationship.

Tarzana, a facility that was part of a for-profit chain, Hyatt Corporation, even before it was purchased by AMI, is a hospital that's doing rather well by industry standards. Located in a wealthy suburb of Los Angeles, it has long had a reputation for quality. Occupancy is high and most patients are well covered by insurance. Still, even there, not all doctors are sanguine. "AMI is a particularly avaricious, ruthless corporation," says one physician who practices at the Tarzana facility. "When they came in, they drastically cut personnel to try and improve the profit margin, and prompted the nurses to bring in a union. Staffing there is still terribly thin."

Asked why, if all this were true, some physicians were so obviously satisfied, this doctor replied, "It's a matter of becoming progressively more dependent on the company. These guys that say they're happy, what's happening is that every day they become more and more dependent, even if they don't realize it. They're losing more and more the ability to make their livings on their own. Then one day, they won't be able to say no, and AMI will control their destiny. To me, the time to say no is right at the first juicy carrot. These guys have already eaten the first carrot, and the second and the third."

Not-for-profit hospitals, too, are paying more attention to the way their affiliated physicians practice, but the pressures are not as great as they are at the big chains. One reason for this is that the not-for-profits have for years had two often conflicting goals: serving the needs of a community, or a segment of a community, and staying economically viable. That dual mission serves as a wedge to permit physicians and other health-care professionals to press their own concerns, even if they conflict with the economic interests of the hospital as an institution. Hospital administrators do not usually suggest the opening of a burn center or an oncology department, for instance, because of the extended intensive care required by victims who often exhaust any insurance benefits. But as such a facility could contribute to the incomes of some staff physicians, their interests would coincide with those of the community and might be argued in terms of the institution's community-service goals.

As Stephen Shortell, a professor of hospital and health services management at the Kellogg Graduate School of Management, Northwestern University, wrote in a paper published in 1986 by the National Academy of Science's Institute of Medicine:

> Investor-owned hospitals are likely to face somewhat more computational and judgmental decisions, while voluntary hospitals are likely to experience somewhat more compromise and inspirational decisions. . . . This is more likely to be true in investor-owned hospitals both because they are a part of systems typically characterized by the centralized influence of corporate offices and because of the more homogeneous group of defined constituents in terms of stockholders. In contrast, voluntary community hospitals have many different constituents to serve. They also tend to have high turnover in upper administrative ranks, and, therefore, many lack strong continuous managerial direction. In brief, there are likely to be more debates about the preferences for different kinds of outcomes in voluntary community hospitals than in investor-owned hospitals. As such, in voluntary hospitals, the decision-making process may be somewhat more complex and indeterminate than in investor-owned hospitals.[15]

Dr. Arnold Relman, past editor of the *New England Journal of Medicine* and one of the most vocal critics of the corporate hospital chains, describes the difference another way: "The for-profits tell their doctors what to do in a much tougher way than the not-for-profits. They tell them not to admit elective patients who can't pay. In most community not-for-profit hospitals, administrators tend to defer to the doctors by tradition."

Says one doctor with staff privileges at both a Humana and an AMI hospital, "The companies themselves rarely come out with rules and regulations for the staffs. They usually arrange to get the most malleable doctors on the executive committee of a hospital. Then the administrator can say, 'Wouldn't it be great if we had a rule saying you have to have x admissions a year or lose your privileges?' and these pigeons will go along."

With corporate chain hospitals owning only some 21 percent of the hospitals in the U.S., it might seem that such a situation would be unusual. Actually, in some parts of the country it isn't uncommon at all. The for-profit chains are expanding in growing, upscale areas where the doctor surplus is most evident and consequently the doctors' bargaining position is weakest. Hence, the corporations' impact on physicians in these regions is far greater than this nationwide percentage might indicate.

According to a 1985 study by the American Medical Association, the most recent for which data is available, nearly one in seven physicians with hospital admitting privileges admitted their patients primarily to a proprietary hospital. Since the chains owned only 15 percent of the nation's hospitals back then, the figure is certainly higher today. Although the AMA study found few differences between proprietary and nonproprietary hospitals in terms of the way doctors were practicing medicine, where there *were* observable differences, they pointed to doctor vulnerability to hospital company pressure. Specifically, in proprietary hospitals the percentage of female doctors was almost twice as high—10.4 percent of staffs compared to only 5.7 percent for nonproprietaries. Also, more than 27.8 percent of medical staffs at the proprietaries were found to have been in practice for less than five years, compared to only 18.6 percent of physicians practicing in nonproprietaries.

This might be good news for young doctors and women physicians in general, but from another perspective these statistics suggest the corporate chains are more likely to have young physicians with small, poorly established practices. Under those conditions, one would expect medical staffs to be more responsive to incentive programs aimed at molding practice habits to conform with corporate goals. At the same time, physicians with newly established practices and relatively few loyal patients would also be vulnerable to more coercive tactics aimed at achieving the same ends, especially if they had already become dependent upon the largess of those same corporations.

Meanwhile, the for-profit hospital companies are not the only ones leaning on physicians. As pressures mount on all hospitals to compete, not-for-profit institutions are also turning the screws, after striking their own deals to become "preferred provider" facilities for insurance companies and HMOs.

When a group of New York City teaching hospitals run by the Federation of Jewish Philanthropies negotiated an agreement in 1986 with Maxicare, at the time the country's largest for-profit HMO company, it was clear that the physicians at those five facilities would lose some control over their medical practices. "For two years, the hospitals negotiated with Maxicare," said a disgruntled physician on the faculty of Mount Sinai School of Medicine who practices at Mount Sinai Medical Center. "During that whole time, they never mentioned to the staff that as part of the deal, they would set aside 20 percent of each doctor's pay until the end of the year, which would only be paid out if he was 'profitable,' in other words if he didn't order too many diagnostic tests and didn't request too many consultations with specialists." Adds the physician, who requested anonymity, "The problem is that doctors are all so inert. We don't know what's happening to us, so we don't fight back. And patients just don't realize what it all means. Do they really want their doctor to be thinking about that other 20 percent of his annual income when they come in with a health problem that calls for tests and consultations? I doubt it. It's all being shoved down people's throats in the name of reducing health costs." (Of course, as long as a physician remains self-employed, the Maxicare strings are only attached to that portion of his or her income derived from Maxicare-covered patients. Other patients' fees, paid by Blue Cross/Blue Shield or some other insurer, would be unaffected. Still, that 20 percent bonus for many physicians can be a princely sum, especially given prevailing fee schedules in New York City.)

In what is becoming a frequent development in the not-for-profit hospital sector, as part of its deal with Maxicare, the Federation of Jewish Philanthropies was to hold a 49 percent equity position in the joint venture that was to be created to operate the new insurance program at the hospitals. Far from simply doing a favor for Maxicare shareholders, the hospitals would thus have had a direct interest in aggressively applying economic sanctions and incentives to gain physician compliance with cost-cutting procedures.

In the end, the deal collapsed because Maxicare went bankrupt (much of Maxicare's business was later purchased by Humana), but the system being negotiated is typical of what is ahead for the nation's physicians and their patient-consumers.

Turning the Screws on Doctors . . . and Patients

"We foresee a rather gloomy future for the doctor," says Dr. Sanford Marcus, a practicing physician who serves as president of the small but growing Union of American Physicians and Dentists, which represents medical practitioners, both employed and self-employed. "What's happening is that the doctor as entrepreneur is finished. We're all being reduced to de facto employees, whether we're actually on salary or not, with the real control over delivery of health care shifting into the hands of the new business of corporate medicine."

Says Marcus, "It used to be that the good doctor was the old-fashioned careful guy who ran all the tests and took care of his patients. That's a bad doctor now. The good one is the one who can bring in a lot of short-turnover, easy-care patients. Of course, the hospital companies act differently depending on where their hospital is located. If the environment is competitive, they'll be accommodating. If not, doctors had better stick together."

He adds, "All the vanity and the preening in front of the mirror by doctors hides the fact that there are really no independent private-practice physicians in America anymore."

An indication of how the pressures by corporate hospitals on physicians can jeopardize patient care comes from Dr. Calvin Fisher at Humana Hoffman Estates. "I'd say bottom-line concerns do compromise quality of care in 10 to 15 percent of cases. Sending someone home sooner can cause problems, say in the case of bleeding in the eye, or a lung. In the hospital you'd detect the problem sooner. It seems to me that Humana plays it very close to census on staffing, and that does cause problems. Louisville *does* have strong influence in this hospital—it's just like McDonalds telling each outlet how many ounces of meat to put in a hamburger. Our administration insists that our statistics are good, but Humana is like the mafia in terms of our actually getting any *access* to statistics on performance."

In a 1989 interview, Fisher cited several examples of where he sees corporate cost-saving measures posing threats to patients. "I have a perception that the staffing in the X-ray department is too low," he explained. "Things take too long to come back. And even when it isn't health threatening, it does mean people have to take a day off from work unnecessarily. Nurse morale is low also, because of low staffing levels. Nurses haven't had a raise in three years, and [in 1987] 120 nurses out of a total of 350 left. As a result they use a lot of agency nurses—even in ICU [the intensive care unit]."

Fisher, a family practice physician, also claimed that Humana had shown "blatant favoritism" to profit-generating members of the physician staff. "In surgery, we see they don't buy new or adequate instruments, which can mean, for the patient, unnecessary time under anesthesia. If it's a high-volume surgeon, though, they'll do anything for him, get him whatever he asks for. The other, lower-volume surgeons can call for days and get nowhere."

Fisher said the problem isn't finances. "We know this is one of Humana's more profitable hospitals. The profits are going somewhere, though. They don't stay here."

A nurse who has worked at both an AMI and NME hospital says the same kinds of things are done there. "To save money on nurses, AMI put me in charge of both the ICU and the Recovery Room. So in the same small space, I was doing recovery and day surgery. I had fresh general anesthesia patients recovering plus day surgery patients coming in. It was not safe. How am I going to take a patient coming in to a recovery room, give [another patient] pre-op instructions, get them to the lab, and still pay attention to [the] recovering patient who needs to be reminded that the operation's over and everything else. That shouldn't happen anywhere. It would never happen in a not-for-profit hospital. There was no lunch break, no bathroom breaks. I ate crackers for lunch. We had meeting after meeting. I'd complain, and the response was always, 'If you don't like it, leave.'" After a year, she was "burned out" and did quit. At the same hospital, this nurse says AMI pressured the hospital to keep its purchase of supplies and equipment at a minimum. "The result, especially if the company got a bad quarterly report, was that we had days in surgery without the right supplies—things like [surgical] sponges [designed to show up in an X ray if left inside a patient inadvertently]. We'd have to use towels instead. I think operations definitely took longer because of poor or lacking equipment, and that's a threat to patients."

At a neighboring NME facility, the situation was similar, she reports. "In November 1987, they had a department-head meeting. They said it was year's end, and they wanted to improve the financial picture, so we were told not to order anything for the rest of the year. It lasted eight weeks."

At AMI, the pressure on doctors to get Medicare patients out of the hospital under DRG limits was intense, she says. "The hospital had a 'DRG person' who went around every day putting notes on a patient's chart saying things like 'The patient is five thousand dollars over DRG.' It would be written in big red numbers. That kind of behavior puts the docs between a rock and a hard place."

All this shifting of the nexus of power from the physician to the hospital, with its potential for conflicts of interest, is not to suggest that there weren't already conflicts of interest when physicians were in the saddle and were paid, as most still are, on a fee-for-service basis (the more they see and do to you, the more they earn). As the Princeton economist Uwe Reinhardt wrote in an exchange of letters with then *New England Journal of Medicine* editor Arnold Relman published in the 1986 report of the National Institute of Medicine titled *For-Profit Enterprise in Health Care:*

> What, in the history of the American medical profession, aside from that profession's own rhetoric, should lead a thoughtful person to expect from physicians a conduct significantly distinct from the conduct of other purveyors of goods and services? I do not deny that there have been grand and noble physicians among the lot, just as there have been grand and noble financiers, lawyers, and even economists. Rather, I am referring here to central tendencies, to the mainstream of American medicine as it has revealed itself through the ages to a paying public. What, then, in the conduct of mainstream American medicine should have led a thoughtful person to expect from physicians a conduct distinct from other ordinary mortals who sell their goods and services for a price? . . .
>
> Surely you will agree that it has been one of American medicine's more hallowed tenets that piece-rate compensation is the sine qua non of high quality medical care. Think about this tenet. We have here a profession that openly professes that its members are unlikely to do their best unless they are rewarded in cold cash for every little ministration rendered their patients.[16]

Nor have the existing traditional conflicts of interest failed to produce their share of scandals and malpractice. Newspapers are larded with accounts of physicians who have bilked their patients and the taxpayer by overmedicating and overtreating patients, giving and taking kickbacks from everyone from lawyers and other doctors to pharmaceutical and medical equipment companies, or just simply overexamining Medicare patients. The argument has been made in some quarters that physicians on salary, as is the case with public hospitals and some HMOs, are in a less compromising environment. Even if that were true, though, the newly evolving arrangements with their bonuses are hardly simple salaried positions. Nonetheless, as with virtually every other aspect of the new marketplace medicine system, the new relationship between hospitals and physicians is being forged with little public discussion. As Marcus and many others note, it is not even being seriously examined by doctors themselves, much less the average health-services consumer and potential patient.

From the point of view of the doctor, the historic status of the physician—self-employed or part owner of his or her own corporation, independent authority on patient treatment, well-paid, and usually respected—is so close to ideal, that any change *has* to be for the worse to some extent. But some doctors grudgingly accept loss of power to the hospital as a lesser of evils. As one doctor at an AMI facility commented dryly, "At least it's better than the alternative: nationalized medicine."

There may also be some sense that the profession will come out OK in the end, as it did with Medicare. That program proved to be a fountain of wealth for physicians, though it was bitterly opposed by the AMA which initially saw it as the first encroachment of the dreaded state. (Back in 1963, when talk of Medicare was the rage in Washington, the AMA hired a grade-B actor named Ronald Reagan to broadcast an advertisement warning of this new "socialist threat," referring to a program that now provides the bulk of many physicians' income—and which the ex-president himself now uses.)

Because the hospital corporations' move into insurance programs and volume discount arrangements as well as their assertion of power in both the external political and the internal administrative arenas are still new, it's not easy to anticipate all the tensions and problems that will develop, but develop they will. Already, doctors who practice at chain hospitals that have insurance plans or PPO arrangements with outside insurers are finding it almost essential to accept the terms of those plans, despite disadvantages, which often include significantly lower fee schedules than other insurers. As the surplus of physicians continues to grow and the hospital industry gains in its efforts to control patient flow, making it less and less dependent upon the whims of physicians for its revenues, doctors who resist efforts at control may find themselves facing competition trucked in by a hospital.

Indeed, this is beginning to happen already. A Harvard Medical School graduate from the 1950s who had an established practice in an area of Wyoming served by a major chain hospital reported, "They've screwed around for a year and a half about giving me staff privileges, and haven't given it to me yet because I'm not a conformist. And now they've brought in a physician to compete with me, who does have staff privileges. Look, I won't kid you. Of course this puts pressure on you, even if you do have an established practice. What would it do to a younger doctor just out of medical school?" A year after that interview, this doctor gave up and moved to California to set up a new practice.

A number of physicians around the country, especially in one-hospital towns where a chain hospital has taken over a local facility, have expressed anxiety about having competition imported by the hospital. That anxiety alone is probably almost as effective in terms of producing physician malleability as the reality of competition. The establishment of company-owned HMOs is also a kind of physician competition.

No one except a doctor would be likely to argue that something like increased competition among physicians, or just lower physician fees, is bad. And certainly the traditional situation, in which the doctor controlled everything from selection of patient to fee, type of treatment and choice of hospital, has left a lot to be desired. Of course, if the patient/doctor relationship is a good one, at least the quality of care is ensured (assuming physician competence). But it also presents the risk of overtreatment, overcharging, and the like. Still, the new environment, in which hospital chains become central to health-care decision-making, only *seems* to preserve the freedom of patient choice. Typically, in a hospital company insurance plan or hospital/insurance joint-venture PPO, the patient chooses his or her doctor as long as the doctor has staff privileges. *Actually*, by placing hidden controls on physician behavior, the new system to some extent negates the value of even that limited freedom. And as much as the hospital companies try to project a caring humanitarian image, there can never be anything at all approaching a "patient/hospital relationship," that is, one between a health-services "consumer" and a health-services corporation.

Meanwhile, for better or worse, the power shift is taking place. "The hospital companies are slowly turning the screw," laments Dr. Fisher. "And they will continue to turn it so that they can dictate to their physicians."

5

Competition as Health-Inflation Rx: Pain but No Gain?

Although the words *competition* and *consumer choice* are freely used, they have an ambiguous content. The new language of American medicine is not patient care, but marketing strategy.
> —Geof Rayner
> in *Banking on Sickness: Commercial Medicine in Britain and the USA*

Your blood pressure and temperature are way up, but your Medicare coverage is way down. Looks as if you can go home today, Mrs. Fitch!
> —Stayskal
> from a political cartoon in the *Tampa Tribune*

When American Medical International purchased York General Hospital in Rock Hill, South Carolina, residents thought their community had wangled a good deal. The old facility had an overcrowded emergency room, a leaky roof, and suffered from frequent equipment breakdowns. Rather than fix the facility and expand where necessary, AMI built a new hospital called Piedmont Medical Center from the ground up for $28 million. The community didn't have to pay a cent.

It seemed too good to be true, and indeed it was. The community didn't have to pay collectively, but patients and employers *did*, as charges jumped 35 percent the first year, and the cost of supplies for an average inpatient admission soared 133 percent. In the past, there may have been a lot to complain about at York General, but at least most people could afford to go there. Now the facility looked nice and offered an attractive ambience—AMI introduced a "stork" program that included steak dinner by candlelight, with wine, for new parents—but the cost had become prohibitive for some. As one local employer commented in the *Wall Street Journal*, referring to AMI's introduction of amenities, "It's icing on the cake, [but] it's getting so we can't afford the icing—or even the cake."[1]

In 1989, six years after the arrival of AMI, York County, which had the foresight to include a five-year repurchase right in its original sale agreement, was having serious second thoughts. As complaints continued in the community about the hospital's charges, the county legislature had decided in 1988 to seriously consider exercising its option. Widespread local dissatisfaction was bolstered by a statewide comparative hospital costs survey conducted that year by the state's Joint Legislative Health Care Planning and Oversight Committee. This survey showed AMI's Piedmont Medical Center to be charging more than surrounding hospitals for each of the ten most common hospital procedures. For normal childbirth, for instance, Piedmont Medical Center charged an average of $2,900, compared with $2,540 at Lexington Medical Center, a similar competing facility in the same region, and $2,340 and $2,220 at Chester County Hospital and Elliott White Springs Memorial, two smaller facilities. AMI's hospital also charged most for admissions for asthma, heart attack, abnormal heart rhythm, cesarean section delivery, chest pain, gall bladder removal, congestive heart failure, hysterectomy, and gastrointestinal inflammation.

Repurchase of the hospital from AMI was never a very likely option, since under the company's purchase agreement, it could insist on a price that included an inflation adjustment and the cost of improvements and debt financing, all of which tended to make such a transaction much too dear for local taxpayers. Still, a competing not-for-profit institution across the state line in Charlotte, North Carolina, the Charlotte Mecklenburg Hospital, was also offering to step in and buy the facility from York County and run it following a repurchase, promising a much lower schedule of charges, should the county ultimately decide to take it back from AMI.

In pursuing that bid, Harry Nurkin, president of the Charlotte Mecklenburg Hospital Authority, made an interesting point. In 1987 alone, AMI corporate headquarters withdrew some $7 million from Piedmont Medical Center for such things as income tax payments, dividends to shareholders, charges for central planning, accounting and home office staff, and intracorporate borrowing. Having your hospital owned by a corporate chain, he argued, was no bargain.

In the end, York County grudgingly decided in 1989 not to make any ownership changes, but still hedged its bets by agreeing to continue the existing arrangement with AMI for only another five years. At that time, in 1994, the county will once more reconsider AMI's ownership.

Habersham County, Georgia, residents had a similar experience with corporate medicine at their local hospital. There, the county invited Hospital Corporation of America to manage the public hospital, which was running at a chronic deficit and gobbling up local tax revenues. HCA did the job it was assigned, bringing the hospital's budget from a 7.8 percent loss in 1978, when HCA came in, to a 3.3 percent surplus in 1983. But a county grand jury examining the situation in 1984 as part of a study of health-care costs in that community concluded that it wasn't so much HCA's vaunted managerial efficiency and skill that turned the trick; it was the firm's higher charges to patients. During the same five-year period, HCA upped patient charges by 235 percent. Even HCA's major selling point—that as a large corporation it could buy supplies at a discount—was questioned. The grand jury found that of thirteen items analyzed, HCA paid more for nine—passing the higher costs on to patients—than did a consortium of other independent non-chain Georgia hospitals.[2]

Right Place, Right Time

There's no question that hospital costs have to be controlled, but all the available evidence suggests that turning hospitals loose in the marketplace is not going to do that job. According to Sam Mitchell, a researcher at the Federation of American Health Systems, hospitals accounted for 44 percent of the nation's health bill in 1990, and as we have seen, the inflation rate for hospital and related services has consistently been above that for health care in general, and nearly double the overall consumer price index rate of climb. Despite years of experimentation with the deliberate fostering of competition in the hospital field, despite concerted efforts by employers to reduce health-care costs, and during a continuing trend toward corporatization of the hospital industry, not only has the cost of a hospital stay continued to soar, but the pace has actually accelerated.

It wasn't supposed to be like this.

When the corporate hospital chains burst onto the national scene in the late 1970s with a sudden rush of acquisitions and construction, they were quick to proclaim themselves as the answer to the nation's health cost crisis. Some industry leaders, like Humana's Chairman David Jones and HCA Chairman Tom Frist, routinely declared their intention to be the low-cost providers of quality health care. Others spoke of being more "efficient," an economist's term that is fraught with ambiguity and hard to quantify. As early as 1971, Richard Eamer, founder and president of then fledgling National Medical Enterprises, wrote in the April issue of the magazine *Modern Hospital* that chain-owned proprietary hospitals were "measurably more efficient" than the not-for-profit competition. Saying, "Now I concede that efficiency is not an easy thing to measure," Eamer went on to cite statistics suggesting that for-profit hospitals use "10 to 12 percent less labor expense" than nonprofits of the same size. In California, where NME was then entirely located, he claimed "profits do it [provide the same quality and quantity of service] for 20 to 25 percent less labor expense."

His explanation:

> I submit that successfully controlling payroll costs without compromising quality of care represents merely the introduction of modern management technics (*sic*) in to the hospital field, not a change to some 'unknown system,' as some observers seem to think.[3]

A companion rebuttal on the same page of the magazine by management consultant Richard L. Johnson of A. T. Kearney,

Incorporated, in Chicago countered that while for-profits had 13 percent fewer employees, they also contributed little space and few resources to medical education, unlike the not-for-profits. They also provided less comprehensive health services.[4]

Wall Street analysts were quick to jump on the corporate-hospital bandwagon. In 1976, in a Heard on the Street column in the *Wall Street Journal* headlined "Hospital Management Industry Is Favored by Analysts as Healthy Area for Investments," industry analyst John Westergaard of Cyrus J. Lawrence, Incorporated, said the hospital companies were attractive investments because "it's within the current trend to put into private hands important sectors of the economy, particularly the service areas, for efficiency and success."

Where hospitals are concerned, efficiency is defined as the most appropriate use of resources in meeting the demands of the marketplace. The problem with this concept when it is applied to medicine is that no one has been able to determine exactly what the demands of a health-care marketplace are. Many of the patients are so poor they can't get into a hospital, and most of the others—insured employees and their families, or the elderly on Medicare—don't pay for their own care, or if they do, it is done through employer benefits or taxes and they don't realize it. Efficiency is also a questionable concept for another reason. In the service sector, particularly in industries like health care or education where quality is especially important, it is not at all clear that, for instance, a more efficient use of labor means more students per teacher, or in the case of health care, more patients per nurse. Put another way, if that *is* efficiency, it's no virtue.

Despite such ambiguities, the explosive expansion of the corporate hospital chains during the decade between 1975 and 1985 came at a time when Washington was looking first with favor and then with fervor at the marketplace for solutions to economic and social problems. President Carter's White House inflation fighters pushed the idea of competition in trucking and air travel and began, after an initial timid experiment with the idea of cost controls, to consider it for health care. (It was the Carter administration that initiated the idea of prospective payment for Medicare, which was seen as a way to make hospitals more cost conscious.)

With the arrival of the Reagan administration in 1981, competition in health care became the unquestioned official policy for controlling health costs. During that year, hospital costs, the largest single component of medical care expenditures, leapt by a record 19 percent, which focused Washington's attention mightily on the industry. Two years later, prospective payment for Medicare, which accounts for over 40 percent of hospital revenues, was signed into law. At the same time all talk of federal controls over hospital charges ended. In the new zeal for applying market solutions to what were once considered government regulatory responsibilities, state after state also began to dismantle controls over hospital construction and expansion, eliminating health planning agencies and the requirement of certificate-of-need permits (a kind of license to build, or to buy expensive medical equipment).

No wonder Michael Bromberg, executive director of the Federation of American Health Systems, the for-profit hospital industry's lobbying organization, so glowingly described the new Reagan presidency as

> an administration opposed to government regulation of our industry, opposed to comprehensive national health insurance, opposed to cost controls, opposed to planning, and receptive to new ideas. . . . We have never been in a better position in our history.[5]

Bromberg's rosy industry outlook for 1982, as published in the federation's 1981 annual report, was based on the conviction that because for-profit hospitals were by definition concerned first and foremost with profitability, they were certain to be more interested in and adept at controlling costs than the not-for-profit competition. They would thus be at a competitive advantage as regulatory controls over hospitals were loosened or dropped altogether. Bromberg's view was shared by Wall Street investors and government policymakers alike, with the former seeing investment opportunities in health care and the latter assuming that a dose of competition from the for-profit side of the industry was what the not-for-profit hospitals needed to become cost conscious. As health-industry analyst John Hindelong of A. G. Becker argued in a 1983 *Wall Street Journal* article after the enactment of a prospective payment system for Medicare:

> The for-profit hospitals are so much more efficient in providing services than non-profit hospitals that they will

be able to improve their profit margins as a result of the new system.[6]

Washington policymakers needed little prompting to get as caught up by the idea of letting businessmen attack the hospital cost spiral as they were with giving free rein to the financial industry. As early as 1974, speaking to a convention of the for-profit hospital industry's trade organization, then called the Federation of American Hospitals (later the FAHS), James Cavanaugh, associate director of President Gerald Ford's White House domestic council, told assembled for-profit hospital managers that "the innovation, talent and managerial expertise that brings about the planning and development of institutions like yours is a key element in our national health strategy."

Not to be outdone, Congressman William Roy, speaking as a Democratic health policymaker that year, told the same group: "I think the attitudes and programs of the Federation of American Hospitals are a model for other groups in the health industry."

As recently as 1985, as a decade of dramatic growth was drawing to an end, the for-profit hospital industry itself was still confidently asserting that it was the most efficient provider of health-care services. David Jones of Humana, for instance, who was becoming a popular speaker at gatherings of health professionals (in part because of his company's high-profile artificial heart experiments, but also because of his blunt advocacy of free-market solutions to the health-care cost crisis), was regularly proclaiming that his hospitals were 18 percent more efficient than the national hospital average. This assertion was based on purported labor productivity and on a claim that his company was the low-cost provider of acute medical care. Jones made both claims to me in an interview in his Louisville office that year, though he offered no substantiation for either. Meanwhile, study after study seemed to show, if anything, the opposite to be true.

Studies Raise Questions

In 1984, the Hospital Alliance of Tennessee, a trade group representing almost all the not-for-profit hospitals in that state (one where HCA now owns or has an interest in 20 percent of the hospitals, with other proprietary hospitals accounting for another 16 percent) hired the consulting firm of Booz, Allen & Hamilton,

Inc., to do a cost study of the state's facilities. It found that over all, costs and charges were "substantially higher" at for-profit hospitals in Tennessee than at not-for-profit hospitals, regardless of the size of the institution. The study found, for instance, that among medium-sized hospitals of 200–299 beds, the charges per admission were 64 percent higher at for-profit hospitals than at not-for-profits. The figure drops to 50 percent when adjusted to account for case mix differences between the two hospital types (in general the study found that not-for-profits handled a greater variety of cases). On a per-patient-day basis, charges by the for-profit sector were still found to be 30 percent higher.

An interesting observation of the Booz, Allen & Hamilton study was that on average, patient charges were higher for the for-profits in rural areas, where a hospital is generally the only hospital in a community, but that in urban areas, the not-for-profit hospitals lost their charge advantage. The study found this not to be because of the for-profits' better competitive abilities, however, but because of the higher percentage of nonpaying patients in urban areas, and the greater proportion of such patients admitted by the not-for-profit sector. Costs incurred by nonpaying patients were shifted onto paying patients by raising room rates. In all cases, the study found administrative costs to be a higher percentage of total costs at for-profit institutions, further suggesting that predicted savings as a result of mergers and acquisitions may be illusory.

Like most subsequent studies, the Booz, Allen & Hamilton study did find the for-profit sector to be more *profitable* than the not-for-profit competition. But it said this phenomenon could be traced not to better cost controls, as free-market theorists had predicted, but rather to thinner hospital staffing practices and to higher markups in four major ancillary service departments: medical supplies, pharmacy, inhalation therapy, and laboratory services.

The Tennessee study concluded that "significant and consistent differences do exist between for-profit and not-for-profit hospitals, and . . . in almost all cases, not-for-profit hospitals deliver care at lower cost."[7]

A year later, in 1985, the Blue Cross/Blue Shield organization in North Carolina published a survey of hospital charges in that state, and similarly found for-profit chain-owned hospitals there to be the highest-cost institutions in their market areas.[8]

As one part of its study, the Blue Cross/Blue Shield researchers looked at four hospitals that had recently been taken over by proprietary chains. In three of the four cases, per day average costs of treatment rose much more rapidly after the takeover than before. Costs also rose more rapidly than they were rising the same year at similar not-for-profit facilities.

The North Carolina study attributed most of the increases to higher markups for pharmacy and medical supplies, and to a lesser extent to higher operating room and anesthesia charges. In looking at six for-profits and similar groups of not-for-profits, the study also found that specific procedures cost more.

In another 1985 study for the Foundation for Health Services Research, health economist Robert Pattison, executive vice president of the Hospital Council of Northern California (a trade organization including most for-profit, not-for-profit, and public hospitals in the northern half of the state), and research associate Piruz Alemi, examined 240 hospitals over a four-year period. They concluded that "for nearly all financially important daily and ancillary services, charges per service unit [prices] were highest in the [investor-owned] sector and lowest in the public sector."[9]

Additionally, and somewhat surprisingly, given the chains' claims that they are "more efficient" than the not-for-profit competition, Pattison and Alemi also found that "administrative and fiscal costs were higher as a percent of operating expenses for the investor-owned than for the not-for-profit sector." In large part, they said, this was because of internal charges to support giant headquarters offices.

Discussing his report with me, Pattison said, "There is simply *no evidence* that I know of that these [for-profit hospital] companies can produce a day of service less costly than another hospital. [Humana's] David Jones says his company is eighteen percent more efficient. I say, just show me. One problem for them is that any efficiencies of scale are just overwhelmed by increases in capital costs and overhead."

In "Cost without Benefit," an article published in the February 13, 1986, issue of the *New England Journal of Medicine*, Dr. David Himmelstein, an internist at Cambridge City Hospital in Massachusetts and an instructor in medicine at Harvard Medical School, reported that headquarters costs were significantly higher for the for-profit chains—and rising. Discussing his findings in an interview in 1988, he said, "What we're finding is that, as part of the so-called drive for efficiency and competition, the health bureaucracy is mushrooming in the private sector . . . at all hospitals, but especially at the for-profit chains. When people talk about efficiency and competition, they really mean more bureaucrats to decide what medical care should be. Increasingly hospitals are being run by people with MBAs who view people as widgets, and you need more and more people and computers which do little for health care but do turn hospitals into businesses." He added that "costs of billing for health care in this country are staggering already: $40 to $50 billion a year." That's almost a tenth of the total annual national health-care bill for that year just to do the paperwork to ensure payment, and Himmelstein, in 1990, said that administrative costs are continuing to keep pace with overall health-care costs.

Of course, there are probably exceptions to the rule. The chief financial officer of an AMI hospital in a rural North Carolina community argues that his facility is flat-out cheaper than the nearest competition, a not-for-profit hospital some twenty miles away. "It all comes down to how you measure costs," he says, "and they are very hard to measure. If you separated out our income taxes, we would definitely be cheaper, and that's not because we don't have a heavy charity care load. AMI takes anyone who comes in the door of the emergency room. That's corporate policy—it would be foolish for us to turn away people if we're the sole provider in an area."

The argument that not-for-profits are cheaper because they don't have to pay taxes, and in effect are subsidized by taxpayers, is one that the for-profit sector has been making. The problem with this theory, however, is that when the corporate chains were growing rapidly, between 1975 and 1985, their effective tax rates, thanks to depreciation write-offs, interest deductions, and invest-ment tax credits, were extremely low—often below 10 percent—yet their patient charges were nevertheless much higher than the not-for-profit competition.

A fourth study, done for the Blue Cross and Blue Shield Association by the San Francisco–based consulting firm Lewin & Associates in 1985, came to conclusions similar to those of the Pattison/Alemi and the Blue Cross of North Carolina studies. The Lewin study looked at 1980 data for a random sample of 561 hospitals (roughly 10 percent of the hospitals in the country), divided into five categories: chain-affiliated investor-owned, free-standing investor-owned, chain-affiliated not-for-profit, free-standing not-for-profit, and government-owned. They found that investor-owned hospitals had patient-care charges per admission that were 18 percent higher than charges at not-for-profit free-standing hospitals and 21 percent higher than charges at not-for-profit chain hospitals. Contributing to the higher costs, they said, were home-office charges of the for-profit chains, which they found to be *five times* as great as the not-for-profit chains.

Despite claims to communities whose hospitals the chains were interested in buying that mass purchasing of supplies would help cut costs, the Lewin & Associates study found

> no evidence that in 1980 either ownership type of multi-institutional system (investor-owned for-profit, or not-for-profit) was able to translate the potential scale economies of system membership—such as purchase discounts, better access to capital, or centralized management, marketing and strategic planning—into lower overall costs for patient services.[10]

This particular observation has some support in the investment community. According to Per Lofberg and Eric Schlesinger of the Boston Consulting Group, about 90 percent of the costs of providing health care are local in nature, with only 10 percent susceptible to national or even regional management. If savings can only come in that 10 percent of costs, the total savings could at best only be a few percentage points off total costs. If that were to happen, it would certainly be welcome in most quarters, but it hardly constitutes a cure to rising health costs.[11]

A fifth study, done in Florida by the state's Health Cost Containment Board, looked at even more recent data, from 1983, as DRGs were being put in place and presumably when hospitals were finally in a competitive mode. The Florida study is particularly interesting, because that state has the highest percentage of for-profit hospitals of any large state (56 percent of all facilities in 1989). What Florida researchers found, based on a survey of all hospitals in the state, was that the phenomenon observed in earlier studies was still going on in 1983. Almost across the board, the for-profit sector was charging more. Looking at a list of sixteen common services, procedures, or supplies provided by hospitals, the study found charges were often substantially higher at for-profit hospitals. For only two services were they lower. In one category, medical/surgical intensive care, the figures were the same. In the case of pediatric intensive care, no comparison was possible. Typically a money-losing activity, few for-profit hospitals even offered the service.

Among the areas where the Florida study found for-profit hospitals to be charging substantially more than the not-for-profit hospital competition were (1) drugs (marked up an average of 227 percent by the for-profit sector, 165 percent by the not-for-profit sector); (2) lab services (marked up 151 percent by for-profits, 97 percent by non-profits); (3) medical supplies (marked up 124 percent at for-profits, 73 percent at non-profits); and (4) physical therapy (marked up 79 percent by the for-profit industry, 27 percent by not-for-profits). The two areas where the for-profit industry charged less were for use of CAT scanners (58 percent over costs for the for-profits versus 158 percent for the not-for-profits) and for clinic services (apparently a losing operation for both classes of hospitals, but it accounts for only 10 percent of for-profit hospitals' costs versus 71 percent of the not-for-profits' costs).[12]

Many of the studies on relative costs of hospital care have relied on the most readily available public data: Medicare charges. This might tend to leave insured middle-class health consumers unconcerned. For one thing, they are for the most part not on Medicare. For another, the higher costs for treatment of the elderly are largely borne by the government and are only indirectly passed on to taxpayers. But the National Academy of Sciences' 1986 report *Implications of For-Profit Enterprise in Health Care*, developed with the participation of both critics and members of the investor-owned for-profit chains, concludes that the difference in costs between for-profits and not-for-profits if anything *increases* when it comes to treating privately insured patients. Where the cost differential for Medicare patients on a nationwide basis was found by the report to be only "slight," for patients covered by private insurance plans, it was found to range as high as 24 percent.[13] That of course means higher insurance premiums, copayments, and for employers, higher employee health costs.

Backing and Filling

The initial response of the corporate hospital industry to the barrage of unflattering cost comparison studies in the early and mid-eighties was to fund its own studies, but that offered little solace. As Frank Sloan, a professor of economics and business administration at Vanderbilt University, in Nashville, and author of the most detailed study funded by the Federation of American Health Systems, told me, "They funded one of our studies—I regret that they did—and we found a one-dollar difference." He added, "There's a lot of mystification going on. Economists think that if something is for-profit it must be more efficient, however when you look at the evidence, you don't find that they're less costly. Some studies show them to have higher charges to patients, some the same, but no one shows them to be lower. Maybe if you rewarded efficiency, you'd get more efficiency, but we just don't know."

When research failed to support their claims, the for-profit industry began to backpedal on its assertions. Instead of simply proclaiming themselves to be cheaper or more efficient, its executives and advocates began to blame the unfavorable results on the lack of any incentive to make them perform like real capitalists.

In 1986, HCA's Tom Frist pointed out that most of the studies were done using pre-DRG hospital data, or at best data from the first year of operation of prospective payment in Medicare. "The critics are saying we're not the low-cost provider. Well, the incentives weren't there," he said.

In other words, the hospital companies might have shown a canny ability to maximize profits, but they have not had to demonstrate much skill when it comes to minimizing costs. Indeed, while they often describe themselves as health-care entrepreneurs and praise the application of "marketplace discipline" to the health-care industry, the founders of the big hospital chains are hardly entrepreneurs in the classical sense. Unlike Stephen Jobs of Apple computer fame, or the early car makers, they didn't get their starts by inventing a better mousetrap and taking the world by storm. Rather, in a manner more akin to the defense industry, they saw, perhaps better than most, the opportunity to feed at the Great Society's health-care trough. They reaped Medicare and Medicaid payments that were calculated on a cost-plus basis, and grew fat on the guaranteed profits. Even FAHS Director Bromberg agrees that past experience offers little evidence of future performance. Referring to the founders of the big-four for-profit hospital chains, HCA, Humana, AMI, and NME, he said in one interview, "These guys faced very little downside risk, where most entrepreneurs are more engaged in a crapshoot."

Once quick to claim his industry would soon usher in a new era of cheaper, better medical care, a chastened Bromberg was speaking much more cautiously by 1987, and he seemed less certain about how soon the issue of relative costs between for-profits and not-for-profits would be settled. Indeed, in a 1990 interview, he said, "We've been seeing hospitals compete for physicians, and for market share. Whether that competition will turn to prices is a good question." Conceding finally that charges to patients almost invariably rise significantly when a hospital is taken over by a for-profit chain, he explained, "If you buy an old house and modernize it, the mortgage goes up, and if you rented it, so would the rent." He went on to suggest that because on average the age of the for-profit industry's facilities are about half that of the not-for-profit sector's, costs are higher, but that "over a twenty-year period, we'd look more competitive."

The question is, is that a wish or a fact?

Bromberg's metaphor of the housing market is more enlightening than he perhaps intended. For as any real estate agent will report, with each house sold, the price tends to ratchet upward, with or without improvements, as each new owner tries to recover financing and closing costs *and* earn a return on investment. In fact, in the case of the hospital industry, once a facility is acquired by a for-profit firm, it may, like a New York City apartment building, change hands frequently, as corporate managers alter strategies, determine that specific hospitals are not meeting company profit goals, or simply find that a particular facility has used up the bulk of its depreciation value. In the meantime, with each change in ownership, more debt is piled onto the facility—and onto the whole industry—that must be repaid out of patient revenues (and interest that will be subsidized by taxpayers, since it is a deductible business expense). The reason the for-profit sector's newer hospitals cost more is not because operating costs are higher. If anything, older facilities cost more to operate. What costs more is all the debt financing. By the third quarter of 1988, the four largest chains had piled up $6.3 billion in recordable debt according to *Standard & Poor's Register of Corporations, Directors, and Executives,* and several billion more in bank loans and revolving debt. A fifth privately held hospital concern, HealthTrust, had another $750 million in face value debt, according to *S&P* researcher William Reed, who estimated that the company had "at least that much again" in bank debt, making the five-company grand total a whopping $7.8 billion. (The bank debt is all at floating interest rates, making the companies—and patients' bills—vulnerable to interest rate volatility.)

Twenty years seems like a terribly long time to have to wait to determine the validity of Bromberg's prediction, especially if it turns out he is wrong. But even if time did show his industry to be cost competitive, that would be small consolation to people in the many communities across the country where local nonprofit or public facilities were taken over by a chain and costs soared immediately heavenward.

Meanwhile, hospital corporation executives like Frist and Jones claim they are finally ready to show their real entrepreneurial stuff. Medicare after all, with the DRG system now well established, offers hospitals a chance to earn a profit by providing care for less than the assigned reimbursement amount for each category of treatment. They get to keep the difference, but conversely must take the loss if treatment of a patient in a given DRG category costs more than the designated reimbursement rate. Will DRGs suddenly turn the for-profits into low-cost providers?

The first major set of post-DRG statistics, gathered by the state of South Carolina in 1988, suggests that the introduction of such incentives has done little to change things.[14] Those data, covering the year ending June 1987, list charges for twenty-five of the most common types of hospital stays. It turns out that for-profit institutions on average again charged significantly more than the statewide average. Here is what the data revealed about the two chain institutions in the state: HCA charged more than the regional average 87 percent of the time, AMI 59 percent of the time. And in the case of both companies, for treatments that cost more than the average regional price, the difference was substantial, while for treatments that cost less than the average, the difference was minimal.

In the case of normal births, for instance, where the level of medical care is likely to vary very little from one institution to another, one AMI hospital in Spartanburg had no obstetrics department, while both its other two facilities' charges were substantially higher than either the state average or the average for that hospital's region. And AMI's Piedmont Medical Center in York County, which introduced this chapter, charged an average of $1,646 for 195 deliveries that year compared to a regional average cost of $1,563. The other AMI hospital in South Carolina, AMI East Cooper, charged an average $1,924 for 119 normal births, compared to a regional average cost of $1,229. HCA's Aiken Regional Medical Center charged $1,954 on average for 76 normal deliveries during the period—25 percent more than the regional average. The statewide average cost of a normal delivery during the study period was $1,316. *No other competing hospital of any ownership type charged as much as AMI and HCA in their respective regions.*

Health Care's Peculiar Market

When competition was encouraged through deregulation of such industries as airlines, trucking, or communications, the results were mixed as some prices to consumers rose and others fell. But in each instance the reason for any *failure* to meet the expectations of free-market economic theorists has generally been clear: After a rough-and-tumble competitive start, there inevitably follows a period of concentration in the industry which again reduces competition. To be sure, there has been plenty of concentration going on in the hospital industry too, but nowhere near enough as yet to explain easily the lack of price competitiveness. So what's going on here?

It may be that promoting competition among hospitals just can't be a particularly effective way of bringing down costs, since for Adam Smith's free-market "invisible hand" to perform its healing work on the cost spiral, consumers have to be able to shop. This is something that few patients do in a peculiar market in which the actual user of services (the patient) pays only a small portion of the cost of the product (health care), and has only an indirect role in choosing the major purveyor of services (doctors usually select the hospital). Except in the case of the uninsured poor, of course, the decision as to which doctor to use has largely been made by patients. This is changing, though, with the growing number of clinic-type HMOs, where the doctor you get is often the one on duty at the time. But in any event, selection of a *hospital*, when a choice is available at all, is usually the prerogative of the patient's physician. And even there, choices are probably made more in a long-term way, based upon where the physician has staff privileges, rather than on a case-by-case basis. Moreover, to the extent that physicians are "shopping" for hospitals, patient cost is unlikely to be high on the list of factors they consider, if it is reckoned at all. Far more important to a doctor will be such considerations as hospital bonuses to physicians, availability of back office services, inexpensive office rent, and a hospital's reputation, both overall and in her or his particular specialty.

Some hospital companies like Humana create their own captive insurance program; others tie in with existing health insurance plans, as HCA did for a time with Equitable Life. Either way, insured patients of those plans must use physicians with staff privileges at particular facilities in order to receive full benefits. As the purchasers of those plans, employers will also play a major role in the selection process. In that case, it may be argued convincingly, hospital costs will be a major consideration, as employers look for the lowest cost provider, but only in areas where there are competing hospitals in a geographic area. Furthermore, if insurance costs are cut by reducing patient access, as many plans are doing by posing hurdles for patients to cross before reimbursement for a hospital admission can be approved, there may not be much impact on actual cost and efficiency in the operation of the hospital industry itself. As Michael Watt, project director for the Lewin & Associates study discussed earlier, observes, "The hospital industry health plans *all* work *not* through lowering the cost of producing a day of hospital care, but through lowering the number of days of hospital care that are used."

When a patient does decide on a hospital, again cost probably has only a minor role to play in the decision-making process. More important are such considerations as reputation and proximity.

The latter factor particularly interferes with the idealized workings of a free market. Consider what happens in the case of supermarkets and grocery stores in a large city like New York, where most residents don't use cars. The sheer number and density of food markets is impressive, yet prices are astronomical, service for the most part awful, and responsiveness to customer needs minimal. Viewed superficially, places like Manhattan should be hotbeds of competitiveness, putting suburban malls to shame, but the reality is different. In such a setting, it turns out that each supermarket can in effect operate like a minimonopoly because no one wants to, and few can, walk five blocks with six bags of groceries (and many bus drivers won't even let riders on with that much baggage).

Similarly, free-market theory suffers in the case of hospitals, which in most localities are too widely dispersed to offer much effective competition. Patients concerned with being near family members and friends are unlikely to consider relative costs if the cheaper facility is prohibitively remote. And in the case of some medical procedures—emergencies, births—distance from home is the paramount factor considered. In my own case in New York City, a locale thick with hospitals, my family always made use of the nearest hospital for real emergencies, despite its relatively poor reputation and high cost, because we could reach it in three minutes in a cab, compared to fifteen minutes at *best* (assuming no traffic jams) for the nearest first-rate emergency room.

Costs *do matter* to patients and their families, naturally, and many health-care consumers these days are doing their own cost comparison studies. That, indeed, was the motive for the 1988 South Carolina hospital cost survey, one result of which was a state handbook on relative charges for consumers called *Health Choices*.

Some people have acted on their own, too. In 1985 Frank Murray wrote a letter to the editor of his local paper, the Las Vegas *Review Journal*. Murray, a kidney stone sufferer, reported that he had had two bouts of kidney stones less than a year apart. The first time, he went to Southern Nevada Memorial Hospital, a local public facility. The second time, he went to Humana Sunrise Hospital. The treatment, he says, was "almost identical," but not the cost. Humana Sunrise's bill, according to Murray, was 50 percent higher.

He wrote:

> As I was curtly informed by administrative personnel at Humana, the costs were higher because Humana is a "private" hospital, and Southern Nevada is a county hospital. Now this is a point well taken, and probably could account for a 15 or 20 percent difference, but 50 percent! Come on, who does Humana think they are fooling?[15]

Murray's solution to Humana's pricing was to resort to the competitive system praised by Humana's David Jones:

> I would strongly urge all Las Vegans to do their part in helping correct health-care costs in Las Vegas by avoiding Humana hospitals whenever possible and going elsewhere. I know I will. To those who have employers paying for your health insurance, remember, higher costs mean higher premiums your company has to pay; thus, less [is] available to give you in wages.

Of course, if Murray's employer had purchased a Humana insurance plan, he wouldn't have had much of a choice. Going to Southern Nevada Memorial Hospital would be prohibitively expensive, since Humana's insurance would require a high deductible from users of non-Humana facilities. It might also mean Murray would have to get another doctor, if his own doctor didn't have admitting privileges at the competing facility, a situation many of the hospital chains apparently are attempting to promote. Indeed, Humana's 1989 annual report carried a polemic on America's health-care crisis, which endorsed the repeal of *all* state laws that ban the placing of limitations on choice of doctor and hospital, on the grounds that such laws "effectively prohibit managed care."[16]

The truth is, Humana's insurance plan, from the employers' point of view, as opposed to the employee/patients', might be cheaper, but not because Humana's hospitals are necessarily cheaper per visit. Rather, to the extent that it is cheaper, it is because the plan makes it harder to win approval from a utilization review process for hospital treatment.

Explaining the shortcomings of free-market theory where hospitals are concerned, Lewin & Associates' Watt, an alumnus of Stanford University's Graduate School of Business who has worked in hospital management, says, "For all the talk about more competitive markets, there are a lot of ways health care doesn't meet the classical definitions. There are information imbalances among hospitals, doctors, and patients. Besides, people get involved in buying health care episodically. It's not something they do regularly and often. It's more like buying a car. Also, you don't have the psychological distance that you get in buying other things. When it's your body and your health, there's more concern about quality and less about cost, but even then, people have a hard time judging quality. Even the industry itself hasn't been able to come up with a way of measuring that."

Admitting as much, HCA in 1987 embarked, at considerable projected expense, on a ten-year project to define quality of care and establish ways of measuring it. By 1990, that project had been quietly scuttled and forgotten.

The trouble is that improving quality of care wasn't the idea behind the introduction of competition into the health-care field. The *quality* of health care services in the U.S., at least for those with insurance, has for decades been first rate; it is the *cost* of that

care that has been concerning the public, employers, and government policymakers alike. As health industry investor Charles
Reilly, formerly senior vice president for development at AMI,
explained to me in a 1986 interview conducted while he was still
working at American Medical International, "The current system
is excellent in terms of clinical care and accessibility, but it has
serious deficiencies in other areas." Specifically, he said, there
is "a lot of redundancy and that means a lot of excess cost, with
the result that the payers aren't getting full value."

This being the case, the goal of any reform of the health-care
industry, whether regulatory or competitive, *should* be to cut costs
as much as possible without reducing either quality or access.

Clearly, as reported in chapters 3 and 4, the growth of
corporate hospital chains has raised concerns about quality of
care, particularly among physicians. And as will be seen in
chapter 7, the expansion of corporate chains has significantly
reduced access for the poor, especially in the South and Southwest
where they are most prevalent. If this jeopardizing of both quality
and access were occurring in return for lower overall medical *costs*,
there might be room for debate on the merits of the new approach
to hospital operation, at least in cold cost/benefit terms. But so far,
the record suggests that the trade-off for the expansion of corporate medicine into the field of acute care has been a one-way
street.

If competition to date has done little to control hospital costs,
future developments are only likely to worsen the situation, not
improve it. Most health industry analysts, not to mention many
leaders of the for-profit hospital industry, agree that the entire
health-care industry is moving into a period of consolidation.

In a 1989 study contracted by the American Hospital Association, Gary Ahlquist and Andrew Greene, research associates
with Booz, Allen & Hamilton, Inc., looked at three hundred
hospital mergers and acquisitions that took place between 1986
and 1989. Noting that mergers have been hailed in some quarters
as a panacea promising "lower costs, market leverage, critical
mass for technology advancement, and *synergy*," they found that
instead "few mergers appear to fulfill even part of this promise."[17]

Saying that hospital mergers were increasing in frequency
between 1986 and 1989, and that by 1993 almost every "moderate
to large" market was "virtually certain to undergo consolidation," they warned that most resulting mergers would be "more
disease than cure."

In a 1990 interview, Ahlquist, a vice president of Booz, Allen specializing in strategy development for the hospital industry, said his study showed that hospital competition tends to lead to *higher* rather than *lower* health costs because it is seldom based on price. "You see situations where in two-hospital towns, costs [are] higher on a per-unit basis than in one-hospital towns, because the hospitals compete for physicians, not patients, and the way you compete for physicians is by having the latest equipment and facilities. The costs of that competition you pass on to the consumer." Even where mergers do make economic sense, Ahlquist and Greene said they are no cure for the endless health-care cost spiral. "True merger-related savings," they wrote, "are at a maximum 10 percent of operating costs, and are less than 5 percent in most cases." Savings of that magnitude, after all, are more than cancelled out by the financing costs that inevitably accompany mergers.

Economically advantageous for society or not, however, consolidation is in the cards for the hospital industry. FAHS Director Bromberg himself, the for-profit industry's chief spokesperson, once predicted that by the middle to late 1990s, some ten or twelve giant concerns could dominate health care in the U.S. Candidates would probably come from the pharmaceutical, the insurance, and the for-profit hospital industries. William Giles, a senior vice president at Grey Advertising, the company that in 1985 was awarded a $20 million contract with Humana, saw even more concentration. He suggested that by the late 1990s, "three or four companies will dominate health care."

Whatever the number, it appears that the health-care industry is undergoing a process similar to that of the steel and automobile industries at earlier periods in this century, with mergers reducing the numbers of competitors to a handful, perhaps a small enough handful that the "free market" won't be all that free. The implications for health-care costs of such a development are enormous.

Consider the U.S. steel industry. After a series of mergers at the turn of the century, it did very well in terms of growth and return on equity to shareholders, but it didn't do so well over the years in terms of price or quality. While nominally competitive, the industry actually became cooperative, with individual steel companies agreeing tacitly on prices and competing in less costly and dangerous ways. Protected by government import quotas, it ultimately became hugely inefficient. The auto industry, which consolidated later in the century, went through much the same process, and even now, after over a decade of renewed competition from foreign imports, manages to use its political and economic clout to keep what competition exists more in the realm of advertising and styling rather than price and quality, in the view of many industry critics.

What would a parallel development mean in health care? That the much heralded age of competition for patients' and doctors' hearts, minds, and health-care dollars might never really even take place at all in the realm of the hospital bill. Rather, it could all come down to a rivalry among advertising agencies, marketing strategists, and architects, thus staying in "safe" areas that would not jeopardize profit margins as price competition might. Just as soft-drink makers compete vigorously to link their names with those of popular entertainers, while selling their flavored sugar water at the same price, and just as automakers jump at the chance to raise prices collectively rather than reduce them to gain market share, so a hospital industry dominated by a few major corporations may do little or nothing to lower the cost of health care.

It's not for nothing that Grey Advertising fought for and won Humana's advertising account. Advertising a company's product as the cheapest is easy and doesn't require much money, but image advertising, the attempt to create a brand allegiance among consumers, is another story—a lucrative one. Humana and Grey in 1986 laid plans for a $20 million one-year ad campaign aimed at creating the first American example of "branded" health care, making Humana a household name. The idea, in the words of Grey Advertising Senior Vice President Thomas Aydelotte, was to make it so that "if someone twists his ankle at Disney World, he might look in the phone book and be reassured to see Humana listed."

The campaign never got off the ground. In 1987, just as Grey was set to go with its novel coordinated ad campaign, Humana cancelled, citing temporary earnings setbacks from its insurance operation. The company went back to its old system of advertising in local markets. But the dream of branded care is only deferred, not forgotten, and will surely be renewed before long as Humana's insurance plan success leads it to aim at a national market.

"Competition," says Lewin & Associates' Michael Watt, "has a definite effect on the health-care industry, but it is not any more of a panacea in terms of solving the cost problem than other things that have been tried. The for-profit hospital industry may continue with higher prices. They may be quite happy being known for higher prices but more amenities. If they have specialty services, like say plastic surgery or alcohol dependency programs, then maybe lowering costs just isn't so important to them in reality."

6

Buying Respect:
The Corporation Goes
to Med Schools

As [academic medical] centers face this host of issues, they often find their governance process is gravely
influenced by the external sources of funds and the
strings that are tied to them.
                    —Irving J. Lewis and Cecil G. Sheps
                    in *The Sick Citadel: The American Academic
                    Medical Center and the Public Interest*

Nineteen eighty-four was the year that the corporate hospital
industry suddenly vaulted from the back pages of the *Wall Street
Journal* onto the front page of the nation's daily newspapers. That
year, Humana, in a well-oiled public relations effort designed to
make its name a household word, bought its way into the forefront
of the new and controversial field of artificial heart technology. For
most people, the stories that poured out of Louisville, Kentucky,
represented the first time they had heard of for-profit hospitals.
And the stories were *exciting*. Millions of people read about or
watched on television the drama of terminal heart-disease victims

146

being restored to at least some degree of health by having their failing hearts removed and then replaced by a pneumatically driven mechanical heart implant. Although Humana was the star of the show, the spotlight was also thrown for the first time on the for-profit hospital chains as an industry. Before Humana's artificial heart program, many people, even in communities where the hospital was owned by a chain, probably didn't know there *was* such a thing as a hospital run on a for-profit basis. Now the corporate hospital chains were being portrayed as the site of the pinnacle of medical research.

It was exactly what Humana's David Jones had hoped would happen. As the company's feisty chairman and CEO recalled the story in a 1986 interview, the program took shape in a 1984 conversation with Dr. Allan Lansing, head of the Humana Heart Institute International at Humana Hospital-Audubon, the company's premier facility in Louisville. "He was telling me how Dr. William DeVries, who had done one artificial heart implant at the University of Utah School of Medicine, couldn't do another because first he would have to raise $180,000," said Jones. "I was frankly appalled that such a talented doctor would have to raise that money himself. Right away, I suggested to Dr. Lansing that we invite him down and offer to cover his expenses. After all, we had the hospital beds [the company's average occupancy rate in 1984 had fallen to 54.4 percent], so it wouldn't be that much of an incremental cost for us. He came and talked, and I offered to finance one hundred operations. That was it." In an interview with the *Wall Street Journal* in November 1984, a few months after Dr. DeVries signed on with Humana and only days before the first artificial heart implant at the Heart Institute, Jones said candidly that he hoped the Jarvik-7 heart implants would provide a major boost toward his "modest goal of becoming a national brand of health care." He added:

> It's realistic to suppose and hope that if this goes well, people will consider Louisville and Humana along with other eminent centers for the treatment of heart disease. If we mess up or if the experimentation doesn't work, our reputation might go the other way. That's a risk we take.[1]

DeVries and Humana received Food and Drug Administration approval to conduct six permanent implants of the Jarvik artificial heart, and they immediately forged ahead, preparing for the first new operation. There were many questions already being asked in the medical community about the ethics of the program, however, a reaction to the dismal results of Dr. DeVries's first heart implant in Utah two years earlier into dentist Barney Clark. Clark had lived only 112 days, all of that time tethered to the first Jarvik-7 machine. And during those sixteen weeks he suffered seizures, periods of mental confusion, severe lung and kidney problems and had to endure additional surgery. Many doctors and scientists argued that the pump itself, dependent on external power and requiring infection-prone hose connections through the skin and into the thoracic cavity, was at best a transitional device and that the experimental implants should be limited to animals.

As Richard Landau, chairman of a committee that determines research policies at the University of Chicago's Medical School, said at the time, "I don't see any value in continuing a life that is artificial."[2] Dr. David Olch, a member of the judicial council that determines the AMA's ethical policies, said of the Clark experiment, "It's hard to rationalize, other than merely being a pioneer, what value this had as far as the patient was concerned."[3]

Dr. DeVries and Humana never did one hundred implants. They never even got to do the six originally approved operations. After stroke problems also developed in their first two patients at Audubon, William Schroeder and Murray Haydon (a third Jarvik-7 recipient, Jack Burcham, died of bleeding complications ten days after the operation), the FDA changed its mind. On January 8, 1986, the agency rescinded its earlier blanket approval for DeVries and Humana to conduct six implants, saying it would permit them only on a "case by case" basis with approval required in advance each time—a significant pullback of support. Permanent implant experiments halted, with DeVries claiming that advances in transplant capability meant that many people who would have been "ideal candidates" for a Jarvik heart a year or two earlier were now able to get a human heart successfully. There were rumors, denied by Humana and DeVries, that the company had told him to stop implanting permanent artificial hearts because of mounting criticism of the procedure. In 1988, DeVries, saying he wanted to go into private practice, resigned from the Humana Heart Institute International, without attempting another permanent artificial heart implant.[4]

The experiments were clearly not an unqualified success, but

Jones was nonetheless proved right in his gambit. The Jarvik heart operations did boost Humana's name recognition dramatically, and his company may not have even had to pay a price in lost image when the experiments turned sour. There's no doubt that the whole artificial heart exercise had indeed made Humana a household name, and people were more likely to recall the initial drama of the implants than the later stories of the device's problems.

It is fair to ask, though, whether the human experiments with the Jarvik-7 device at Humana added much to medical knowledge. The Jarvik heart and other similar artificial hearts or partial heart-pump devices have subsequently proven useful as bridges for patients who have to wait for a donor, but it was clear from the start that they were unsuitable for permanent use because of the size of the external pumping equipment and the need to have air hoses connected through the skin. But for Humana's experiments, the Jarvik-7 might never again have been installed as more than a short-term "bridge" device in transplant patients awaiting a donor, following DeVries's first operation on Barney Clark. Indeed, one reason—besides simple lack of funding—that DeVries moved to Humana was that the internal review board at the University of Utah was reportedly dragging its feet in granting him approval to do another human implant there.

At the nation's other major academic medical centers, DeVries would likely have faced a similarly tough time winning approval from medical research committees to continue with his artificial heart work. He had in fact rejected affiliation with the University of Louisville's medical school—which would have been a logical relationship since Humana was leasing and running the school's teaching hospital—because of disagreements over such review requirements. At Humana Hospital-Audubon there were no academic impediments; if anything, there was a bias toward forging ahead. Not only was there the public relations angle; if the Jarvik device worked, Humana and DeVries, both shareholders in the Utah-based company that made the Jarvik-7 device, stood to profit handsomely. (Both the hospital company and the doctor finally sold their holdings on November 8, 1984,[5] after criticism surfaced, of what industry critic Stanley Wohl has rightly termed a "clear conflict of interest." DeVries reportedly used the proceeds from the sale of his stock to buy a white Mercedes.)[6]

The public relations focus of the entire Humana artificial heart venture was evident from the outset. During the three months between the time it signed on DeVries in August 1984 and the first Jarvik-7 implant operation on November 25, the company spent at least as much time preparing to promote itself as it spent preparing to operate. Not that planning wasn't called for: So many reporters showed up from media outlets around the world for the first operation on Schroeder that a specially built press room at Audubon had to be hastily abandoned in favor of the city's convention center.[7] There was a carnival atmosphere to the whole affair—openly encouraged by Humana's public relations team— which left many medical experts wondering if the patient himself wasn't getting second billing to the company. For instance, where much of the day-to-day medical information about Barney Clark was withheld for reasons of privacy by doctors in Utah, the medical informed consent form given to Schroeder to sign by Humana essentially made the patient public property, giving Dr. DeVries the authority to release to the public any information "within generally accepted bounds of good taste."[8] Since at the time he signed Schroeder was on his deathbed, and since his whole future depended on Humana's and Dr. DeVries's willingness to perform an enormously costly experimental operation on him at their expense, the voluntary nature of this type of release has to be questioned, even if in Schroeder's particular case, the patient had no objections to the public attention.

A New Strategy: Buying a Reputation

Publicly, Humana's human tests of the artificial heart were the big medical story in 1984 and 1985. But while Schroeder and Haydon were battling for life tethered to their heart pumps, the big for-profit hospital chains, including Humana, were each privately embarking on a much bigger experiment in the realm of state-of-the-art medicine: the acquisition of entire teaching hospitals.

The pell-mell expansion of corporate hospital chains over the last decade has certainly stirred up controversy in the fields of politics, public health, and economics. But it was only when the big hospital companies all decided to buy into the nation's teaching hospital system that the medical profession itself really entered the fray. With the first forays by the chains into academic medicine, the issue of for-profit health care suddenly penetrated the core of the nation's medical system, the place where standards are set, where entire generations of doctors are trained, and where most medical research is conducted. Now even the most prominent physicians and medical researchers have been compelled to contemplate the notion of health as a commodity, and of themselves as "revenue producers" or "cost centers."

The general public got a glimpse of this corporate/academic conflict as early as the summer of 1983, when HCA made a bid to buy McLean Psychiatric Hospital, a teaching hospital owned by Massachusetts General Hospital, the Harvard Medical School's teaching hospital system.

HCA's interest in buying McLean was clear. The company, in step with several of the other big chains, was at the time just making a major move into the lucrative new psychiatric hospital market. It already had twenty-four psychiatric hospitals in its stable, but it still had to deal with the prevailing public perception of psychiatric hospitals as "nuthouses" or "loony bins"—not the place to send your kid for a behavioral problem, or to commit yourself for treatment of an alcohol or chemical dependency. HCA hoped that by buying McLean Psychiatric Hospital, the company could add the luster of Harvard Medical School to its new venture, and thereby change the public's view of private inpatient psychiatric facilities.

HCA approached McLean and the trustees of the Massachusetts General Hospital system at a critical moment: the parent hospital complex was trying to devise some way of raising the $250 million considered necessary to rebuild its aging plant. Renovation of McLean alone was expected to run about $35 million. It was an enormous project, and the Massachusetts General Hospital board of trustees had been looking for solutions to the financing problem with only limited success for two years (during that time it had only raised about $60 million), when the HCA proposal came in that summer.

Operating behind the scenes, hospital board chairman Francis Burr, a respected Boston lawyer, negotiated what he and the board thought was a solid contract with HCA. They claimed the agreement would protect academic freedom at McLean, guarantee the poor access to the hospital, and at the same time provide the needed funds to rebuild the hospital. While the total price HCA was offering to pay was never disclosed, Burr did say the company was ready to finance the complete $35 million renovation of the facility, to establish a governing board that would include only one-third HCA representatives, and to donate $6.25 million directly to Harvard.

It seemed like a dream come true to the board of trustees, but it was greeted with a firestorm of criticism by medical faculty when the proposed takeover was announced in August. The Harvard Medical School publishes the *New England Journal of Medicine*, whose editor at the time, Arnold Relman, has had a running feud on the editorial page with the for-profit hospital industry. His arguments against the corporate chains became a rallying cry for opposition to the sale. In a September 4, 1983, interview with the *New York Times*, he explained his position saying:

> Here is the bastion of academic medicine, with the most distinguished teaching hospital in the country, if not in the world, face-to-face with the biggest, richest hospital company in the world. They want Harvard's imprimatur. It's going to be an important bellwether of where our society is going to go.[9]

Relman may have been sought out for comment by journalists, but opposition to the sale was also reflected widely among the less prominent doctors and medical school professors at Harvard. Even though under the proposed agreement HCA generously promised to underwrite the entire academic staff of the hospital, to maintain the existing level of teaching and research, and to allow a committee composed of two-thirds Harvard faculty and one-third HCA personnel to run academic affairs, the faculty recoiled. Many immediately expressed concern about the precedent being set by the sale of part of one of the nation's leading teaching hospitals to a corporate chain.

Almost as soon as word of the negotiations between HCA and the Massachusetts General board of trustees got out in late August, the medical school faculty demanded a say. The dean of the school, Daniel Tosteson, responded by appointing a committee of nine senior faculty members to study the proposal. Meanwhile, other faculty members organized hearings and did some research into HCA and the behind-the-scenes bargaining that led to the proposed sale.

Dr. Ed Shapiro, an early critic of the proposal, was an organizer of faculty opposition. Explaining the vehemence of that resistance, he said, "First of all, there was the process dilemma. A lot of the storm came because the thing was managed so badly. Here the hospital had been discussing its future for two years, and in August, when many people were away, the board of trustees suddenly announced plans to sell the hospital to HCA, ignoring all the planning that had been going on."

Shapiro added that faculty members were concerned about rumors that one official who would be involved in any sale decision had ties to a company with a financial stake in HCA, as well as the possibility that someone in a leadership position at McLean might be offered a position in HCA after any sale agreement. This latter concern was supported by HCA's history of frequently retaining senior managers when it acquired a hospital. Even if the practice makes sense in terms of maintaining institutional stability, it proved disconcerting to an already suspicious faculty worried about any hint of conflict of interest.

Once the Harvard Medical School faculty organized, it was clear to both the hospital board of trustees and to HCA executives that nothing would happen quickly. The committee appointed by Dean Tosteson ultimately recommended in November that the medical school reject the sale of McLean. Though the committee had surveyed seventeen HCA hospitals and reported finding no problems with excessive costs or quality of care, it said the "overwhelmingly negative reaction of the medical staff" was paramount. It also said that organizational arrangements designed to separate the faculty from the hospital company would be "too cumbersome."

In the end, said Shapiro, "the struggle came down to a matter of deeply held values, because the pragmatics argued for affiliation."

The prevailing sentiment was probably best expressed by Professor Rashi Fein, a health economist at Harvard. Speaking at a medical school faculty meeting just before a straw poll on the issue, he said:

> As a graduate of another university I confess there have been times when I've been taken aback by the arrogance of Harvard's presumed leadership. But it is true, Harvard is a leader. Its actions are watched and its behavior provides legitimization. We cannot claim that leadership and act as if the sale of McLean is a purely internal matter to be judged solely by its impact on the [Massachusetts General Hospital] and on Harvard. We help set standards. We *are* the custodians of a proud and useful tradition, one which others have emulated: that

the practice of medicine does not rest on the quest for profit, but on the quest for cure and care and equity. If we abandon that tradition—the marketplace does not seek equity—and legitimize that abandonment, so too will others. Some of those others, perhaps many, will be too weak to strike as good a financial bargain or to ensure the academic freedom we all prize. Some of them will be less concerned about justice and fairness. We will have provided legitimization for a certain kind of behavior—that, of course, is what HCA seeks—and now the debate, to put it crudely, will be about the price.

When a formal vote was taken in November, the faculty came down 81 percent against affiliation with HCA and six percent in favor (the rest abstained or were absent), a stunning defeat for the company and for the idea of corporate ownership of teaching hospitals. Though the faculty of the medical school legally had no control over the sale of McLean, it was, after all, the Harvard connection that most interested HCA. Without faculty support for the purchase, the company lost interest.

Undaunted in its quest for a reputation for quality medicine, HCA went on to buy two midwestern teaching institutions, Wesley Medical Center in Wichita, Kansas, and Methodist Hospital in Oklahoma City. More recently, in late 1986, the company announced a much looser affiliation agreement with another Harvard Medical School teaching institution, Brigham and Women's Hospital, the nation's sixth-largest obstetrical facility and a major center for cardiac and orthopedic care. Under the latter agreement, Brigham and Women's agreed to develop continuing medical education courses for use in HCA's hospitals nationwide and to assess quality of care in the company's eighteen New England–area hospitals, at HCA expense. In return, the 720-bed hospital gets to make use of the company's purchasing system. There is, however, no HCA ownership or involvement in the management of the hospital. Nor, as a result, was there any faculty opposition.

Adding a New Link to the Chain

Why the sudden interest by the corporate hospital industry in academic medical centers? After all, the companies had been expanding for almost a decade and a half without showing any interest at all in these medical behemoths. Are the corporate hospital chains interested in research and physician education? Do they think they can turn a profit or make use of the admittedly massive cash flows at such major facilities? Or are they less concerned with making money and more interested in acquiring the reputation for quality of the hospitals they buy? The answers to these questions are not simple, and in fact seem to vary from situation to situation, and company to company.

Teaching hospitals, or academic medical centers, as they are often called, are clearly distinct from other hospitals, public and private. They are generally much bigger, but they stand apart in a number of important ways besides size. While many of the patients they care for could just as easily be treated in a community hospital, teaching hospitals are also the place where state-of-the-art medicine is practiced, and where much of the care of the nation's poor is provided, particularly when serious illness or injury is involved. These poor and uninsured patients—and to some extent insured private patients as well—have served as research subjects, on the one hand, and as "teaching fodder" for generations of interns and residents, on the other.

Prior to Humana's artificial heart experiments, critics of the for-profit hospital industry routinely charged that corporate hospitals did little medical research and education work. Indeed, in the late 1970s and early 1980s, it was often suggested that one reason the not-for-profit sector was having trouble competing was that many not-for-profits *did* engage in research and teaching—both notorious money-losing activities. In the early and middle 1980s, perhaps in part to answer those charges but more importantly to capture some of the reputation for quality medicine that teaching hospitals have attained, and to position themselves as full-service providers of health care, all the major hospital companies began buying or leasing large teaching hospitals.

Today, Humana has a forty-year lease on the University of Louisville's teaching hospital and owns another, the Michael Reese Hospital and Medical Center in Chicago. HCA, in addition to its hospitals in Kansas and Oklahoma, has close links to Vanderbilt University Hospital in Nashville (as of mid-1991, HCA Chairman Tom Frist, Jr., was a member of the Vanderbilt board of trustees, while Joe Wyatt, chancellor of Vanderbilt, sat for years on the HCA board of directors). In 1984, AMI purchased St. Joseph's Hospital in Omaha, Nebraska (associated with Creighton University Medical School), and Presbyterian–St. Luke's Medical Center, a multihospital system in Denver that includes two teaching hospitals connected with the University of Colorado. Two other AMI efforts—to purchase or build teaching hospitals at George Washington University in Washington, D.C. and the University of California at Irvine—were dropped when the company ran into financial difficulties in 1986. For its part, National Medical Enterprises decided to build a new $150-million 275-bed teaching hospital, due to open in 1991, which it will own and run for the University of Southern California Medical School in Los Angeles.

As recently as 1983, even as people outside the investment houses on Wall Street were beginning to notice the rapid expansion of the corporate hospital chains, few observers expected the companies to show any interest in teaching hospitals. The high and unpredictable burden of unreimbursed indigent care, an unusually complex management structure involving multiple lines of authority at hospital and medical school, and the often precarious financial condition at these institutions, all seemed to obviate such a tactic.

In 1982, sociologist Paul Starr, an astute observer of the development of corporate medicine, wrote in *The Social Transformation of American Medicine* that it was unlikely that the hospital chains would buy up teaching institutions, because of their high operating costs and the large number of indigent patients.[10] And Irving Lewis and Cecil Sheps, coauthors of *The Sick Citadel*, a 1981 book specifically about the academic medical center and what they called its "crisis of identity," wrote:

> The most prevalent attitude among medical school and teaching hospital leadership today is one of "gloom and doom." Teaching hospitals feel seriously misunderstood and disadvantaged because the emphasis on cost containment hurts them more than other hospitals, and are concerned about how they will fare in a period of market competition.[11]

But Lewis and Sheps did not anticipate that one response to those concerns would be outright sale to the for-profit competition. Rather, they wrote that "efforts to institute a competitive strategy are likely to founder." In a 1988 interview, Lewis said, "I have to say, I was prepared, even when the first interest was being expressed by the hospital companies [in teaching hospitals], to take the point of view that the competition kick and the for-profit takeover kick would be short-lived. Now I'm not so sure about that."

Indeed, shortly after the publication of those two important books, corporate acquisition of a number of major academic medical centers and close tie-ins with others became almost *de rigueur* in the industry. Concern began to mount in some quarters that medical education, research, and indigent care would all suffer.

Richard H. Egdahl, director of Boston University Medical Center, outlined some of those concerns clearly. Speaking at the Hirsh Symposium on the Implications of the For-Profit Hospital in Health Care, held in 1984 at George Washington University when that institution itself was in the thick of considering a sale of its hospital, he said:

> Profit can be a powerful engine for the efficient operation of health-care institutions, a useful incentive for cost control and improved performance, and a stimulus for raising patient satisfaction with the health care provided. But even among those who acknowledge the potential benefits of ties between educational institutions and for-profit chains, there is concern about close links between groups with the seemingly disparate goals of return on equity to shareholders and the promotion of education and research. Under what circumstances are these goals competitive and under what circumstances are they supportive of each other? What potential dangers and possible conflicts of interest do medical schools and their associated teaching hospitals face in forming financial and management ties with for-profit corporations? Under what conditions will a for-profit partner, acting on economic motives, seek to pull out of an arrangement, and what protection will the nonprofit partner have? Finally, what are the risks or potential drawbacks of linkages between for-profit and educational institutions?[12]

More pointedly, he asked further:

> Are there ways the for-profit partner could "milk" an institution over the short-term, reducing its economic

viability, and then withdraw? Short of actual withdrawal, are there pressures that might entice a for-profit entity to alter the patient mix or treatment patterns of patients in ways that undermine the teaching and research goals of the institution?

What *are* teaching hospitals and why are they commonly held to be so central to the American health-care system? According to the American Hospital Association, about one in six of the nation's hospitals has at least some sort of relationship with a medical school, though in most cases only a minor one. There are 435 hospitals that are members of the Council of Teaching Hospitals (COTH), which requires at least four major residency programs and "close"affiliation with a medical school, but only some 100–175 of these are considered to be "major" institutions. According to the AHA, as of 1989 only 68 were actually *owned* by a medical school.

Teaching hospitals provide the bulk of all so-called "tertiary" care, or advanced treatment for those who are seriously ill. They also serve as the main training ground for physicians and other health-care personnel, and a proving ground for new equipment and techniques. In addition, and in part because of their educational and research roles, teaching hospitals serve disproportionate numbers of the poor. Probably equally important is the role of the teaching hospital in setting overall standards for the medical profession.

Lewis and Sheps, in *The Sick Citadel*, offer this definition:

> The academic medical center is at the core of the nation's health system. It feeds it, fuels it, and overtly runs a substantial part of it. It fully controls the most specialized medical care; at the same time, it is the doctor to much of urban America, rich and poor alike. It produces tomorrow's physician and profoundly influences current and future medical practice. It shapes the future of our health services. . . . The universities and the public tend to see the center as an academic research institution, but it is more than that. Its broad range of functions gives it the power to determine the scope, pattern, availability, and cost of health services.[13]

Teaching hospitals, then, have traditionally played a number of critical roles, whose impact on the larger medical community, and on the nation's health system, has been mixed. As the centers for clinical research, technological innovation, and education, for instance, they have served as referral locations for treatment of patients whose ailments were beyond the capabilities of community hospitals. At the same time they have compelled those very community hospitals to make ever greater capital investments by establishing standards for quality of care and treatment that can be ignored by smaller hospitals only at the risk of losing the support of local physicians and patients. Assuming an insurance plan that will pay most of the bill anyway, who for instance would want to have an operation for kidney stones at a local community hospital when the nearest teaching hospital could do the job nonsurgically with an expensive lithotripsy? What parent, for that matter, would want a child operated on for a tonsillectomy at a small hospital with no intensive care room?

Given their large size and accordingly large overhead, teaching hospitals have always been the most expensive places for the provision of medical care, but as long as most patients were having their treatment reimbursed on a cost-plus basis, such facilities did very nicely, thank you. When the government tossed out Medicare's old cost-plus reimbursement system and substituted the DRG system, though, it hit the teaching hospitals particularly hard. For one thing, a disproportionate percentage of their patients—compared to most community hospitals—are on Medicare. For another, as tertiary-care hospitals, they were by definition treating the sickest and therefore most expensive patients, a fact that the DRG calculus didn't adequately take into consideration. Held, at least initially, to cost standards set by the overall hospital industry for DRG reimbursements for Medicare patients, they also saw Medicaid reimbursements decline as both state and federal government agencies cut back funding. Further, in the face of a growing nationwide property tax rebellion, local governments were also balking at paying the bills of indigent patients. All of this left teaching hospitals with the unenviable choice of either cutting back on care for the poor (resulting in a decrease in patients for medical students to practice on) or running at a loss while trying to develop new sources of revenue. Finally, the federal government began in the late 1970s to reduce funds for education and research, both of which traditionally were mainstays of the academic medical centers' finances.

For some teaching hospitals and medical schools, corporate chains have seemed like a painless cure for the problem of diminishing revenues from government and private insurance sources. As Egdahl said, what the hospital companies offer "at least in theory" is "a vital new supply of funds: dollars for building and research, money for the salaries of both faculty and nonacademic personnel, and the like." He added, "They may obtain access to the generally well reputed management of the for-profit companies, their marketing skills and their operational efficiencies," as well as "extensive patient data bases that may be of use in academic research and training."

Just when teaching hospitals were feeling a financial crunch, the hospital industry started hurting too, in part because of the same Medicare reimbursement changes. The double whammy of a fixed-rate DRG-based system for Medicare in 1983 and efforts by private employers to trim their health benefits costs was pushing hospital occupancy rates down to levels that alarmed administrators. Corporate chain managers were desperately casting about for new ways of bringing business into the admitting office. The specific strategies varied a bit. Humana, as usual a bit bolder than the other companies, opted in 1984 for a captive insurance plan that essentially required subscribers to use Humana facilities. NME expanded into long-term (nursing home) care, free-standing ambulatory facilities, and other elements designed to make the company the provider of a broad continuum of care and also to lessen its dependence on hospitals for revenue and earnings growth. HCA looked for ways to win health-care supply contracts with national employers. Whatever the variant, however, each strategy called for the development of regional company-owned systems centered around a major tertiary hospital, thereby establishing the company as a (or if possible the only) full-service operation in a given geographic market area. Since for the most part, each of the corporate chains tended to consist of masses of small-to-medium-sized community hospitals—planets without a sun so to speak—the new regional approach meant buying tertiary-care teaching institutions around which such smaller facilities would "orbit." For the hospital companies, buying or in some way hooking up with teaching hospitals offered instant acquisition of those institutions' reputation for quality. It also filled an important gap in the creation of what one hospital company executive has referred to as the "seamless web" of a vertically integrated health-care system. As researchers Howard Berliner and Robb Burlage wrote in a paper delivered at the American Public Health Association's 1986 annual meeting:

Up to the present, patients in chain institutions that need more intensive services or particular types of technology have had to be referred out of the [corporate] system. The chains face potential loss of those patients [if they become attracted to the hospital to which they were transferred], and they lose the associated revenues from the tertiary services. . . . The chains may find that the ability to shift patients up and down the continuum of care is not only a convenient mechanism for locking patients into their systems, but also a useful way of keeping revenues within their systems.

They added:

The concept of vertical integration stresses that the system is more important than the particular institution. The theory is that it is not the prestige of any particular hospital that is being marketed (although there is no reason why this cannot be) but rather the ability of the chain itself to fulfill all the medical-care needs well. Thus it is not necessary to own the most prestigious teaching hospital so much as it is necessary to own any teaching hospital. To the extent that the system is interested in revenues and retention of patients and market share, the best tertiary hospital may not be the one with the best-known research program or the best educational program so much as the one with the best local reputation for patient care.[14]

To date, there has been little experience with the recent wedding of corporate health care and medical education and research. As the 1986 report *For-Profit Enterprise in Health Care* of the Institute of Medicine notes of those new ties:

Investor-owned companies have only begun to have substantial involvement in education and research . . . [and] because there are so many unique aspects of each institution and each agreement, it may be a long time indeed before general conclusions can be drawn. . . .[15]

To carry the marriage analogy a bit further, the relationship is probably still at the honeymoon stage; any incompatibilities have not had a chance to appear. With everybody concerned about putting on a good show, the prevailing attitude still seems to be "Gee whiz! Don't they make a beautiful couple!" The report includes a note of caution:

> It is . . . likely that the experiences of the first few teaching hospitals to be acquired may not be good predictors for the long run, because of their visibility, and because of the interest of the investor-owned companies in achieving legitimacy and avoiding negative reports (and the hospitals in having made sound decisions). Both the terms that can be reached between the companies and the hospitals (or their owners) and the consequences of involvement of investor ownership in teaching hospitals may be different in the future.[16]

Still, there are enough examples around now for a few evaluations to be made, and these suggest that while corporate purchases of teaching hospitals are helping out certain troubled medical schools, they are no panacea. And there are some undesirable side effects that could get worse over time.

Humana Makes a Deal

The University of Louisville was the first to plunge into the vortex of corporate medicine, signing, in 1983, a renewable forty-year lease with Humana. In the months that followed, Humana Chairman David Jones was effusive in touting the agreement at speaking engagements all over the country as a cure-all for local communities' indigent care problem, and as a solution for teaching hospitals' funding crisis. As he told a meeting of the Massachusetts Public Health Association in 1985:

> There's nothing about that solution that's unique to Humana or to the city of Louisville. It's the kind of solution that could work well here in Boston if you have a problem that's anything like the one that I described.[17]

This is quite an overstatement, for there were at least two aspects to the deal that made it unique: it occurred in Humana's home town, and both Jones and CEO Wendell Cherry were

University of Louisville alumni (Jones was at the time of the agreement a member of the school's board of trustees). Jones has also overstated the extent to which the company's takeover of the University of Louisville's teaching hospital has solved the city's indigent health-care crisis. He told me simply, in one interview, that "in Louisville, we don't have a problem with indigent care." Historical experience suggests, however, that Humana has figured out a way to profit by providing some of that care, and when not profitable, Humana has also figured out how to pass patients and the cost of their treatment off onto others, or to avoid admitting patients.

The whole idea of that corporate takeover began in the early eighties, as the construction of a new $73-million public hospital neared completion in Louisville. The 404-bed future teaching site for the state-owned University of Louisville's School of Medicine, was to replace aging Jefferson County Hospital, which through a quirk of politics and finance was being subsidized by the university at a loss of some $4 million a year. In 1979, the old facility was deeded by the city to the university, making the university formally responsible for the whole losing operation. As Jones recalls, that arrangement could not long endure, given the university's paltry endowment of only $25 million at the time.

While the new hospital would make for better medicine, it was also likely to add to the university's losses. The cost of debt repayment on the new building would have to be covered, while reimbursement for the hospital's indigent and Medicaid patients was on the decline. Indeed, a 1982 study by the accounting firm Ernst & Whinney had projected that in the first year alone the new hospital would lose $10 million or more. At that rate, the entire university endowment would be gone in less than three years!

It was at this juncture that Humana entered the picture, offering to assume operation of the hospital (minus a few obvious money losers: pediatrics and a cancer center), providing that the city and state came up with funds to pay for treatment of indigents. Given Humana's political—and economic—clout in Louisville, and Jones's friendship with then governor John Y. Brown, Jr., the promise of funds for indigent care ($20 million a year) was easily obtained, and on remarkably generous terms. As the deal was worked out, poor people with no resources and no Medicaid would get admitted at the new Humana hospital as they had been before at the old general hospital. But where the old hospital received nothing for its treatment of such patients, at the new facility, Humana would be reimbursed for 95 percent of its billed charges. Competing voluntaries in town are still forced to admit indigents as before on an emergency basis with minimal reimbursement, and they are not being allowed to transfer them to Humana University once stabilized, as they could have done at the old public hospital. Thus, to the extent that this contributes to the financial weakness or threatened closing of some of the city's medical institutions, there *is* still an "indigent care problem."

Getting the university behind the proposal took some doing. As the largest employer in Louisville, Humana was simultaneously respected and feared in the city, and there was a definite wariness among the faculty at the notion of striking such a major deal with the company. A key ally in Humana's push to overcome this reticence was Donald Swain, the new president of the university. Jones and Swain were on the best of terms. Jones had cochaired the board of trustees' search committee and had reportedly wooed Swain from his position as academic vice president of the University of California. What was not widely known at the time the deal was being hammered out was that a house provided by "an anonymous donor" for the new president (who had already received a generous moving allowance), was in fact supplied by Jones himself. Technically, he made a donation to the university, which then purchased the house, offering Swain an option to buy it in the future at the original purchase price.[18] Jones later explained that he was just "an alumnus doing his part." It was an unusually self-effacing response, since neither Humana nor its key principals, Jones and Cherry, have been at all shy about being identified for their expansive local charity activities in Louisville.

In an interview with the Louisville *Courier-Journal* in 1981, before the idea of a Humana takeover of the university hospital first came up, Jones said that he had turned down an offer by Swain to serve on a board that set policy for the hospital, saying it would not be a good idea because public reaction would not be favorable. The article stated that:

> Because Humana owns three hospitals in Jefferson County that operate for profit, Jones said an appearance of a conflict of interest has kept him out of issues involving U of L's non-profit teaching hospital. . . . The *Courier-Journal* would "write something nasty about it," Jones said.[19]

Yet according to most accounts, the deal to have Humana take over the university hospital was pretty much drawn up by Jones and Swain and then presented to the twenty medical departments for rejection or approval. Unlike at Harvard, that approval was overwhelming: According to Donald Kmetz, dean of the Medical School, 76 percent of those voting favored the takeover.

Given the plight of the university hospital, and by extension the Medical School, such a favorable vote is not surprising. Besides, viewed strictly from a financial perspective, Humana was offering the university an excellent deal. Humana agreed to pay a lease fee of $6.5 million a year, which was recycled to the company as a fee for indigent care. The state agreed to provide $8.5 million a year more for indigent care, with the city and county putting in an additional $5 million. The company also agreed to turn over to the university 20 percent of the hospital's annual pretax profits (in 1986, the first year of full operation, this came to $532,000), and to give the university a grant of $4 million at the end of four years. In the interim, the university got the interest on the grant money ($489,000 the first year of the contract).

It was a daring and dramatic play on Humana's part, since it committed the company to cover any indigent care beyond the $20 million, freeing the other parties to the deal of any liability. Of course, it was as shrewd as it was bold, for Humana was getting quite a deal too. In effect the company gained control of a spanking new hospital for less than the prevailing interest rate on the bonds it would have had to sell to finance an equivalent institution (at the same time eliminating that hospital as a future competitor). And it was getting $20 million a year (inflation adjusted) thrown in to meet any indigent care expenses. As Tim Harrington, administrator of Saints Mary and Elizabeth Hospital, a local Humana competitor, grumbled, "All of us would be willing to provide indigent care if we had a huge subsidy and were able to collect on 95 percent of charges!" (In 1991, following passage by the Kentucky state legislature of a measure to reimburse hospitals for indigent care, a dispute arose because Humana's university hospital, by participating in the new program, seemed to be "double dipping." According to an article in the Louisville *Courier-Journal*, Humana would recieve $8 million in 1991 and as much as $11.2 million in 1992 under the new Hospital Indigent Care Assurance Program at the same time that it was already getting paid to treat indigents [$17.6 million in 1991].[20] Humana, for its part, denied that it was getting paid twice, saying that the two sources of funds were for different purposes. Dean Kmetz assured legislators that a committe overseeing the fund would meet to assure that the two reimbursement programs did not overlap.)[21]

Meanwhile, behind the seemingly overwhelmingly favorable medical faculty vote, there was considerable dissension. At least one department that voted heavily in favor of the deal, pediatrics, wasn't even going to be part of it. Humana had opted to leave pediatric care separate from the hospital, aware that NKC, owner of Norton-Kosair Children's Hospital, where the pediatric teaching facility is located, had been absorbing almost $9 million a year in unreimbursed indigent pediatric care bills, with the county only providing NKC with $200,000 a year in reimbursements. In contrast, four departments that *were* very much impacted by the takeover—surgery, pathology, neurology, and anesthesiology—voted solidly *against* the plan.

The lopsided overall vote was not much of a mandate from the faculty for other reasons, too. As one faculty member explained, "There was not much time for discussion. It was bulldozed through. And among many faculty members, there was an attitude that it was a fait accompli. Then, since the voting was by department, many people felt that it was easy to tell how someone voted, so to some extent people were intimidated." (According to Swain himself, the 350-member medical school faculty was only given one week to discuss and vote on the issue.)

And dissension remains, though Kmetz, a Swain appointee, downplays its significance. "The arrangement has been very successful," asserted Kmetz in 1987 (four years into the program), adding, "Sure there have been complaints from the faculty, but they get resolved. When we had the initial agreement, four departments voted against it. I predict you'd still find several departments in opposition, but they might not be the same ones." He declined to name departments that were complaining about the new corporate arrangement.

If Kmetz soft-pedaled any opposition to Humana's takeover within the faculty, Jones denies it entirely. "No one has complained to me about anything," he asserted in an interview. Although surgery was one of the departments that not only voted against the takeover of the new hospital by Humana, but also has complained since, in a February 1985 address to a national meeting of the Society of University Surgeons, Jones made no mention of any problems past or present. The surgeons at the gathering might, for instance, have wanted to hear about how, once the agreement was signed, Humana fought before the state's Certificate of Need and Licensure Board *against* the awarding of a CON for a $2-million magnetic resonance imager at Humana Hospital University. The company argued that the hugely profitable and important diagnostic device should instead go to the company's flagship hospital, Humana Audubon, where the high-profile Humana Heart Institute is located (and where, incidentally, it is of little or no use to the city's poorer residents, who are steered to Humana University where the company can count on 95 percent reimbursement of its charges).

That particular feud between Humana corporate offices and the University Medical School faculty, which Humana won, apparently convinced University of North Carolina radiologist Edward Staab to remove his name from consideration for chairmanship of the University of Louisville's radiology department. According to the Louisville *Courier-Journal*, after learning of the MRI fight, Staab backed out as a candidate, saying, "I guess the bottom line was I couldn't tell who was running that medical school. Were we going to talk about academics or were we going to talk about profit margins for the company? I'm not sure they know the answer to that in Louisville."[22]

Staab, who instead joined the faculty of the University of Florida Medical School in Gainesville, recalled his experience in a 1986 interview with me:

> They offered me the world at Louisville, and were very gracious, but I confess I was a little concerned when, during the course of my one-day interview process, the vast majority of the people I met were accountants and lawyers. From what I could see, Humana had two major hospitals in the area, University and Audubon, and the company quite frankly uses Audubon as a showcase. As a showcase it gets precedence. At least in the field of radiology, University Hospital is not a first-rate institution compared to the hospitals around it.
>
> My big concern was not over quality of care, it was over academic freedom. I asked the people at the hospital who makes the decisions. For instance let's say we just don't have enough money in the pot and it's an academic/quality-of-care issue? Who decides? I was talking with the hospital director, and the answer, it turns out, was [Humana Chairman David] Jones. It became

clear to me in every conversation I had there that bottom-line concerns were being applied to each issue. Now, I know that if you have a guy doing research at a teaching hospital that is run by a medical school, and he's not paying his way, he might be dropped, but the decision will be made by academics. That wasn't true at Louisville. They couldn't even answer me when I asked if they would look beyond a department that was losing money to the overall financial picture. At university-run hospitals, you have losing operations, but you have them for *academic* reasons. *They* have loss-leaders for *profit* reasons.

In a series of interviews conducted by the Louisville *Courier-Journal* in 1985, ten of forty-one medical school faculty members questioned were critical of Humana and the corporate operation of the hospital.[23] Although most of those interviewed had tenure, all asked to remain anonymous. (This is a common feature of corporate-run academic medical centers. In my experience, scarcely anyone with a critical word to say feels safe speaking on the record. Whether or not the corporate managers would retaliate for such criticisms, in terms of freedom of speech, the culture at those institutions seems to have much more in common with industry, where employees typically are afraid to be openly critical, than with academia, where faculty members generally show no such caution.)

For Steven Smith, a professor of law and the 1987 president of the university's faculty senate who opposed the takeover, academic freedom was a critical point. "The senate expressed some serious concern about the contract over the issue of academic freedom. Humana absolutely refused to address the issue of tenure, saying only that academic freedom would be one factor considered in making its decisions," he said.

A member of the medical school faculty added, "The issue of control over professors was well understood: If faculty members weren't granted privileges at the Humana hospital, their employment at the university would be in jeopardy, since they are supposed to be 'contributing to medical knowledge.' The faculty asked for a phrase in the contract saying that academic freedom would not be abridged. Humana refused to include that, and instead only said they would 'respect' academic freedom."

So far there has been no confirmed example of such academic

freedom being abridged or threatened. A number of faculty members have separately claimed off the record to me that several professors have been "punished" for being critical of Humana but none would provide details. Humana denies the charge.

Like all the hospital corporations involved with medical schools, Humana insists that it isn't involved in academic decisions. Dr. E. David Rollo, senior vice president for medical affairs at Humana and a practicing physician himself, said "The docs practice in our hospital because they want to. They don't work for us." In fact, Humana has enormous clout in another way. According to university staff members, early in 1990, the hospital company threatened the medical school and the university because faculty physicians were not sending sufficient numbers of insured private-practice patients to the Hospital University. The company reportedly told them it would stop rebating a share of its profits at the hospital unless they stepped up such admissions. By late 1990, the company had made the payment but it was too soon to see what effect the threat had had on the faculty doctors' admitting practice.

Although Humana is correct in saying that, legally speaking, doctors are not Humana employees, in any arrangement where people's incomes and working conditions are determined by an institution, they *are* at least de facto employees. The unwillingness of most medical faculty members at any such institution to speak critically on the record is ample evidence of this power relationship. In the case of Humana and the University of Louisville, the medical faculty members in some departments, such as pathology, earn from 50 to 80 percent of their salary from Humana through their clinical practice at the hospital. But where medical schools in most traditionally run academic medical centers have a major hand in the running of their hospitals, in the Louisville case, physician access is determined by the company, not the medical school. The same is true for availability of hospital equipment and facilities for research, upon which promotion and tenure decisions are based.

Dean Kmetz has asserted that the company's position on tenure and academic freedom is irrelevant. "Tenure is a medical-school, not a hospital, issue," Kmetz said, adding that the medical school's safeguard is a provision that department chairs double as department chiefs at the hospital.

Yet as radiologist Staab observed, "If they take away your

space for research at the hospital, you may as well leave the school, and that's a decision being made by Humana."

In any event, concern about academic freedom is not the only area of criticism. Said one disgruntled faculty member, "When the university ran the hospital, faculty doctors could bring in patients with interesting cases but no money. You can't do that so easily anymore." Said another, "It used to be in pathology that if you needed to do some research, you just sat down at a bench. You can't do that anymore."

Humana's no-nonsense attitude toward nonrevenue-producing medical school faculty members, even on petty matters, was quickly demonstrated. Almost immediately after the company assumed control of the hospital, it closed a popular parking area at the hospital to those with no clinical responsibilities there, ending the earlier and more collegial approach in which all medical school personnel were considered part of the same broad endeavor. Similarly, medical school employees and students, accustomed to eating at discount prices at the hospital's cafeteria, suddenly discovered they couldn't have the discount; only those with specific hospital duties were eligible. After a hue and cry among students, the discount was extended to include third- and fourth-year medical students, on the grounds that they were contributing to patient care.

More seriously, there are, in the words of another faculty member, "concerns about academic practice." As she explained, "The atmosphere has changed. For one thing, Humana is paying a lot of the salary of the clinical faculty, which makes them sensitive to pressure from the company and keeps them from complaining." Indeed, the agreement's provision that medical school department chairs (or their designees) double as clinical department chiefs at the hospital, hailed as a protective measure by Dean Kmetz, is seen by some faculty members as more of an encroachment on academic independence than a bulwark. As one professor explained, "The clinical chairs are evaluated not only on how they are running their [academic] departments, but on how profitably they manage their hospital departments. If they don't run a tight ship at the hospital, they won't stay long as chairmen at the medical school." That being the case, he asked, how strongly can they expect to stand behind their faculty members in hospital-related matters?

Even the pediatrics department, which back in 1982 thought it was not going to be involved in the new Humana experiment, has had complaints about Humana. Specifically, it seems the company tried to lure insured tertiary-care pediatric patients away from Kosair, where the medical school faculty practices, to the company's own Audubon hospital. Says one pediatrics faculty member, "Audubon always had a pediatric ward that provided primary and secondary care, and it was always liked if you weren't very sick. Then they started thinking of doing tertiary care. Now all the subspecialists were here at [Kosair] Children's [Hospital], and people had to commute. We decided we couldn't practice good medicine that way and wouldn't practice there. In open-heart surgery for infants, for instance, there are guidelines, and they didn't always meet them, didn't always have all the subspecialists on hand. If you believe in the guidelines, which I do, you have to say that's not good medicine."

On the matter of quality of patient care, there are other questions. In 1986, Humana Hospital University was reaccredited by the Joint Commission on Accreditation of Healthcare Organizations (JCAHO), but Humana officials have consistently refused to release the contents of the report. (State health department officials and officials of JCAHO, as well as those in Dean Kmetz's office, all say release of the report is up to Humana—a curious assertion since the hospital is only being *leased* by the company and is actually publicly owned.) There are rumors at the medical school that the report was critical of staffing levels. Nursing staff was slashed by the company when it took over operation of the facility. In Jones's words, "Our productivity management system lowered the number of full-time equivalent employees per patient day from 5.5 to 4.1 bringing about a seventeen-percent reduction in payroll expenses per patient day." Whether that reduction in staffing means unsatisfactory, or even less than excellent, care cannot be determined from the available evidence (most of which is being withheld by the company as "proprietary information"). What it inevitably means, though, is less attention for patients than they would have gotten with more nursing staff.

While the commission's objective appraisal is being kept under wraps even years later, a more subjective view of Humana's reduction in staffing comes from one of those "full-time equivalents" referred to by Jones, a nurse who says she left the hospital in dismay over "a rising workload and declining patient care." Asking to remain anonymous because she still finds herself having to work at Humana facilities in a community where the company runs four hospitals, she said she had worked at the old

General Hospital and then at Humana University. She claimed that in addition to adding to nurses' workloads, cutbacks in nursing staff, particularly in intensive care, were "not safe." She also charged that in an effort to encourage insured patients to use the new hospital—a key strategy the company developed to make the hospital a paying proposition—the company was attempting through room assignments to segregate these paying patients from indigents. In Louisville, as in other cities where the poor are overwhelmingly black, any such effort would result in racial segregation.

Both the company and the university vigorously denied the charge of segregating patients by race when asked. They also both claimed levels of care haven't been hurt by what they called "more efficient use of staff." At the same time, the nurse in question admits that other colleagues who have stayed on have praised Humana as an employer, citing improved company benefits.

To be sure, Humana has accomplished a lot at the helm of Humana Hospital University. Instead of losing $10 million their first year, as had been projected before the takeover, the hospital turned a nifty $2.5 million profit in 1984, of which 20 percent went to the university under the agreement. At the same time, according to Humana, during the first sixteen months of operation the hospital cared for an average of ninety-four indigent patients a day, about 11 percent more than the average a year earlier at the old county hospital. That, plus the money flowing into the university, has made for a good deal of community contentment. "Humana has the ability to move rapidly when they want to, which can be excellent," says Dr. Roger Shott, head of Humana University's newborn nurseries. "If for instance there's a need for a piece of equipment, bing! they can fill it, whereas if you're at a not-for-profit, you'd need to apply for state funds, put it out to bid, and so on."

But there are nagging questions. Explains Dr. Shott, "The other side of it is that you are *not allowed to forget* the bottom line in everything you do. If you're in a low profit-making unit, a decision about that same piece of equipment will be sent 'downtown' [to corporate headquarters], and that will be the last you'll hear of it. The hospital won't have anything to do with the decision."

Perceived problems at Humana's teaching hospital in Louisville and dissatisfaction among members of the medical school faculty may in part stem from the relatively weak position both the university and the municipality of Louisville held going into the deal. Humana certainly wanted the university hospital, but it didn't *need* it. The university, on the other hand, desperately wanted someone to take the hospital off its hands, and Jefferson County wanted help with its indigent care expenses. That lead to some very one-sided bargaining.

Helen Deines, a member of the University of Louisville's Department of Sociology, was a consumer representative during the sessions that led to the Humana takeover. "It was a really funny way to negotiate," she recalls with a laugh. "We'd say we wanted something, and they'd just say no. No bargaining, no counteroffers, just no. The medical faculty had the same experience.

"When we said we wanted to have an ombudsman position to deal with people who had problems getting care at the hospital, they agreed but gave the position no authority, and they refused to let the ombudsman have an office at the hospital. That, of course, meant that the ombudsman had nothing to do. People who got turned away would be sent to another hospital, and then they didn't complain."

Even when Deines wound up working as the ombudsman, a position she kept for two years before quitting in frustration, she says she had little to do. "The ombudsman was the best kept secret in Louisville. All they had was a little bitty three-by-five [inch] card taped on the admissions desk!" That may explain why, in its 1989 annual report, Humana was able to boast that the ombudsman for its university hospital operation, "empowered to adjudicate any conflicts as to eligibility, has never had to rule." One has to suspect that *something* is amiss if an ombudsman has had nothing to do for half a decade. No system could be that perfect!

Humana had enormous leverage in the initial contract negotiations with the city, county, state, and university. Since any delay in opening the hospital was costing the university hundreds of thousands of dollars for security and maintenance, the company, at no cost, was in effect holding the opening of the hospital hostage. It could win concessions it wanted just by waiting. One of the one-sided terms it won by just sitting on its hands was a clause that permits Humana to cancel the lease *without cause* at any time, with three years' notice to the school. The university, in contrast, for the initial fifteen years, can only get out of the agreement for academic cause. "The threat of a cancellation of the contract by Humana means that we always have to have contingencies. That's a concern to me," says Dean Kmetz. He notes that Humana started out in the nursing home business, dumping that when hospitals became more profitable. "They could always decide that the economic situation has changed again," he suggests, "and just get out of hospitals, including ours."

Finally, there are indications that Humana, now firmly ensconced in its teaching hospital, is reneging on its indigent care agreement—the key reason the various government bodies went along with the deal in the first place. Over the summer, in 1987, the Louisville *Courier-Journal* reported that the hospital had been "turning away emergency patients in unprecedented numbers." The evidence: The city's emergency medical service records showed that nearly three hundred ambulance patients brought to Humana University were turned away and sent to other hospitals. Humana claimed they were rerouted because its beds were full, but both EMS service workers and legal aid attorneys report that 80 percent of those who were rerouted were not in need of hospitalization in the first place, only ambulatory care. They were treated as outpatients at other facilities on which they had been "dumped."[24]

Moreover, because Humana uses a large number of on-call registry nurses to staff the hospital, the number of "available" beds at any given time is really an artificial figure which can be manipulated at will by hospital administrators. The company regularly shuts down beds and reduces its nursing staff to maintain a high occupancy rate on paper. At the time it was refusing emergency patients, the hospital reportedly had one hundred beds temporarily closed in that manner. Technically they weren't available, but they could easily have been "activated" with a call to a contract nursing agency.[25]

What the transferred patients that summer did seem to have in common was a lack of insurance. In a study of 53 transfers by the city's EMS, 30 were found to be without resources or Medicaid. Another nine were Medicaid patients. And according to a legal aid attorney close to the situation, "that was one thing that Humana always knew before they made a transfer." Typically, the emotionally charged issue of patient "dumping" has been a case of private hospitals—for-profit and not-for-profit—unloading poor patients without resources on public facilities. The situation in Louisville in the summer of 1987 represented something unprecedented: the dumping of patients by a public hospital—for Humana Hospital University is legally a public facility being run on a long-term lease by a private firm—on area not-for-profits.

The problems with emergency patients being turned away from Humana Hospital University led to efforts to find a solution in which EMS crews would attempt, sometimes in consultation by radio with Humana Hospital University physicians, to determine in advance whether individual patients were likely to need critical-care beds, so that those who didn't need such special treatment would still be taken even if the hospital's critical beds were full. Still, Humana critics charge that the problem of patient "dumping" has continued to crop up.

Other Takeover Examples

Where teaching hospitals have entered into purchase agreements with hospital companies from a strong financial position, the agreements have been more even-handed than that between Humana and the University of Louisville, but the new corporate-medical school relationship is still problematic. One illustration of this is the 1984 sale of St. Joseph's Hospital in Omaha by the Sisters of St. Francis to American Medical International.

Creighton University's School of Medicine and the Catholic order selling the facility both won strong protective clauses in the agreement because the hospital and the university were in sound financial shape at the time AMI approached them with an offer. As Medical School Dean Richard O'Brien reports, AMI, which paid $100 million for the hospital, simply accepted the same agreement regarding faculty academic freedom that the previous owner had had. The company also agreed to a buy-back clause that permits the university or the order to repurchase the hospital with 80 percent financing from AMI guaranteed (at the current prime interest rate, and for the prevailing market price, less depreciation). AMI also agreed to having only four of eighteen positions on the hospital board of trustees, though it obviously still controls the purse strings from Beverly Hills.

"We weren't in financial trouble at the time we sold the hospital to AMI," says O'Brien. "We were just looking out five to ten years and recognizing that in a rapidly changing environment for health care it would be very difficult someday to raise needed capital."

The first few years of the arrangement, he says, were good,

and the hospital is rumored to be AMI's second biggest source of cash flow. Still, there is a certain amount of grumbling by the faculty because AMI has not increased its reimbursement for house staff teaching activities since the takeover, and O'Brien says staff morale has been hurt by rapid management turnover.

And if what Creighton wanted was more certainty about the future, they didn't get it. Between 1985 and 1989, AMI was periodically on the ropes, and it was almost always a rumored takeover target. In August 1988 a group of financiers including the Bass brothers, Sid and Lee, and a Florida physician named M. Lee Pearce bought major positions in AMI. They successfully demanded positions on the board. While they didn't succeed in taking over the company, they did succeed in pressuring the company's full board of directors to oust AMI Chairman and CEO Wally Weisman and to begin a program of divestitures of hospital holdings, all of which understandably left the Medical School shaken. "We're no longer dealing with any of the same people, and quite frankly I don't think the new people at AMI have the same commitment to academic medicine," said a "worried" O'Brien in a 1989 interview.

Later in 1989, Pearce and the Basses were defeated in an effort to buy out the company, which was instead taken over by an investor group headed by the Pritzker family of Chicago, a move which has done nothing to allay O'Brien's fears. By mid-1990, O'Brien said things had reached a point of confrontation. "The change in ownership at AMI has created real concerns for us," he said in an interview with me. "Given the extent to which the company was indebted for the LBO [leveraged buy-out], we're worried about whether they can continue to finance the program at the hospital." Already, he said, the new capital budget offered by AMI has created a storm of protest. "It was considerably less than reasonable for a hospital of this size," said O'Brien. "On the basis of meeting with the medical staff and the local board, the proposed budget was revised upwards, but it's still not adequate." He reported that the new AMI management in Dallas has also challenged the terms of the original sale agreement. "The sale agreement gave all operating authority to the local governing board," he said. "But the new owners are challenging that, saying that the local board is only advisory. We believe this violates the sale agreement."

Given the growing conflict with AMI, and concerns about its commitment to St. Joseph's Hospital, Dean O'Brien said in July

1991 that the school and the church order were exploring their repurchase option.

There are similar concerns in Wichita, where another teaching institution, Wesley Medical Center, was sold. Again, compared to the University of Louisville situation, this sale of a teaching institution to Hospital Corporation of America was made from a relative position of strength. Wesley Medical Center, owned by the Methodist Church, was a growing hospital complex in 1984 and was clearly the major institution in its region. A teaching hospital for the Wichita branch of the University of Kansas School of Medicine, it was earning an annual rate of return on equity that year that made it one of the top performers in the Voluntary Hospitals of America group, and all signs pointed toward further growth.

But Jack Davis, who had just taken over as chief executive officer of the facility upon the retirement of his mentor, Roy House, was still anxious. He looked at two aging teaching hospitals in town, owned by two different Catholic orders, and suspected that one or both would eventually turn to one of the big hospital companies for help. He worried that a big chain would take over one of those two hospitals and use its financial clout to start a price war that his hospital might lose. "We were exceedingly strong," he recalled in a 1989 interview, "but we were concerned by what could happen in the future." The answer, he told the hospital's board of trustees, was to sell out now and beat them to the punch, while a good price could be had for Wesley.

Even before he assumed control of Wesley, and without the knowledge of either House or many members of the hospital's board, Davis had already been in contact with HCA, which was interested in acquiring a big-name teaching institution with a good reputation and a healthy bottom line. As Davis had suspected, the company was willing to pay top dollar to get it, particularly after running into problems in its effort to acquire Harvard's psychiatric hospital. HCA was still hunting for some prestige properties to add to its system and agreed to pay $260 million, about $100 million more than the hospital was really worth, according to House, who as chairman emeritus had fought a losing battle to prevent the sale.

"I'm not a fan of the proprietary hospital movement," explained House in a 1987 interview. "I had picked Davis myself and trained him for over twenty years. We all thought he was committed to strengthening the existing system." Wesley, House noted, was a charter member of the Voluntary Hospitals of America network.

Still sounding betrayed in a 1988 interview, House said, "Davis and his colleagues conspired to make this sale. There were golden parachutes, high positions in HCA. I really think it was all because they were *afraid* to compete. Even the church was bought off. It got $32 million in the form of a foundation for 'good work,' and $32 million looks like a lot of money to a bunch of Methodist preachers." He snorted. "Quite frankly, they sold out."

Whether HCA or one of the other big corporate chains would ever have bought Wesley's competition will never be known. In any event, with Davis at the helm as an HCA executive, Wesley is now the one applying the competitive pressure in Wichita. Davis has fulfilled his own prophesy, but in reverse.

The academic physicians and the Wichita community have felt the change from religious to corporate ownership already. Sandra Parker, administrative director of the United Methodist Urban Ministry, says that HCA simply dropped a program the hospital had run before the sale to treat indigent Hispanic patients in need of surgery. "There's no interest in doing that kind of thing anymore," she says.

Dr. Thomas Houston, residency director for the School of Medicine's family medicine program at Wesley, is also less than happy with HCA's support. "Under HCA there is all this attention to the bottom line," he said in a 1989 interview. "The hospital seems driven via Nashville to be fiscally responsible regardless of the effects on the medical education program. There has been a tightening—gradual and subtle, but definitely a tightening— particularly where indigent patient treatment is concerned, and the family practice program attracts indigents." Houston says his department tries its best to keep indigent care levels under control, but adds, "We need the patients for teaching; that's essential."

He criticizes HCA and Wesley management for not being more supportive of family practice. "We have a shortage of family practice physicians in this area, and I could easily find enough patients and jobs to support ten residents a year," he says, "but because of fiscal pressures I can only train six. The problem is that it costs about $100,000 a year to train a family physician, and viewed over the short term, family practice programs are costly because they don't generate expensive operations. That's how

HCA perceives it. I try to explain that over the long haul family practice programs are a good investment because physicians bring in patients who will keep coming to the hospital, and because doctors who go through the program and stay in Wichita are likely to send patients to this hospital. But they don't take a long view."

In contrast, he notes that the two Catholic hospitals in Wichita, which also have family practice residency programs, have had the foresight to expand them. In the case of St. Francis Hospital, $1 million was spent in 1987–88 to construct a new family practice center. "We do take a long view," explains St. Francis President and CEO Sister M. Sylvia Egan. "The sisters have a mission and they carry it out within the confines of economic conditions, but we *are* able to take a longer-term view. Our focus is not at all related to the bondholders."

As in the case of AMI's purchase of St. Joseph's in Omaha, HCA's purchase of Wesley Medical Center has ironically done nothing to enhance stability of the community's health delivery system. Like AMI, HCA came under pressure from investors in 1986 and 1987 to do something about increasing its share value. The company responded by selling off nearly half its smaller hospitals, and scaling back plans to create regional systems. Then in 1988, company management, led by founder Thomas Frist, Jr., made a successful bid to buy up all the firm's outstanding stock and take it private, in the process piling up $4 billion dollars in debt in the form of bank loans and junk bonds. Now many people at the hospital are worried about the company's commitment to Wesley, and about its ability or willingness to provide the kind of financial support that originally had been assumed. Even Davis— who speaks in the first person plural when referring both to HCA and to his own hospital—admits to some concern about the future. "Hopefully, we'll be more stable as part of HCA, but who knows?" he said in a 1989 interview. "When I heard about the [management] leveraged buy-out, I thought, Hopefully they'll leave us alone. I have mixed feelings about LBOs, yet we [the parent company] were undervalued and were a potential takeover target, so I was in that sense glad to see a dedicated founder take it over. But some of our medical staff is still concerned, because you just don't know what will happen."

National Medical Enterprises was the last of the major corporate hospital chains to buy into the nation's teaching hospital sector. But it has made up for lost time by agreeing to build and run at a cost of some $150 million a spanking new 275-bed teaching hospital to be affiliated with the University of Southern California School of Medicine in Los Angeles. What makes this unique venture, slated to open in 1991, particularly interesting is that the Medical School is already affiliated with the giant Los Angeles County Medical Center (a favorite setting for Hollywood hospital dramas) in east L.A., which depends on the school for its entire physician staff.

A tie-in between the USC Medical School and NME was viewed positively by both the company and the medical faculty from the outset. From NME's perspective, the new hospital makes good business sense: In the words of Gerald G. Bosworth, NME's chief executive officer for what will be called the Richard Eamer Medical Plaza, "It will make us available to the three thousand physicians in Los Angeles who are clinical faculty members of the USC Med School." With that kind of lucrative referral base of insured patients, Bosworth says NME expects the new hospital to break even in a matter of years and to begin quickly turning a profit. There will be no danger of the company's getting swamped with low-reimbursement Medicaid or charity patients at this peculiar teaching institution. Perhaps unique in the universe of teaching hospitals, it is being designed with no emergency room and no pediatrics or obstetrics wards, so all patients must be referred by their physicians. Any emergency or uninsured patients from the largely poor and Hispanic area will go to the existing underfunded and overcrowded County Medical Center.

From the perspective of faculty doctors at the Medical School, they have everything to gain from the new hospital, since for the first time they will have a place to refer their own private patients, an important source of income for academic physicians. The aging county hospital, where patients with intravenous tubes attached can often be seen languishing in hallways for want of a spare bed in the wards, has long been viewed as anathema to middle-class Angelenos. USC doctors have consequently had to maintain staff privileges at a variety of community hospitals all over the Los Angeles basin in order to run a private practice because of this attitude.

The one note of concern about the new teaching hospital comes from Jerry Buckingham, executive director of the L.A. County Medical Center. "For the county hospital to be successful, we must have a good medical school, and for the medical school to thrive, it has to have a teaching institution, so our destinies are intertwined. From that perspective, we are supportive of the idea," he says. "The fact that they turned to NME is an interesting development, but it's not overly disadvantageous." But Buckingham admits that at times he does worry about the new hospital. "The potential is there for a natural tendency of the faculty to lose some of their current focus on county patients," he says. "Right now, much of the faculty's attention is focused on patient care in this facility. We have to be concerned that they will begin to refocus on the NME hospital when it opens. It's not that they will skim private patients away from us; the private patient doesn't exist here *now*. But with their private practice so nearby, you could imagine them paying less attention to our patients."

The potential for the development of just such a graphic two-tiered health-care system within the USC Medical School was demonstrated when the announcement was first made in 1986 that NME would build the hospital. At that time, Allen W. Mathies, dean of the Medical School, explained the need for a new 275-bed hospital across the street from the County Medical Center (in a region notoriously overbedded) by saying that while the county hospital had provided a "marvelous experience for understanding the diseases of the poor and uneducated, . . . students and house officers have the need to gain experience with patients whose approach to illness from a cultural and sociologic perspective is different. They need to take a medical history from a college graduate, a businessman, or a housewife who has some knowledge of disease and disease prevention."

Such a classist attitude toward medical education, while perhaps understandable on one level, raises the spectre of research focusing on middle-class needs, a de-emphasis of any instruction in the traditional ethical commitment toward healing the sick, and unavoidably a clear withdrawal of support from the county hospital, where the bulk of Los Angeles's poor—those on Medicaid and the medically indigent—are treated for serious illness. As Morrison Chamberlain, administrator of Hollywood Presbyterian Hospital in Los Angeles, put it, "As far as I knew, when God created rich people and poor people, He made them alike." Chamberlain, who prior to his Hollywood Presbyterian job was head of the Los Angeles Department of Health Services, which operates Los Angeles County Medical Center, said he was "dumbfounded" by Mathies's argument.

In any event, an equally telling explanation for the construction plan and the corporate takeover came in a later remark by Mathies, when he suggested that having a teaching hospital for private patients "enhances the ability" of the school, a private institution, to raise money from the private sector.

Not every effort by the hospital companies to forge links with medical schools through the purchase of teaching hospitals has succeeded. Some overtures have been rejected by the schools or hospital boards of trustees in question. Explaining the decision his school reached after considerable internal debate and discussion in 1986 not to sell its teaching hospital to a corporation, Georgetown University Chancellor Matthew F. McNulty said, "In looking at the role of a teaching hospital, it was not at all clear to us that the future was in the for-profit sector. The only benefit we could identify was that a lot of money would flow to the university. That's not a perjorative; any university getting $150 million for its hospital could use it to improve its role in service to society. But we have a basic mission of patient care and didn't want to jeopardize that. The medical staff also expressed apprehension about a loss of academic freedom. The attitude was, 'Why change what we've got?'"

Where Georgetown's decision not to sell its teaching hospital to a hospital company was the result of a rather gentile intellectual debate, a hard political battle had to be fought at the Irvine campus of the University of California, where the state almost agreed to have AMI buy its financially ailing medical center. The local university administration, worried about losses that by 1985 had reached a rate of $9 million a year at its teaching hospital, was initially very receptive to a takeover offer by AMI. As proposed by the company, the UC Irvine Medical Center takeover would have resembled NME's arrangement with the University of Southern California, with the company building a brand new private teaching hospital in Irvine for the treatment of private patients, and also negotiating a lease-management contract to run the medical center. Medical center workers would become AMI employees under the proposed takeover plan, with faculty continuing to work for the university.

As Dr. Howard Waitzkin, a UC Irvine Medical School physician and a leader of the opposition to the sale, wrote in a November 1986 article in the *New England Journal of Medicine*, a majority of the Medical School faculty supported the idea of a sale. Because of the medical center's deficit, funding for physician services had been "frozen or reduced," along with ancillary services needed to support their private practice and research.[26] But a minority of the faculty was opposed, as was the American

Federation of State, County and Municipal Employees (AFSCME) Union, which represented the medical center workers.

AFSCME workers certainly had the most to lose under the proposed agreement. Their current contracts called for the state to grant them all wage increases and benefits set in statewide bargaining, regardless of the Irvine Medical Center's uniquely weak financial position in the UC system. Worse still from their perspective, the proposed contract allowed AMI, after a one-year grace period, to fire employees without cause and to abandon prior salary, seniority, and benefit agreements. There was even some doubt about whether AMI would have to recognize the union.

Critics of the plan—faculty, workers, and students—began to meet regularly in 1985 and organized a coalition, which had the advantage of the lobbying resources and knowhow of AFSCME national and state headquarters. While antisale faculty members and student activists researched information about AMI and about other corporate takeovers of academic medical centers to develop a philosophical argument against the proposal, the union went into action in Sacramento. One of the most powerful labor organizations in a state where unions are critical to Democratic party control of the legislature, AFSCME had an easy time winning the ear of key legislators. Some of those elected officials were already concerned about a plan that would permit state funds allocated for clinical teaching support and other services at the UC Irvine Medical Center to pass through to AMI.

AFSCME's success in the legislature was bolstered by opposition to the AMI takeover at other University of California branches. Chancellors and hospital administrators at UCLA and UC San Francisco both decided to oppose the AMI proposal, fearing that the idea might spread. Ultimately, in 1986, UC President David Gargner decided to oppose the deal, saying the university was committed to maintaining direct authority over all five of its teaching hospitals.

Waitzkin says that the union played the central role in blocking the takeover, but adds that the concerted efforts of a coalition of academics, workers, and students was essential. He also suggests that AMI's own financial weakness, apparent by 1986, made it much easier to convince key administrators and legislators than it might have been had the company been rolling in profits.

"What was important in the end," he says, "was that in

turning down the AMI proposal, the state agreed to increase funding for the UC Irvine Medical Center," including some $40 million for capital improvements and funds to cover operating deficits in the future. "It shows that there *was* a public funding alternative."

What Lies Ahead?

The last actual completed takeover of an academic medical center by a hospital company was NME's 1986 deal with Los Angeles County and the USC School of Medicine (though this won't really be complete until the new facility opens in 1991). Since then, with all the companies reefing their sails and restructuring to face a stormy reimbursement environment, any similar plans have been placed in drydock. Still, over the longer haul, the corporate hospital chains do want to buy into the American academic medical system. They cannot stay on the margins of the health system forever, running smaller secondary-care health centers. At the same time the financial crisis at America's academic medical centers, which has made them willing targets for acquisition in the first place, is not going away. If anything, the same pressures that are being felt in hospital corporation boardrooms are being felt more strongly by trustees of universities and administrators of teaching hospitals.

This leaves the academic medical centers—the schools and their hospitals—with a big problem. As Harvard's Rashi Fein put it in his appeal for a faculty rejection of HCA's McLean bid:

> Is there no other option? Are we so weak that we must consort with those whose standards are not our standards, whose goals are not our goals, whose criteria for success are not our criteria? Are we so impoverished that we must act to legitimize acquisitiveness in place of altruism, and competition in place of cooperation? I am not privy to the books. I do not know. But this I do know: that we dare not underestimate the costs that others will bear if we act only in terms of our self-interest.

For some medical schools there may in fact be no other option, particularly if they are affiliated with a private university. But it also seems clear in looking at cases like the University of

Louisville hospital or UC Irvine that going to a corporate hospital chain was a first, not a last, resort. In the Louisville case, there's no doubt that Jones, with the clout that Humana's political action committee money can command, was much better able than the university alone would have been to wring increased indigent care funding from state and local governments. But the prospect of a failure of the state school's new multimillion-dollar hospital would likely have won the same commitment in the end and allowed the university to continue running the facility, perhaps with a management firm's assistance.

Whatever the arguments, it seems inevitable that there will be more examples of mergers, affiliations, and other linkages between the growing corporate hospital sector and teaching hospitals. The companies need access to these facilities for the purposes of vertical integration of their operations and for the enhancement of their reputations as places where quality health care is delivered. Even if they can't get what they need from a university, they will go ahead with research that offers the potential for profit or name recognition, just as Humana did with its controversial heart program. And that raises the threat of more academic researchers and their projects being bought away from the medical schools, as DeVries was lured away from the University of Utah.

For university trustees and academic medical center administrators, the hospital corporations offer an easy solution to a seemingly intractable problem: It is they who can raise the astronomical sums necessary to stay at the cutting edge of an increasingly technological medical system. This alone will make many university hospitals pursue such links, especially in cases where, as at McLean or the University of Louisville, the maintenance of a teaching hospital is a crushing burden.

To be sure, the idea of corporate sponsorship of research at medical schools, like corporate sponsorship of research in other academic fields, is not anything new. Long before HCA tried to buy McLean Hospital, Hoechst AG, a German chemical and pharmaceutical company, had provided $50 million to underwrite the molecular biology department of Massachusetts General Hospital, reportedly with no complaints from the faculty at Harvard. And U.S. pharmaceutical firms have long funded applied research at teaching institutions, albeit not always without controversy. What makes the takeover of academic medical centers different from, and more controversial than, the typical investment in research is the element of control over academic and medical affairs that ownership or even just management implies.

As Lewis and Sheps wrote in *The Sick Citadel*:

> The governance of the academic medical center differs sharply from that of the typical business corporation. The classical concept . . . is essentially collegial. Faculty members are not simply employees of the university in the usual sense of that term. For understandable reasons, they have a great deal of autonomy as individuals and as departments and subunits. . . . In the typical business corporation, the hierarchy of control is much clearer. While professional and technical expertise among its employees is sought when needed, the power of decisionmaking rests with the top administration of the corporation.[27]

It is possible, of course, that the corporate takeover of teaching hospitals will be a limited phenomenon, involving only a small number of the nation's major tertiary-care institutions. This was the conclusion of the National Institute of Medicine's Committee on Implications of For-Profit Enterprise in Health Care, which stated in its 1986 report that

> because of the formidable amounts of capital required, the complexity of the institutions and their long traditions, and their questionable profitability, the committee does not expect to see a large number of teaching hospitals coming under the control of investor-owned companies in the near future, although more limited relationships, involving specialized facilities or programs, may continue to proliferate.[28]

Berliner and Burlage, in their American Public Health Association paper, also argued that it "does not seem likely that" hospital corporation purchases or leases of teaching hospitals "will increase significantly." But they also ask whether the tie-ins between the hospital corporations and a few large teaching hospitals might be leading many other teaching institutions to "reshape more basically internally as 'corporate restructurers' . . . in apparent competition with and imitation of them." They wonder, in other words, as did Harvard's faculty, if the impact in the teaching hospital field of several takeovers might be far greater than their numbers might at first suggest (as it has clearly been in the broader not-for-profit hospital realm).[29]

Whatever the case, the companies themselves already express some frustration at the resistance to their proposals for academic takeovers. Typical is NME's John Bedrosian. "We used to be criticized by [Arnold] Relman and others for not being involved in research and education," he lamented in a 1986 interview. "Now, when we do get involved, they criticize us too! Granted, Humana may have mixed motives for its artificial heart research, but it *is* research."

Maybe so. But it is research with a *difference*. What makes that difference hard to see is that the medical schools themselves are not being taken over; rather it is the teaching hospitals at which the faculty and students do their clinical work. As Stanley Wohl, a staff physician at Stanford University's medical center and author of the book *The Medical Industrial Complex*, put it in an interview I had with him, "Universities are supposed to be independent. University departments—and a medical school and teaching hospital is basically just another university department— should also be independent. What would people say if GM bought the Harvard philosophy department? It looks ridiculous. But here are shareholder-owned corporations owning or running medical centers."

When Lewis and Sheps wrote their controversial critique of the American academic medical center in 1981, their main argument was that the institutions, central to the whole system of American medical practice, were too unwilling to perform the function of community service and were instead geared toward research of benefit primarily to the physicians who worked in them. They saw as a hopeful sign the increasing role of government in funding medical centers, whether owned by the state or by private universities. As they put it:

> One prominent difference between public or private sponsorship [of an academic medical center] is the degree and immediacy of public accountability. Clearly a private university trustee board which has the final responsibility for policy and financing of its medical school, as dedicated, knowledgeable and farsighted as it may be, is generally not as directly concerned about public needs and perceptions, particularly in the state and region, as a

state university board or the state legislature is likely to be. This difference, while still present, has been sharply reduced in the past two decades, largely because of the heavy investment of tax funds in the support of medical schools. . . .

Certainly there have always been a few voices in medical schools urging that more overt and organized attention be given by their institutions to the immediate and long-term needs of their region and the nation. The great increase in the importance of tax funds in support of medical schools helps to strengthen these voices at least a little.[30]

The entry of the corporate hospital chains into this arena is a move in exactly the opposite direction, away from accountability and away from meeting regional and national needs.

A Cautionary Tale

It was 1986, and AMI executives had just provided me with a guided tour of Tarzana Regional Medical Center, one of their flagship hospitals in Los Angeles, and a luncheon interview with several key members of the hospital's medical staff. The reports from the three physicians had been glowing: The company was doing a superb job of running the hospital and was very solicitous of doctors' needs. But the next morning, I met one of the same trio (I never could determine whether by chance or design) outside my hotel, which was a good fifteen miles from the hospital. He called me over to his car and told a different story. "I'm happy with the way the company runs Tarzana," he said, explaining that his praise of the company the day before had been sincere, "but I'm worried about the future. Where will the teachers come from when the system is run on a for-profit basis? These hospital companies aren't interested in the future of medicine. They aren't interested in research, and they aren't interested in education. I'm afraid they're riding on what's already been done. Next, they'll start closing the unprofitable operations, and then, when we realize that it was a mistake, it will be too late to do anything about it. Society won't have the resources to rebuild what was lost." He shook his head sadly, and then drove off to work.

7

Corporate Hospital Chains: A Prescription for Inequality?

My task, every day throughout my life, is to try to make sure that in our country we have unimpeded, universal access to high-quality, necessary medical services at affordable prices.

—David Jones, Chairman
Humana, Inc.

We spent $176 million [in 1984] on uncompensated care—about four percent of our revenues. That's about what four thousand not-for-profit hospitals do.

—Thomas Frist, Jr., Chairman
Hospital Corporation of America

AMI spends $200 million on indigent care. And overwhelmingly that uncompensated care comes from ERs [emergency rooms]. We have a firm company policy of treating anyone who comes in the door.

—Walter Weisman, Former President and CEO
American Medical International

In fact, we are doing as much indigent care as the not-for-profit community hospitals.

—John Bedrosian, Sr. Executive V.P.
National Medical Enterprises

Most Americans still believe that in this country, everyone who needs medical care can get it. A generation after the Johnson administration began its War on Poverty with the passage of Medicare and Medicaid legislation promising equal access to health care for all, and after the past decade of cutbacks in those once ambitious programs, it is still widely assumed that lack of money will deny no one access to a hospital or physician. The reality is something else entirely. According to the American Hospital Association, in 1990 nearly 60 million people—or nearly one in four Americans—were at risk of being without access to medical care in a crisis, because of lack of or inadequate insurance.

Who are these unfortunates? Not the "Bowery bum," derelict, or welfare recipient that many people automatically envision, for such people *are* for the most part covered by the government's Medicaid program. Their ranks only account for 10 to 15 percent of the nation's 37 million uninsured. Rather, the medically indigent constitute a more diffuse group, one whose resources are inadequate to meet the cost of needed care. Some 75 to 80 percent of the total are working people and their families, people who are too well-off to qualify for state Medicaid assistance, yet too poor to buy private insurance. They are not old enough to retire and receive Medicare coverage, but are either temporarily unemployed, or working for an employer too parsimonious to offer employee medical benefits. They may even be relatively well-off but have been confronted with a medical bill greater than their combined insurance coverage and personal assets. Until a health crisis, many seem to be getting by like the rest of Middle America, making enough to live decently as long as everyone in the family stays healthy. But when well, they and their families probably didn't get adequate preventive care. And when sick, if they went for treatment, they probably got it late, often too late. In fact, the indigent often have to fight hard to get care at all, using public pressure and the assistance of Legal Aid lawyers to get them through the door of a hospital.

That's the way it was for Joe Allen Bennett. A poor dirt farmer from rural Tennessee stricken with lung cancer, Bennett needed help that in his region only Hospital Corporation of America could provide. But when he tried to get that help, he found HCA's doors closed to him. His story says much about what is happening in health care in America and about the differences between voluntary and investor-owned hospitals. It is also a tale of the conflicting pressures on hospital corporations, which must be sensitive to public relations while at the same time not frightening shareholders by exhibiting too much costly compassion.

Bennett had always had a tough time making ends meet on his rocky fourteen-acre farm, but when his breath started getting short, things became impossible. With his health rapidly failing, he and his wife, herself a victim of emphysema, were forced to get by on just her $328 monthly Social Security check. Then the family doctor said he needed to go into the hospital for a biopsy to see if he might have lung cancer.

His physician referred him to not-for-profit Baptist Hospital in Nashville for the operation, where the admitting office, as has become the rule in most hospitals, profit or not-for-profit, demanded an advance payment of $300. Too exhausted to fight, Bennett was ready to turn around and go home right then, but his sister Mattie Sue Owens contacted his doctor, who told the hospital it was an emergency and got him admitted on that basis without a deposit.

That was the easy part. It was only the start of Bennett's ordeal.

First, the biopsy revealed the worst: He had an advanced case of lung cancer, for which the only available therapy was radiation treatment. That presented a new problem. The doctor said Parkview Memorial was one of only two hospitals in the region equipped to treat Bennett, having been granted the required certificate of need (CON) permit from the state Health Department to acquire the radiation therapy equipment. But Parkview, flagship of the Hospital Corporation of America empire, has a reputation of not admitting patients who have no insurance and no ability to pay. And unlike Baptist, HCA left an emergency room out of its blueprints at Parkview. Though Bennett's physician had staff privileges there, he couldn't use the same gambit he had used at Baptist to get him admitted this time.

Since he could no longer work, Bennett filed for Medicaid coverage. But like welfare and food stamp assistance, Medicaid is not automatic, and it could take twelve critical weeks for Bennett's application to be approved. In the meantime, Parkview, where well-heeled, insured patients and their visitors drop their cars off with uniformed valets and get VIP treatment in plush surroundings, might as well have been surrounded by a moat as far as he was concerned. Hospital officials did say they'd let him in with a $500 cash payment up front, but that was as insurmountable a barrier as a raised drawbridge for Bennett, who probably couldn't even have come up with so much cash by selling his rattle-trap seven-year-old pickup truck. Mattie Sue offered to provide $300 of her own scarce assets, but after consulting with a supervisor, the admitting clerk at Parkview told her no dice. The entry price was $500. Period.

Mattie Sue Owens is a shy, soft-spoken woman, but her brother's desperate plight brought forth a tenacity she didn't know she had. "I couldn't believe that a hospital would do this," she said, sounding more shocked than angry. "I knew that without the treatments my brother would die. His wife just cried and cried, and he just sort of wanted to give up, to just forget it and turn around and go home, but I kept pushing him, saying, 'We're fighting for your life.'"

Bennett's sister says she tried calling the company's executive office, but all she claims she got were expressions of sympathy, no change in company rules.

At that point, with her brother in tears of discouragement and pain, she scraped together the initial money herself, cosigned a promise to pay for Bennett's care, and got him started on a thirty-five-treatment program that the hospital estimated would cost between $1,200 and $2,600. She was told by HCA that the treatments would halt in two weeks unless she came up with another $500, something she knew was an impossibility.

Then she learned about a local poverty law center, Legal Services of Middle Tennessee, that was making something of a cause out of trying to get poor patients into area hospitals. She presented her brother's case there. Attorney Gordon Bonnyman checked out the story and tried to convince the HCA hospital to continue to treat Bennett. Failing to get the hospital to budge (despite a written assurance from the state Medicaid office that it would eventually enroll Bennett and that it would backdate his coverage to reimburse all radiation treatments), Bonnyman threatened to file suit, charging patient abandonment and violation of the state's emergency treatment laws. Bonnyman concedes now that he had a weak case at best, since Bennett had only been an outpatient at Parkview and wasn't technically on his deathbed. But the threat of litigation, coupled with some media coverage of Bennett's plight arranged by Bonnyman, won a change of heart at HCA. Bennett was permitted to continue his treatments for the full term prescribed by his doctor. His tumor shrunken, Bennett lived another nine months, apparently in considerably less pain.

"We were lucky we got the treatments," said Owens. "If it

had just been Joe and his wife, they would have just accepted it all, and he would have died in a month. My brother had no education, and he didn't know what to do. As it is, he had to go through a lot of needless trauma. Who knows whether that made him weaker. I just think it's a shame that a hospital can control and say *you* get treatment and *you* don't. I think they should treat everyone, and you should be able to pay later. It's a shame that the almighty dollar has so much power over health care."

No Real National System for Caring for the Poor

The provision of health care for the nation's poor has always been a haphazard affair at best, but its history is closely intertwined with the institutional history of the hospital. As mentioned earlier, the first hospitals were established for the most part to care for the poor at a time when wealthier segments of society were treated at home.

The first organized effort to arrange for care of the poor on a national basis was the Hill-Burton Act (though this was only incidental to the legislation's main purpose, which was to help finance hospitals). With a proliferation of postwar families living outside urban centers, the growing country needed more hospitals. So in 1946, Congress voted to establish a guaranteed loan program for hospital construction, modernization and expansion. Between passage of the act and 1971, $2.8 billion in federal loans and another $9 billion in matching local and state funds were spent as hundreds of hospitals were added to the nation's inventory, many of which were the first and only health-care facility in the area. As part of the package deal for the loan program, hospitals making use of Hill-Burton funding had to agree to treat the uninsured poor in their area.

To some extent, the idea worked, but even in its heyday, it was clear that the number of medically indigent—those without the resources to pay for treatment—far outstripped the resources of many hospitals. Accordingly, as part of the Johnson administration's War on Poverty in 1965, Medicaid was established as a government health insurance program to finance directly, through state and federal funds, the treatment of the poor.

But Medicaid never covered everybody. With eligibility limited to those whose family income was no more than 33 percent higher than a given state's family welfare grant, many people with only the most modest income or assets were left out (obviously, the lower the welfare grant level in a state, the fewer people are covered by Medicaid, too). And even if Medicaid as originally conceived would have meant health care for many of the poor, within two years it had been slashed. Even before the program's funding was cut during the Reagan administration, Medicaid was only covering about a third of the nation's poor. After 1980, Medicaid coverage was even further scaled back as Washington, and many state governments, sought to reduce welfare outlays. At the same time, the mounting cost of health insurance premiums, combined with a trend toward higher levels of unemployment and part-time employment, produced a steady increase in the number of the medically indigent.

Far from being replaced by Medicaid, by the early 1970s the Hill-Burton hospital finance system, by requiring recipient hospitals to admit those with no resources, had become a crucial factor in the provision of care for those excluded from other programs.

Most hospitals had resisted the indigent care provisions of Hill-Burton all along, or adhered to them only grudgingly, often with more or less impunity, though. There was little effort at enforcement by state or federal authorities, and no penalties beyond a public dressing-down. But with the arrival of corporate hospitals in the 1970s, the situation changed dramatically for the worse. New hospitals built by for-profit concerns to compete with existing Hill-Burton–financed facilities had a competitive advantage. They didn't have any obligation to provide free care. When they built a new facility, the hospital companies were careful to locate it in neighborhoods where they would be unlikely to have indigent patients. And even when they bought a hospital that had been built with Hill-Burton loans, most companies were careful to pay off the facility's obligation to the government at the time of purchase, thus terminating any prior requirement to care for the medically indigent.

By 1981, with a sixth of the nation's hospitals in corporate hands and the rest feeling the competitive heat, Hill-Burton was becoming a frail reed upon which to rest the care of the medically indigent. And the structural change in the nation's economy was increasing the number of those without either Medicaid or private insurance coverage. Between 1981 and 1986, the number of medically indigent rose by 50 percent, while the costs for their care—absorbed by hospitals, local governments, and, as a result of cost-shifting by hospitals and insurers, the rest of the population—doubled to $8.5 billion, according to the AHA. The National Conference of State Legislatures reported that the 1988 cost of indigent care may have soared as high as $12 billion.

Impact of the Corporate Chains

While the corporate hospital sector obviously had little to do with the genesis of the indigent health-care problem, it *has* played a key role in worsening the plight of those millions of families unable to pay for medical treatment.

You wouldn't know it to hear them talk, though.

Surely one would never expect Chrysler's Lee Iacocca or General Motor's Robert C. Stemple to boast about giving away free cars to the poor. Neither do executives at A&P or Safeway supermarket chains proclaim that they regularly provide vast stores of free food to low-income families. (Some food-store chains even have corporate policies against giving away salable food to food banks and limit donations to dated goods.) Most modern executives *do* try to convey an image of public spiritedness and social responsibility, but rarely do they give away their main product to those unable to pay for it, or to those only able to pay with great difficulty. Yet the for-profit hospital industry, which describes itself as tough, entrepreneurial, cost-conscious, and eager to earn a profit for shareholders, seems hell-bent on proclaiming its nobility in providing free hospital care to the needy.

Why this altruistic posture?

This question goes to the heart of the ethical issues raised by for-profit medicine: Is capitalism in acute health care compatible with the availability of quality care for everyone in society? If the answer were simply that corporate hospital enterprises are just like charity hospitals—assuming the claims by the for-profit companies to be true—there would be no major ethical issue presented by the spread of for-profit hospital chains. The claims are, however, for the most part either exaggerated or simply false. And the motives of the companies in trying to demonstrate what would be an extraordinary corporate conscience are complex, involving everything from community image to concern about the direction of national health-care policy and fear of re-regulation.

In fact, at the same time that executives at the big hospital companies proclaim their humanitarian efforts in caring for the poor, they decry a system and a society that expects them to make such efforts. Here, for instance, is what Humana wrote in an application for a "certificate of need" permit in Florida, a document which some states still require before a new hospital or major hospital equipment purchase may be made:

> Public policy of the United States has determined that providing hospital care to indigent patients is a government responsibility. In order to meet this responsibility, various levels of government collect taxes and make funds available to certain hospitals for this purpose. As a taxpayer, Humana contributes to the provision of this care through payment of taxes. As a result of public policy, and their status as taxpayers, Humana hospitals do not have the responsibility to provide hospital care for the indigent except in emergencies or in those situations where reimbursement for indigent patients is provided.

In other words, Humana, in its corporate view, is only as responsible for treating poor patients without resources as the local discount store or fast food outlet is—no more, no less. Like a McDonald's or Burger King franchise, it pays taxes on its profits, and some of those taxes go to pay for public hospitals, and that's enough.

Unlike a franchise operation, however, which for all intents and purposes is a locally owned business, there is reason to question whether all hospitals owned by Humana or the other chains actually pay state and local taxes in proportion to their real level of business activity. Depending on how sales, property, state, and local corporate income taxes are calculated, these companies, like any multistate corporate entity, can allocate revenues, earnings, and expenses within the larger corporation. By such accounting devices as internal pricing and charges for home office expenses, they are able to minimize payments in high-tax jurisdictions. And such venues, like California, Florida, Texas, are often the very ones with the largest medically indigent populations.

Even at the federal level, many if not all of the hospital chains pay taxes at a fairly low rate, thanks to generous federal allowances for depreciation and interest payments. In 1984, for instance, a year when HCA was making a large number of hospital acquisitions, the company paid an effective tax rate on earnings of only 9.6 percent. The official tax rate on corporate profits that year was 46 percent, before taking write-offs into account. But even the median rate paid by all major American corporations, according to Citizens for Tax Justice, a private monitoring group, was 15 percent. This suggests that at least HCA was not pulling its weight where funding of indigent care is concerned. In the latter part of the 1980s, it should be noted that the big four hospital firms' tax rates were much closer to the statutory federal tax rate of 36 percent for corporate profits, because they were doing very little in the way of acquisitions. But once growth resumes, their rates will fall accordingly.

But the corporate chains are not simply businesses that purvey their goods and pay their taxes, at whatever rate. They are *hospital* companies, and *how* they go about doing their business in a community can be much more important than the amount of tax revenues they contribute to the general fund. That was certainly made clear in Pulaski County, Kentucky, where Humana took the local public hospital off the taxpayers' hands and began making it a tax-generating local business operation.

There, Humana wasn't so much preventing poor people from coming to the Humana Hospital Lake Cumberland, in Somerset, as it was keeping them there until they paid their bills (though there are reports that Humana also tried to keep people out altogether).

In one sworn affidavit, Thomas Ray Burton tells how things worked at Humana Lake Cumberland when his wife had their baby there.

> My wife was checked into Lake Cumberland Medical Center at approximately 3:00 A.M. . . . I had made prior arrangements with the Citizens Bank for a loan to cover my hospital bill. When I checked my wife in I told the admitting clerk this. As soon as the bank opened that morning, I went to see about the loan but was told it had not been approved. The following day I talked to [hospital official] Patricia Harris about the bill. When I told her that the bank had not approved the loan, she suggested that I take my wife home and leave the baby there so that my bill would not be as large. I told her that Dr. Nunemaker had not ordered this.
>
> When I got ready to check my wife out of the

hospital, Patricia Harris told me that I could not take my wife and child until I paid a substantial part of my bill. I agreed to sign a promissory note but this was not sufficient. . . .

Although it did not seem right to me, when Patricia Harris said, "You've got to give me so much on your bill or you can't take your baby and wife home," it upset me and I felt that I had to do something about the bill.[1]

According to Jean Munroe, an attorney with Legal Aid in Somerset at the time, her office was deluged with complaints from poor citizens saying that they were informed by Humana officials that they could not take their newborn babies home until they paid their bills in full or signed promissory notes or postdated checks. "They had grown men in tears," Munroe recalls, adding that many women, like Burton's wife, were advised to check out of the hospital after delivery and leave the baby there "to keep the bill down" until they could obtain a loan from the local bank to cover the bill and get the child.

Humana, for its part, consistently denied—and still denies—all the charges. But when the consumer complaints office of the state's attorney general began an investigation into the hospital's billing and collections practices, Jones said that the company wanted "an easy way to dispose of" the matter and Humana agreed to sign a consent decree, without admitting having done anything improper. Still, the language of the decree is clear. In what is called an Assurance of Voluntary Compliance filed with Franklin Circuit Court in Kentucky, Humana agreed that it would:

> • not inform patients or patients' families that patients cannot leave the hospital until the patient makes arrangements to pay. . . .
> • not have any debtor execute a retail installment contract granting a security interest in a motor vehicle when a security interest is not in fact given. . . .
> • refrain from representing to its patients that a document is simply an acknowledgment of a debt and an agreement to arrange financing when, in truth the document is a written promissory note. . . .
> • not call debtors at their place of employment after being notified that the employer prohibits such calls. . . .

• not solicit postdated checks or other postdated payment instruments for the purpose of threatening or instituting criminal prosecution. . . .

In addition, the company agreed to post a sign in the admission and discharge areas of Humana Hospital, Lake Cumberland stating:

Your doctor is responsible for discharging you from the hospital. Prior to leaving the hospital, you are requested to make arrangements for the payment of your bills.[2]

While the agreement between the attorney general and Humana may have resolved the problem of poor patients being unable to leave the hospital, it did not address the bigger problem that faces Kentucky and the nation—getting poor patients *into* the hospital in the first place. Specifically, the agreement states that "refusal of Lake Cumberland to admit nonemergency patients who fail to make the normal preadmission financial arrangements" shall not be considered a violation of the terms of the decree.

That leaves the indigent of Pulaski County with a big problem. Lake Cumberland, the only hospital within seventy miles, was once owned by the county and was thus available to all (in addition to being a public institution, it had been constructed with the help of Hill-Burton funds and so was obligated to care for the indigent). But in a microcosm of what has been happening to hospitals across the nation, this particular facility proved to be an increasing tax burden for local residents. In the end, the taxpayers decided to unload themselves of their expense and sold the facility to Humana, which promptly paid off its federal loans and absolved itself of that particular legal obligation to care for the poor.

As Humana's David Jones explained to me, "If the people in Somerset want to provide for indigent care, they can build a public hospital. I predict they won't. The grievances of people who can't pay their bills shouldn't be with us, they should be with the residents of Pulaski County."

In one sense, Jones is absolutely correct: When Pulaski County officials sold their hospital to Humana, they didn't bother to use the proceeds to establish an indigent care fund, as some more humane or farsighted communities have done in similar circumstances (nor did Humana push the idea at contract time). But even had they done so, it begs the question of what happens when such a fund is exhausted, as happened in Coweta County, Georgia. There, for reasons similar to those in Somerset, city fathers sold Coweta's public hospital to Humana, establishing, at the time of the sale and in the agreement with Humana, a fund for indigent care. The fund was quickly exhausted, leaving the poor with little access, since Humana chose to provide only emergency care to those without resources.

As we saw in chapter 6, Humana signed a forty-year lease agreement with the University of Louisville and local and state officials in which it pledged to handle all the indigent care in the city, even if the volume should exceed the city, county, and state reimbursement for the year. Yet there are still questions as to whether Humana is in practice living up to the terms of the lease. Rejecting many poor patients at the emergency door in the summer of 1987 was not the only thing Humana did. According to legal aid attorney Eleanor Martin, whose office, like most legal aid services across the country, is swamped with poor clients seeking to gain access to hospitals, Humana also threw up "all kinds of bureaucratic requirements" at its university hospital. These requirements, she said, "have the effect of keeping people from getting care." For example, she said, "Humana requires indigent patients to prove they have no resources with things like notarized statements from the unemployment office, notarized statements from a separated spouse, things that can be almost impossible to get, or that take *weeks*. We've had cases of cosmetically necessary care [to prevent scarring] being held up for things like that."

Martin added that under its forty-year lease agreement Humana was also supposed to use 10 percent of its indigent care fund each year to cover poor patients from outside Jefferson County. "Since Humana gets reimbursed by the government under the agreement for 95 percent of its billed *charges*, [fees the level of which are established by the company], that 10 percent [portion of the fund for out-of-county patients] gets used up very quickly. Usually by November, my out-of-county clients can't get in. I tell everybody, if you're going to live outside Jefferson County, get sick early in the year!"

Humana is hardly alone in renouncing any special responsibility to care for the health of the poor. Says HCA's Joe Hutts, "There are some areas we as a society have to address [and] indigent care is one. Maybe a general tax is the answer. But I don't think a tax just on hospitals—whether it's cross-subsidization or an actual gross receipts tax—makes sense."

Similarly, Walter Weisman, AMI president and CEO until he resigned under pressure from several major shareholders in September 1988, said, "There's a lot about health care that causes emotionalism, [but that's because people assume housing and food]. Clearly health care is not more important than water, food, and housing . . . and [those industries] are still more unregulated than regulated." He added, "I think indigent care is clearly a societal problem and has to have a societal solution. I don't have much hope for government solving it, though, so it will probably, improperly, become our problem. We will probably have to continue accepting people and transferring them, if possible, when stabilized."

There is, in other words, something of a contradiction in the public statements and postures of the big hospital companies.

A nurse at an AMI hospital tells one story that dramatically illustrates what AMI's policy is in practice, where poor patients are involved. "At AMI, it's always the bottom line that counts," she said. "And we were told on the ObGyn floor not to take patients who didn't have insurance. We were supposed to examine them to make sure they were 'stabilized,' and then to transfer them. But that's not always possible or safe." She tells of a case on her own shift where a woman came in to the emergency room saying she was in labor. The woman had apparently had a previous cesarean section delivery, and was thus a likely candidate for another costly surgical delivery, and she had no insurance.

"Under the ER system for specialties, there is a doctor and a back-up on call," the nurse reported. "The first physician on call refused to even see the woman, and the back-up did the same. We called the chief of staff of obstetrics and gynecology then, and without his having a physician even examine her, and even though a nurse told him she was six centimeters dilated [very close to delivery] he said to transfer her to the charity hospital. We did it, but sent one of our nurses along with her on our own authority in the ambulance, even though she was putting herself in legal jeopardy by going." The baby was delivered safely by cesarean section at the charity hospital (at taxpayers expense) within an hour of the transfer decision, but the results could have been far different for mother and baby, the floor nurse says, had the birth occurred vaginally in the ambulance. A ruptured uterus, had it occurred, could have been fatal to both mother and baby.

Where There Are For-Profit Hospitals, Care for the Poor Suffers

The reality seems to be that it is precisely in those states where for-profit hospitals have become the most common—Florida, Texas, Tennessee, Kentucky, Louisiana, and Nevada—that caring for those without resources or Medicaid becomes the biggest problem. When a joint commission of the Texas state legislature made a study in 1984 of the indigent care provided by the state's hospitals, it found that the state's for-profit hospitals on average provided charity care that equalled less than one percent of patient revenues. Even when bad debt was added in (patients who were admitted with the expectation that they would pay for their care but who, for whatever reason, later failed to pay for all or part of their bills), the figure was only 3.5 percent. In contrast, the state's not-for-profit sector provided some 6.5 percent of revenues in charity and bad-debt care, a substantial portion of which was actual charity care—people admitted despite a known inability to pay for treatment. For public hospitals, the comparable figure was 16 percent of revenues. Overall, the Texas commission found that the for-profit sector, representing about 20 percent of the hospitals in the state, provided a statistically insignificant amount of charity care and accounted for only 2.7 percent of the bad-debt uncompensated care in the state.[3]

In an effort to counter this kind of damning evidence, the Federation of American Health Systems in 1986 commissioned a research paper by Jack Meyer, an economist with the American Enterprise Institute, a conservative Washington think tank. Meyer argued, with some validity, that figures showing that not-for-profit hospitals in Florida, Tennessee, Texas and Kentucky provided almost twice as much free care as for-profits were skewed because size had not been considered as a factor. Specifically, he observed that some very large not-for-profit hospitals were teaching institutions. Excluding these, he found the difference between the two classes of hospital in terms of the amount of uncompensated indigent care provided diminished somewhat, though not-for-profits still provided significantly more. Then he argued that the for-profit sector's charity care contribution should be augmented by adding in its payment of all state and local taxes, since this was "money available to the community," presumably for indigent care. Since communities and states have much more to pay for with taxes than just indigent care—roads, schools, public safety, welfare, public employee salaries—this is clearly reaching to make a point. Yet even with the adjustments, only in Florida was Meyer able to claim that the investor-owned hospital sector was doing *more* charity care than the not-for-profit sector. All other studies clearly demonstrate that for-profit hospitals, particularly where another hospital—not-for-profit or public—is available, simply don't take care of the poor.

Some states, like Florida, have tried to address this issue by establishing a tax on hospital revenues, called a gross receipts tax, with the proceeds earmarked for indigent care. It is an approach bitterly opposed by the hospital industry, which refers to the idea disparagingly as a "sick tax." In fact, it is a tax that is eventually passed on not so much to paying "sick" patients, a relatively small group, but rather, because the tax is on total hospital receipts, to payers of insurance premiums, a very broad and for the most part healthy group. Others have tried a voluntary approach, in which *hospitals* are each asked to volunteer a certain amount of free care to indigents. In Kentucky this effort was hobbled by lack of participation of the state's largest hospital group: Humana. Saying it disagreed in principle with the idea of "cost-shifting," and also with the way the state determines how much free care each facility should provide, Humana refused to have any of its hospitals in the state participate.

On a more local level, HCA has been similarly intransigent when asked to treat indigent patients voluntarily. When public officials in Knox County, Tennessee, established a fund that would provide at least minimal reimbursement for care of the poor back in 1984, and asked Knoxville's hospitals each to handle some of the load, HCA's Fort Sanders/Park West facility initially refused to participate. Fort Sanders/Park West provided no charity care in 1984, according to the Tennessee Department of Health's Center for Statistics. HCA eventually signed on to the plan, which allows participating hospitals to obtain some reimbursement for the care of pre-approved indigent patients in the county's program. Still, according to the Center for Statistics' accountant, Fort Sanders/Park West reported providing no medically indigent care in 1989.

During an interview conducted in his new executive headquarters office tower in Louisville, Humana Chairman David Jones said, "Is it right for the insured patient to be subsidizing the indigent patients in a hospital? Because that's what is happening if a hospital provides free care to indigents. We think the matter of indigent care is a social issue that should be addressed by government. Our society is abundant enough to provide care for everyone. What is needed is good leadership and clear thinking. There *is* a moral issue here, but it's not indigent care; it's whether people should pay higher prices for health care than what the market would charge."

Intellectually speaking, this is sound logic. It is hard to justify the idea of making the hospital industry solely responsible for the health-care needs of a large segment of the population. This is especially the case in the absence of rigid price controls, as the industry will do the job by "cost shifting" or raising the cost of other patients' treatment and of insurance premiums. But as long as the political system refuses to address the issue and the health needs remain—as has been the case now for well over a decade— Jones's view does little to help the needy poor. It's like saying, don't provide food assistance to the starving citizens of Ethiopia and the Sudan, because the real solution there is land reform and population control. Certainly short of national health care, a general tax on incomes to finance an expansion of Medicaid so it covers all the poor and uninsured, is the best long-term solution to the problem of indigent health-care, just as land reform and birth control are unquestionably the long-term solutions to the Sahel's continuing famine. The problem is that the real solutions are political impossibilities in the short run. And in the long run, as the philosopher John Maynard Keynes once observed, we're all dead.

In any case, all the for-profit chains engage in a kind of cost shifting anyway. As HCA's Tom Frist stated in an interview about indigent care, "We'll have some hospitals that do almost none, and others that do well over four percent of gross patient revenues, so it averages out to about four percent overall." Why, one might ask, if cost shifting is so pernicious and unfair to paying patients, should patients at those HCA hospitals where there is no local indigent care have to pay at rates that inevitably must help cover the costs of indigent care at other hospitals in the chain?

Similarly, in explaining their strategy for operating the University of Louisville's public teaching hospital, Humana officials said the key to success was attracting insured middle-class patients to the facility, instead of just the poor. The obvious reason was so that third-party insurance payments would enable the firm to cover the unfunded care of indigents which it is required to admit under terms of its contract, and to earn a profit into the bargain. This too is a classic example of cost shifting. And of course, critics are quick to point out that Humana's provision of millions of dollars worth of free care to its artificial heart patients is nothing but cross-subsidization again. They point out that that money came from inflated charges to paying patients.

It is indisputable that hospital cost shifting has, as the FAHS observes, become a kind of hidden indigent care tax. It is used to accomplish something that the political leadership has not had the courage to do in the open, and that the taxpaying public has been loathe to pay for. There is no question either that continuation of the cost-shifting approach, which leads to a very haphazard and arbitrary system of care for the poor, postpones a day of reckoning when the real issue has to be faced of whether or not this society has a moral obligation to provide decent health care to its less fortunate. But without any political agenda to deal with the problem head-on, cost shifting is the only avenue available at the moment. The no-care policies of the increasingly powerful and influential corporate hospital chains, besides immediately reducing the availability of care and stressing the finances of those hospitals that continue to provide it, are also hastening a relatively new phenomenon: the creation of a dual-track health-care system. That is, one in which the patients with resources go to a private hospital and the poor go to public institutions. The danger, of course, is that once all poor people get treated in tax-funded facilities and all employed, insured taxpayers get treated in independently financed ones, such support as still exists for public hospitals and Medicaid insurance programs for the poor will dry up. Anyone trying to imagine where this all leads need only look at public schools in urban districts in the North and West, or rural districts of the Southeast, where middle-class white families send their kids to private and parochial schools and then vote against adequate funding for the public schools that poor minority kids have to attend.

Relman's counterargument to that articulated by Jones and the FAHS lobby, while it tends to romanticize the charitable record of the not-for-profit hospital sector in providing care for the poor, is nonetheless largely valid. As he wrote in an article in the April 1984 issue of *Technology Review*:

> In this country, we have always depended on a significant degree of charity and cross-subsidization by the nonprofit tax-exempt hospitals to provide health care

for the poor. Competition from the for-profit sector, which is skimming away a large number of paying patients and profitable services [needed to make cost shifting possible], is impairing the ability of many non-profit hospitals to shoulder their share of the free-care burden. The shunting of indigent patients to public hospitals already suffering from reduced tax support can only mean deterioration in services and less care for the poor.[4]

The "Tipping" Problem: Making a Bad Situation Worse

None of this is to suggest that refusing to admit or treat the uninsured or impoverished is confined to the corporate hospital chain, or even to hospitals as an industry within the larger medical-pharmaceutical establishment. Rare is the physician who accepts Medicaid patients in his or her office (even in states where Medicaid funding is relatively high like New York, the program only reimburses physicians and hospitals at a rate of about 40 percent of their usual charges), not to mention the tens of millions of poor or temporarily poor who fail, for one bureaucratic reason or another, even to qualify for Medicaid assistance. And even those institutions—a majority of all hospitals in the country—that only exist because of low-interest guaranteed construction and equipment loans provided under the Hill-Burton Act, or more recently to tax-exempt revenue bonds subsidized by the taxpayer, often ignore the law and turn poor patients away. As an investigative reporter in Los Angeles and New York, I discovered that many not-for-profit hospitals not only turned people away, but, in blatant violation of state and federal law, failed even to post the requisite notices in admitting areas announcing that free care was available for those without resources.

The broader nature of the problem was illustrated by the Utah Supreme Court, which ruled in June 1985 that two allegedly charitable hospitals owned by Intermountain Health Care, Incorporated, a *not-for-profit* chain of twenty-one hospitals, should not be permitted to claim exemption from local property taxation. Among the court's reasons: Neither hospital, between the years 1978 and 1980, provided an amount of free care to indigents equal to even 1 percent of gross patient revenues! The hospitals, according to court testimony, "deliberately did not advertise" availability of free care for fear of a "deluge of people," and "even offered assistance to patients who claimed inability to pay to enter into bank loan agreements to finance their hospital expenses."[5]

Still, it is clear that not-for-profit hospitals have been an important mainstay of the nation's "system," if it can be called that, of medical care for the poor. And the growth of the corporate hospital sector is equally clearly undermining that resource.

As Geri Dallek, past director of the National Health Law Program in Los Angeles, put it, "The voluntaries are becoming increasingly like the for-profits, but even now if I had to organize a community [to pressure a hospital management], I'd much prefer to be holding an allegedly charitable institution up to scrutiny than a for-profit hospital with management in Louisville or Los Angeles."

Baruch College's Luanne Kennedy believes that there is a direct causal relationship between the growth of for-profit hospital chains and the increasing emulation of their behavior by the nation's traditionally not-for-profit hospitals. Looking at all the hospitals in a sample of ten states from 1972 to 1982, she said, "I found a substantial change in voluntary hospital behavior after there was a substantial number of proprietaries in a state." She called the phenomenon "tipping," explaining, "Once a certain percentage of beds in a community were in proprietary hands, the voluntaries started to act just like them."

Dr. Quentin Young, internist, professor of preventive medicine at the University of Illinois Medical School, and president of the Chicago-based Health and Medicine Policy Research Group, speaks less politely of a "vampire effect," saying, "Once a corporate hospital comes to town, all the hospitals there start acting alike."

This view is echoed by Linda Miller, executive director of the Volunteer Trustees of Not-for-Profit Hospitals, a Washington trade group and lobbying organization. Says Miller, "When a for-profit hospital comes into town, the rules of competition change. Everyone will be competing for the wealthy patient. What the for-profit companies are doing is squeezing the voluntaries and then buying them. I'm not defending the behavior of the not-for-profits—plenty of them have dumped poor patients onto the public hospitals too—but there *is* a difference between a corporation and a not-for-profit institution. Fifty-one percent of the hospitals in Florida were for-profit in 1985, and only 4.5

percent of the indigent care was being done by them. The not-for-profits were providing 48 percent of the indigent care in the state."

An example of how the dynamics of the "tipping" phenomenon operate was provided recently when Humana built a women's hospital in Tampa, Florida. Thanks to its slick marketing of hotel-like birthing rooms, champagne-and-steak meals for parents, and the like, the new facility quickly attracted what had been the local public hospital's most important financial asset: insured women with normal, low-risk pregnancies. More importantly, it lured away their physicians. Within a few years after Humana Women's Hospital opened the public hospital, Tampa General, once the main choice of pregnant women of means, was in the position of having 90 percent of its deliveries unfunded. Only the poor were going there, or people with birth complications for which the teaching staff was better equipped. The county hospital found itself on the rocks. It was already having to accept medical transfers, those with severe complications, and "economic transfers," those whose insurance coverage has been exhausted, from Humana and from AMI, which also owns a hospital in the area. But now it couldn't even use cost shifting to cover the costs of their treatment. There were no paying patients onto whose insurance carriers costs could be shifted.

Tampa General recovered dramatically by taking bold steps on the advice of a local grand jury studying the hospital's financial crisis, but not without fundamentally changing the nature of the public hospital. It hired a marketing executive to promote the hospital to the middle class, and it built a gleaming new obstetrics facility on borrowed money. But where the hospital once treated everyone when they needed treatment, now, under a "business-like" philosophy recommended by the grand jury, Tampa General doesn't perform "elective" surgery on indigents (and even delays elective surgery on patients covered by Medicaid).

What does that mean? "Well," explained Managing Director Newel France, the man credited with turning around the county hospital's fortunes, "for instance, an indigent who needs a hernia operation would no longer be taken immediately." He added, "Lately, we're gradually relaxing on that [policy]. If we find that we're falling a little short of teaching material, we'll admit more elective surgery. If we have a cluster of one hundred men who have hernias and can't work, we'll selectively do them, or if, say, we have women with a history of neonatal babies and they want a tubal ligation—that is elective—we'll do it, because [sterilization is] more cost effective than having them turn up again pregnant."

Counters Adrianne Sundheim, head of the West Central Florida Health Council, "The problem is, everything is elective to the next guy. How can you call a hernia repair 'elective' surgery? The sense I have is that there are a lot of indigent people going around without needed medical care now."

Put another way, at the new "businesslike" Tampa General, hernia surgery on an indigent male is considered to be "medically necessary" if it is forcing him on to the welfare roles by preventing him from working. Otherwise, it's just "elective."

And it isn't always just the indigent who are ignored by corporate hospitals or their not-for-profit and public emulators. Humana Women's Hospital in Tampa also treats very few Medicaid patients, whose reimbursement rates are far below what private insurance companies, or even Medicare, pay. According to the Florida Department of Health and Rehabilitative Service's Medicaid Cost Reimbursement Section, only 2.6 percent of Humana Women's Hospital's in-patient days were for Medicaid patients in 1990. In 1988, the figure was just 1.2 percent. Another way to look at its performance: Of 20,000 babies delivered at Humana Women's in 1988, only 257 were Medicaid cases. That was actually an improvement over 1987 and 1986, when Medicaid patients accounted for only .99 and .58 percent, respectively, of the hospital's total patient load. Humana's acceptance of Medicaid patients is also below the 1990 statewide average Medicaid patient utilization rate of 7.7 percent, according to Section Chief Joyce Barrington. Tampa General, meanwhile, reported that in 1990, 18.6 percent of its patients were on Medicaid.

Such avoidance of Medicaid patients is consistent with the national picture. In 1981, the for-profit chains in Florida, Texas, and Tennessee, where Medicaid reimbursement rates are extremely low, reported that fewer than 3 percent of their patients were covered by Medicaid. By 1990, according to the Florida Department of Health and Rehabilitation, the for-profits in the state were still only able to report 5.6 percent of their patients on Medicaid. (Humana's seventeen reporting hospitals in Florida that year averaged only 4 percent Medicaid patient days.) By way of contrast, the 1990 not-for-profit Medicaid patient days percentage was 9.4 percent, the same as the statewide average for *all* hospitals.

Nationally, the chains have a much smaller proportion of

Medicaid patients than do voluntaries. It's a point that usually gets left out of discussions about "indigent" care, since Medicaid recipients aren't classified as indigent. Yet obviously, any Medicaid patients who can't or don't use Humana and other private hospitals in the region wind up at Tampa General, where any difference between government reimbursement and actual costs of treatment will have to be made up by the taxpayers. More broadly, when for-profit hospitals keep their Medicaid patient census minimal, it adds to the financial weakness of the not-for-profit sector and puts increasing political and fiscal stress on the public hospitals.

In the end, the rescue of Tampa General didn't come free to the middle-class community for another reason: County residents also had to approve a sales tax increase to finance the hospital's new competitive strategy. It was that, says Sundheim, or see their hospital go under.

If not-for-profit hospitals, and even some public hospitals like Tampa General, are acting more and more like for-profits, what then, is so different about the for-profit hospital?

Here, it is important to draw a few distinctions, the most basic being that every nonpublic hospital has to make money. Even the books of the Salvation Army or the Red Cross have to balance at the end of the year, and can't show red ink forever. A hospital, corporate or charity, that operates with a continually growing deficit will not be operating indefinitely. If the institution is owned by a government entity, whether city, county, state, or federal, it inevitably handles a large percentage of nonpaying patients, using tax subsidies to make up the difference. Not-for-profit hospitals, also known as voluntary or charity institutions, traditionally covered their losses from charity care by relying on philanthropy. As philanthropic donations have waned, they have begun setting up profit-making subsidiary operations or entering profit-making joint ventures with outside companies or physician groups. Corporate, or proprietary, hospitals, without access to tax dollars or to significant charitable contributions, make their money like any other capitalist enterprise, by simply charging more in revenues than they pay out in expenses. The difference is profit, or surplus.

To listen to Humana's David Jones, these are all fine points. As he sees it, the only real distinction is between hospitals "that are tax supported and those that aren't." As for the matter of for-profits versus not-for-profits, Jones says simply, "There *is* no difference, except that one pays taxes and the other doesn't."

Is that a fair statement? Not really. A fundamental difference exists, namely that the "profits," or surplus revenues, of a not-for-profit institution are by law re-invested in the institution, while at least some portion of a for-profit hospital's profit is distributed to shareholders in the form of dividends. Arnold Relman noted a further distinction. While not-for-profit hospitals have to earn a surplus of revenues over expenses so as to stay up with medical advances, meet growing demand, replace aging equipment and facilities, et cetera, investor-owned hospitals have a further imperative: growth for growth's sake. As Relman noted in the April 1983 issue of *Technology Review*:

> . . . profit per se is not the prime economic goal of investor-owned corporations. It is the prospect of an increase in the value of stock that attracts investors, and it is the opportunity to acquire profitable stock options that enriches top management.[6]

Incidentally, AMI's ex-president Walter Weisman listed stock options as one of the advantages held by corporate hospital chains over not-for-profits in the competition to attract "top quality managers." It was by exercising stock options that David Jones managed to become the second-highest-paid corporate executive in America in 1984, when he earned $18 million.

Corporate Hospitals Are Different

The difference in the way for-profit and not-for-profit companies deal with profits, or "surplus" revenues, may seem like a subtle distinction, but it is not. One direct result of this need to see the company's share value grow has been the for-profit hospital industry's incredible acquisition binge—even when society's need is clearly for fewer hospitals. Whenever a new hospital was acquired (or built), its annual patient revenues were added to the corporate total. The other result has been the industry's equally dramatic contraction when times got harder.

Like oil companies during the mid-1980s, which found that buying wells and companies that owned wells was cheaper than expanding production by drilling more wells, the hospital companies found it easier to increase patient revenues by acquiring new hospitals than by working to increase occupancy at existing facilities, which would have called for creative marketing and better management. In the mid-1960s, immediately upon the founding of most of the extant major companies, an acquisition "feeding frenzy" began. It continued to accelerate, involving ever larger mergers, for twenty years, at which point several things happened. First, where once the purchase of a hospital or two was enough to boost the relatively small total company revenues significantly, companies like HCA, NME, AMI, and Humana grew so large that even acquisition of a moderate-sized hospital *chain* only increased revenues—which tallied in the billions of dollars—by a little bit. Second, because the costs of some of the acquired properties were so high, they proved to be unprofitable to operate. Third, by 1985 the impact of Medicare reforms, meaning lower reimbursements for elderly patients, was beginning to be felt seriously. All these factors led to lower earnings growth at the big chains. Investors, who need to see both revenues *and* earnings rising to sustain their interest, began to sour on the industry, causing stock values to plummet.

How did the for-profit sector respond to this Wall Street debacle? The faster a company's stock fell, the more quickly it moved in the other direction, to divest itself of those hospitals that were a drag on earnings, and to tighten up on the running of those facilities it retained. HCA sold dozens of hospitals right after its stock fell on hard times. Most of them went to smaller investor-owned firms, where the sudden growth in revenues produced by the acquisition of just a few hospitals was still so dramatic it clouded investors' eyes as to long-term profitablilty. When this didn't satisfy HCA's investors, and the stock continued to languish, the company bit the bullet and in 1987 unloaded another 104 poor performers at one fell swoop. NME's mid-1986 sale of nine hospitals led many Wall Street observers to speculate—incorrectly it turned out—that the company, already more diversified than its major competitors, was essentially abandoning the hospital market in favor of other fields of endeavor, like psychiatric care. Westworld, a smaller company, actually did that, getting out of acute-care hospitals altogether (it owned 33 in 1986) in favor of psychiatric and alcoholism treatment centers. And AMI, besides selling off some fifty of its holdings, including thirty-six at once into an ESOP trust modeled on HCA's Health-Trust spin-off, put the screws to its remaining hospitals; it conducted seemingly random purges of middle management and directed local hospital administrators to try to shift away from more acute patients to those with fast turn-around times. There was no sell-off at Humana, where management had foreseen the problem of reduced profitability and had unloaded less profitable hospitals years before. In fact, by late 1988 Humana was rumored to be looking covetously at HCA as a takeover target, at least until HCA went private to protect itself.

Said Ron Booker, about to lose his job in July 1986 as manager of diagnostic imaging for two AMI hospitals in San Diego during one round of company layoffs, "AMI lives and dies by the [financial] quarter. When things were going well, there was no problem. But when the market turned, we in middle management felt those quarterly reports [of earnings and revenues] as much as they did in Beverly Hills," where AMI headquarters is located.

What did that mean for his department? "As a manager, you feel the pressures. My department was making a profit, but the hospitals, with 40 percent occupancy, were losing money. Beverly Hills looks at the overall picture and ordered us to trim staffing to reach their arbitrary goals. But I was already in the position where I was two people short, and then they sent me a force reduction requiring me to let two more [people] go, which I couldn't do without quality suffering. I was at the edge of the cliff, and they cut back the cliff. In my case, it was easier to let the manager go, because that doesn't directly affect services." Booker was accordingly given his walking papers, and his department, responsible for such services as X ray, CAT scanning, and the like, is now being run, somewhat improbably, by the director of physical therapy for the two hospitals, under an ad hoc system euphemistically called "cluster management."

Meanwhile, Booker said, the hospitals have been told to find a "new niche." He explained, "They're looking for people who handle lighter medicine, like foot surgeons. Real acute hospital care is very draining on the budget, but with something like foot surgery, it's usually not very serious, and people can be in and out of the hospital in one day. It's not intensive care. Our philosophy has changed."

With No Local Input in Decision Making, Whole Communities Can Be Left in the Lurch

What does all this talk about profits and profitability have to do with medical ethics? Plenty, for there is beginning to be some empirical evidence about how health care changes in a community when a corporate chain takes over. The most dramatic change—certainly far more dramatic than any change in behavior and services—is the outright closing of hospitals. According to a March 1988 report by the American Hospital Association, between 1980 and the start of 1990, 513 community hospitals were closed, 299 in the last three years of that period alone. For 1990, the AHA reported another 50 hospital closures and only five openings of new facilities. By far, the majority of these closures were in states where the for-profit hospital sector was strongest, with over 200 closings alone in California, Texas, Florida, Louisiana, Tennessee, and Kentucky. Over 40 percent of these shutdowns were urban community hospitals, where the loss of local medical services is more of an inconvenience than a health threat. But the other shutdowns were almost entirely rural community hospitals, most of which were the *only* hospitals in their area. And a Senate Select Committee on Aging hearing in June 1988 was told that another 600 of the nation's remaining 2,700 rural hospitals could be expected to follow suit.

A salient fact overlooked at the Senate hearing and in the AHA report is that while the for-profit hospital sector only represents some 9 percent of the rural hospital total, nearly half of the closed facilities were for-profit. In 1987 alone, of the record 79 community hospitals reported closed, urban and rural, 35 were for-profit operations according to the AHA. Of the 151 closed facilities examined at the Senate hearing, 48, or 32 percent, were for-profit entities. The situation continues: The AHA reported that during 1989, of 65 hospitals that closed their doors, 44 were rural ones. Twelve of these, or more than 25 percent, were investor-owned for-profits.

The closing of a rural hospital is a particularly serious disaster for a community. Residents of the area are put at risk by being forced suddenly to travel from twenty to one hundred miles for emergency medical treatment. Often the closed hospital was the main source of local employment. Health impacts continue to snowball too, as local physicians, unable to treat patients, drift away to better markets.

When a community-run hospital—public or not-for-profit—falls on hard times, the community can either make a conscious decision to close it, or act to ensure its survival. The latter strategy was taken by the citizens of Memphis, Texas.[7] When their public hospital faced bankruptcy in 1988, the community rallied and raised the $400,000 necessary to keep it open. They knew they needed a hospital, and all that mattered was: could they raise enough money so it could break even? They didn't have to worry about making an adequate return on an investment. If they had to, they probably wouldn't have ever tried to raise the funds to keep the hospital going.

Things are different when a corporation owns a hospital. Then, the community has little or no say over the decision to close, and the decision might be made even though a hospital is marginally profitable, since a 1 or 2 percent return is hardly something to write home about to the shareholders in a public corporation. If the tax writeoff from closing the hospital (and subtracting its book value from company income) is greater than what can be earned by selling it to some entrepreneur willing to take a chance or to the community, it will be closed.

Closings aside, when the soaring hospital business hit an air pocket in 1985, many corporate hospital managers quickly forgot those promises of stability and continuity of health services they'd made to communities when they were buying up hospitals. They turned around and sold facility after facility to small financially risky entrepreneurial ventures, or in HCA's or AMI's case, to huge debt-ridden private trusts, where the hospitals' fates are all at the whim of interest rates. A rash of closures is then predictable.

The same loss of investor confidence in the hospital industry in 1985–86 that caused such a panic in Nashville and Los Angeles had no observable impact on the not-for-profit sector, which didn't have investors nervously looking over its shoulder.

One can imagine a not-for-profit hospital being shut down or driven into bankruptcy by stiff competition, run into the ground by bad management, or even closed down for lack of occupancy, but it's hard to imagine many local hospital boards voting to shut down their community hospital just because the annual surplus was too low. For corporate chains, it's another story. Certainly, shutting down a losing operation could mean some bad publicity, especially locally (ask any steel company!), but that weighs far less heavily in such decisions than the view on Wall Street. The same can be said for less dramatic proposals, such as whether a hospital should operate a money-losing burn or trauma center.

Caring for the poor is not the only ethical issue being raised by the rapid spread of investor-owned hospital chains. Earlier we examined some of the others, particularly the increasing pressures on the physician/patient relationship and the impact on research and medical education. But as far as ethics are concerned, because of their vulnerability and lack of alternatives, care for the poor surely is the most serious issue.

Economists, particularly in the U.S., are wont to talk at length about the contradictory goals of efficiency and equity, generally concluding that the two are opposites: promoting one hurts the other. There clearly has been gross inefficiency in the American medical system, a problem the promotion of for-profit medicine seeks to address. To what extent the new corporate hospital chains contribute to efficiency is open to some question. What is beyond debate is that, cost-effective or not, they are contributing mightily to a decline in equity in the system.

Says Gene Clark, administrator of the Johnson City Medical Center in Tennessee, a not-for-profit hospital that he reports has had to adopt "businesslike" practices in the face of stiff competition on HCA's home turf, "We're going to look back on this age and see it as an age of greed in health care. We've stopped seeing the needs of people. We're too close to it right now to see that, but one day we're going to see all this emphasis on profits as not such a great time."

8

The Unhealthy Politics of the Health-Care Industry

People of the same trade seldom meet together, even for merriment and diversion, but the conversation ends in a conspiracy against the public, or in some contrivance to raise prices.
—Adam Smith
in *An Inquiry into the Nature and Causes of the Wealth of Nations*, 1776

A substantial increase in the for-profit [hospital] sector's share of the health system could . . . create powerful centers of influence to affect public policy. . . .
—From a letter of dissent by several members of the National Institutes of Health's Committee on Implications of For-Profit Enterprise in Health Care, *For-Profit Enterprise in Health Care*, 1986

If we can gain the inside track on these two [hospital] projects, the cost savings would be tremendous. Therefore, I recommend we contribute two tables to the Democratic Presidential Campaign Committee in the amount of $5,000.
—Internal memo from National Medical Enterprises Senior Vice President Steve Dominguez to NME Senior Executive Vice President John Bedrosian, 1983

In the early 1980s, a group of businessmen with political connections in Louisiana teamed up with former governor Edwin W. Edwards to form a company, Health Services Development Corporation, specifically for the purpose of obtaining from the state prized certificates of need (CONs) to build new hospitals. The idea was to acquire the CONs in the name of made-to-order corporations, and then to sell these shell companies—essentially companies whose only asset was a paper permit—to large corporate entities that were anxious to increase their penetration of the state's health-care market. The price: about $1.5 million per approved certificate of need.

The scheme—while not illegal—clearly undermined the purpose of CONs, since a central aim of the certificate process was to give communities and regions some measure of control over important health-care capital-spending decisions. Having a local company apply for such a certificate made it seem that the hospital in question was to be locally owned and run, though the intention all along was to sell the approved CON to out-of-state hospital corporations, over which communities would have little or no control.

According to U.S. Attorney John Volz, the federal prosecutor for New Orleans, there was more to the story than simply a local firm assisting out-of-state companies in obtaining construction permits. In a fifty-one-count federal grand jury indictment of Edwards and several codefendants handed down on February 28, 1985, Volz charged that Edwards illegally profited by concealing his interest in Health Services Development (his brother Marion was an owner of the firm), and that he had aided the operation after returning to the governor's mansion in 1984. He did this, Volz alleged, by imposing a moratorium on new hospital construction while explicitly exempting those five projects where Health Services Development held CON permits. The principals, including Edwards, were all indicted on charges that included racketeering, conspiracy, and wire and mail fraud.

Edwards admitted to having received $2 million from Health Services, but claimed it was for legal services rendered as a private attorney between 1982 and 1984, an interlude when he was out of the governor's mansion. Of the exemptions to the moratorium, he argued that he had agreed to them as governor because of specific needs in each community.

There were two trials, in 1985 and 1986. The flamboyant and garrulous Edwards (he came to court one day in a horse-drawn carriage), at the time surely the most popular politician in the state, took the stand each time in his own defense. He was acquitted in both trials—the first time by a hung jury.

Some observers questioned the way the trials were conducted. Volz never included in the indictment as co-conspirators any of the companies or corporate officers who were paying exorbitant prices for permits that normally cost only a few dollars. In an era when prosecutors routinely cast a wide net of indictments in hopes of winning some cooperative witnesses who wish to escape prosecution, this curious strategy left the prosecutor with no leverage to gain possibly damning testimony from any parties to one side of the transactions. Nonetheless, it was clear from sworn testimony at the two trials that the companies purchasing the CONs from Health Services Development, HCA and AMI, were aware—or thought—that they were involved in something other than a typical business deal (NME was also involved, but ultimately declined to buy one CON for unspecified reasons). As AMI executive Joseph L. Reina, the person responsible for the company's acquisition program in Louisiana, put it simply in his sworn trial testimony, when the company applied for a CON on its own, it was often turned down, but when it applied through local organizations, it got approved. "Here was an opportunity," Reina testified, referring to Health Services Development's activities, "where at no risk to us, we could hire a local company and that's a 'key,' a local company."[1]

Outside the trial, company employees were saying much more explicitly off the record that AMI knew *exactly* what was going on. According to one executive in AMI's Beverly Hills corporate headquarters, "The guys in the acquisition department said doing business in Louisiana was worse than doing business in Mexico. You had to pay for everything."

A management employee in the company's Louisiana region said, "There were people down here who were sweating blood, expecting Volz to call them and question them under oath about bribing government officials." He never did.

During all the time that Health Services Development was gathering up CONs and then demanding enormous fees for the certificates, none of the hospital corporations came forward to state authorities to complain. Instead, they tried to play the game, apparently figuring $1.5 million for a guaranteed, preapproved CON was a price worth paying to ensure entry in a profitable hospital marketplace. Indeed, one company executive testified at the trial that in one instance his firm had purchased a CON just to keep out the competition.

Barbara Sanders was "director of facilities planning" at Health Services Development but left after a falling out with the owners of the company. HCA then hired Sanders as director of its planning and development office. Meanwhile, NME hired a former partner of the two principal owners of Health Services Development as its senior vice president for corporate development.

Left completely out of the corporate calculations of entry costs and relative advantage were the interests of the people of local areas where the new hospitals were to be built. Consider, for instance, AMI's controversial CON permit, obtained for them in the name of Health Services Development, for construction of a 150-bed hospital in Gonzales, Louisiana. Because the existing local 60-bed public hospital, East Ascension General Hospital, was already operating at less than full occupancy, the new facility seemed unnecessary and in fact nearly caused the failure of East Ascension.

Attorney James Cobb III, hired by the community to bring a civil damage suit against AMI under the federal racketeering law, recalled later, "AMI built a doctors' building across the street from the new hospital, and gave the docs everything they wanted up front—cheap rent, more nurses, equipment, you name it—and locked them all up, so no one would bring patients to East Ascension. When we had our last meeting at the hospital in 1987, it had three patients." At that point, he said, the community didn't know if their public hospital would last another year. If it failed, he added, it would have been a local disaster. In 1967, the town had invested $3 million raised in a bond issue to build East Ascension General, and in 1984, the community borrowed another $6 million to modernize and upgrade it. If the hospital were to fold for lack of patients, he said, the community would "be left paying off the bonds, but they won't have the income stream to cover the payments, so taxes would have to go up. You talk about the sacking of Rome!"

In 1988, AMI unloaded its new hospital in Gonzales as part of EPIC, the ESOP spin-off corporation it created that year in response to investor pressure to improve its earnings and share value. Then in early 1989, AMI, without admitting any liability, settled the case brought by the people of Gonzales, for a sum that was ordered kept secret by the court at the company's request. ("I *will* say we're happy with it!" was Cobb's only comment.) Mean-while, East Ascension General solved its low-occupancy crisis by leasing 80 percent of its unused bed space to a small investor-owned hospital company, Vencare of Louisville, Kentucky. Ven-care uses the beds for patients in need of chronic respiratory support—the company's specialty—while the community retains the other 20 percent for emergency patients and minor surgery, plus the right to retake more beds if patient demand increases.

All three of the companies mentioned in connection with the Edwards trials—HCA, NME, and AMI—were attempting to in-crease their presence in Louisiana, a state viewed as a high-growth, high-income market, but one which is also particularly overbedded. It was a classic formula for conflict, pitting these corporate newcomers against a variety of local and for the most part not-for-profit or public incumbents. With the local hospital establishment more or less ensconced in regional and local regu-latory bodies—health systems agencies, parish councils—the na-tional firms had to find political allies as best they could. What they did, with some success, was use money to overcome local chauvinism and other obstacles to growth.

Deus ex Medica

Whether or not free enterprise is a solution to the nation's health-care ills is a subject that can be debated endlessly. Even if one accepts the conservative theory that market forces will lead to cheaper, better medicine, the advocates of this approach have conveniently ignored the role of politics in selectively staying the workings of Adam Smith's "invisible hand." It is a serious omission, especially in the field of health. As Adam Smith himself well knew, economic interests that have sufficient power to control the political environment are able to get government to subvert the workings of a free market to their advantage and to the disadvantage of the consumer. And in recent history particularly, politics and health care have had a very intimate relationship, a relationship that has all too often resembled the kind of "conspir-acy against the public" so presciently referred to by Smith.

As we have seen, since World War II government involve-ment in health care has increased exponentially. Today, the economic health of America's hospitals—profit and not-for-profit, public and private—and of its physicians is largely dependent upon political decisions about federal funding levels. Statehouse decisions about the level of Medicaid funding and local government decisions about reimbursement for care of the indigent also continue to play crucial roles in the financial well-being of hospitals and physicians. Likewise the actions of federal, state, regional, and local regulatory bodies can determine what facilities are to be built and what equipment purchased. The hospital industry has responded by developing strong political connections.

Physicians and hospitals both have a venerable tradition of political activity in their own financial interest. Physicians banded together as early as 1846 to form the organization that later came to be called the American Medical Association. By casting issues in terms of patient care and freedom of choice while it lobbied for legislation that made physicians rich at their patients' expense, the AMA was a trade group that eventually became the envy of Washington lobbyists. In its heyday, it held sway with the National Rifle Association as one of the most powerful political groups in the country. Although public concern over health-care inflation and a decline in membership among younger physicians have weakened its appeal on Capitol Hill, it still remains powerful.

The political activities of hospitals go back almost as far, to 1899, when the Association of Hospital Superintendents, forerunner of the American Hospital Association, was chartered. Both the physicians' and the hospitals' organizations were active politically, particularly in the reformist days of the New Deal, when they stood foursquare together against any talk of nationalizing health care or of government health insurance programs. Never as powerful as the AMA, the AHA was wildly successful nonetheless in the postwar period in winning funds and a protected position. It accomplished this feat in part by riding on the success of the doctors, with whose association it was for the most part allied in interest.

In recent years, those interests have diverged. So too have the interests of the subgroups of hospitals themselves. As the for-profit and not-for-profit hospital sectors have increasingly found themselves on opposite sides of certain issues, the AHA, which includes both types of operations as well as public and teaching hospitals within its ranks, has been accordingly weakened. While it remains an important lobbying organization in Washington, and its various state affiliates remain powerful in their jurisdictions, a new political force has grown: the Federation of American Health Systems, trade group of the for-profit investor-owned hospital industry. A third trade organization, the Volunteer Trustees of Not-for-Profit Hospitals, has also emerged and can sometimes be found lobbying opposite the for-profit group.

In theory the AHA should represent the collective interests of hospitals when for-profits and not-for-profits share the same position, as, for instance, when it comes to pushing for higher reimbursement rates for DRG categories. In practice, the not-for-profit sector itself is torn by dissention, with some hospitals fighting for-profit hospital expansion tooth and nail and others simply waiting for the best offer. Because it has not been clear on where its collective interests lie, the AHA has played less of a role than it might have at both the state and federal levels, according to congressional staffers who have been on the receiving end of the lobbying. It has even acted on occasion in the interest of the for-profit sector. On the other hand, Humana found the AHA so riven by the conflicting interests of its members that the company, in 1986, briefly quit the organization. Humana only returned to the fold when the AHA submissively agreed to reduce the firm's membership dues, reportedly by about half.

Ambivalence and lack of focus at the AHA have tended to work to the advantage of the FAHS, as the for-profit hospital companies have been solidly united in pushing for their industry's advantage in the legislative arena. Despite its much smaller constituency, the federation has raised and spent campaign funds on a scale comparable to the AHA. It has also organized, in concert with the American Association of Retired People (AARP), a grass-roots campaign aimed at preventing budget cuts in Medicare, the industry's life blood. Moreover, the Volunteer Trustees organization, which might seem to be the logical counterweight to the FAHS, has a hard time playing that role because its members, like AHA's, often disagree. Within the voluntary hospital sector, there are those who adamantly resist the for-profit sector's expansion, and those who see themselves eventually selling out to, or in some way entering into a relationship with, that sector. Says Linda Miller, executive director of the Voluntary Trustees organization, with an air of frustration, "I have a hard time getting a lot of my members to realize what's happening to them!"

Still, as successful as the federation has been at the national level, with the for-profit hospital industry—chains and single-hospital companies—representing only 25 percent of the nation's hospitals, slick lobbying can only accomplish so much. This is particularly true where the for-profit hospital sector's interests are in direct conflict with the interests of the not-for-profit establishment.

In certain states, however, the for-profit industry has become either a majority (Florida—56 percent), or a large minority (Tennessee—45 percent, Georgia—42 percent, Texas—39 percent, Louisiana—38 percent, and California—35 percent). In states where the for-profit sector represents a smaller share of the local hospital industry (Arizona—19 percent, Nevada—27 percent, and New Mexico—23 percent), the sheer size of the chains can give them disproportionate political clout, since relatively small amounts of campaign spending go a much longer way. The place to look for a glimpse of what can be expected politically from the for-profit hospital companies when, as most observers expect, they become the dominant sector in the hospital industry, is not Washington, but rather those jurisdictions where the companies are already powers to reckon with.

The view can be disconcerting.

New Mexico and NME

National Medical Enterprises may have had good reasons for backing out of the Louisiana CON game early, but it's unlikely that fear of playing politics—or paying for favors—was one of them. Elsewhere the company has not hesitated to use money in an effort to influence government policy or specific decisions.

In New Mexico, a federal grand jury in 1986 looked into a series of campaign donations made by the company to the former governor of the state, Toney Anaya, and to the state's ruling Democratic party. While it didn't lead to any prosecution, the investigation did produce some interesting information about the hospital business and state politics.

There was speculation that the company was attempting to win approval for construction of a 136-bed, $23.7-million hospital in Las Cruces. In 1983 state health planners had said a new hospital would hurt Memorial General, a local public hospital, and contribute to higher overall costs by adding to overbedding in the state, and on January 30, 1984 the state turned down NME's building proposal. Then, on September 19, 1984, the state health department suddenly reversed itself and granted the application, citing "technical" problems with the earlier decision to deny the NME permit.

In between, and even before the initial negative decision on the certificate, NME had been busy winning friends and influencing people, primarily by scattering campaign money in the right places. Among the NME contributions being questioned was one of $10,000 made to the state Democratic party on June 28, 1984, more than two months before the state decision was reversed.[2] That money was donated, apparently in a lump sum, a month *after* a Democratic fund-raising event held at the governor's mansion. According to documents obtained in the course of an investigation of the donation by then U.S. Attorney William Lutz, the donation was not recorded by the party as a lump sum. Instead, NME allegedly began retroactively seeking $100 tickets to the May event, allegedly to serve as receipts for donations. Since under New Mexico law political contributions of $100 or less can be listed anonymously, this maneuver might have enabled the company's entire donation to go unnoticed outside of Democratic party circles.

Memorial General Hospital, which was threatened by NME's development plans, filed a civil suit in federal court against NME in 1986, charging it with political influence. The lawsuit brought the campaign contribution, and others like it, to light, though ultimately because NME, for economic reasons, cancelled plans for the hospital, the case was not pursued.

According to Alan Konrad, the attorney handling the case for Memorial General, NME's contributions to the state Democratic party and to Governor Anaya, in amounts of $2,500 and $3,000 in addition to the single $10,000 donation, added up to "over $20,000" for the two-year period under discussion. That's a princely sum in a sparsely populated state where total Democratic party contributions in 1984 were only $320,000. An internal NME document obtained by Konrad lists five contributions totaling $18,750 between June 1982 and June 1984. One of the checks from the company, in the amount of $1,250, was made payable to Toney Anaya.

Both NME and now ex-Governor Anaya have denied that the company's contributions had the real or intended effect of altering a health planning agency decision. Nonetheless, top company officials clearly had unusual personal access to the governor and his appointees in the health regulatory apparatus, which approved the company's application and ultimately granted a permit for a key hospital project. Whatever the actual impact of the NME money on the decisions of New Mexico regulatory authorities, a series of memorandums obtained from NME by attorneys for Memorial General in the course of the public hospital's lawsuit provides a remarkable inside look at a corporate hospital chain's political machinations.

Among the documents obtained by Memorial General in its suit was one NME memo on the Las Cruces hospital project which conceded that feasibility studies for the region showed "a questionable need" for the hospital "based on planning factor considerations alone." But the memo then suggested that there could be a "feasible project depending on significance of political factors as well as the gain [to NME] from probably adverse impact on the existing hospital, together with a creative approach" to the necessary permit application. Among the political factors cited by the NME memo was a "substantial dissatisfaction among Las Cruces physicians" with the existing hospital, where they "have to treat the medically indigent patients that they are required to admit through the (emergency room) at Memorial, free of charge." That requirement, the memo noted, "would be eliminated for physicians using" a new NME hospital.[3]

Three months after that memo circulated in the company, on December 1, 1983, NME Senior Vice President Steve Dominguez wrote a memo to his boss, company cofounder and Senior Executive Vice President John Bedrosian, suggesting that two current projects—the permission to build a hospital in Las Cruces and an agreement to purchase a potentially highly profitable two-hundred-bed not-for-profit hospital, St. Vincent's, in Santa Fe—could be facilitated through a timely $5,000 contribution of two tables at a Presidential Campaign Committee function being held by the state Democratic party. Dominguez said the purchase of at least one table was suggested to a local NME executive in New Mexico by Dan Lopez, a state government official whom they had approached for "help" in winning approval for the two controversial projects.[4]

Lopez had run Governor Anaya's successful campaign and then headed the state's employment security office. It was not the first time he had received a hefty campaign check from NME. On June 12, 1982, he was sent a contribution for the "Toney Anaya Campaign for Governor—'82" campaign, with a lettter from NME's vice president for legislative and regulatory affairs, Michael Farien, who wrote pointedly that "NME has been very interested in expanding its business operations into the state, which falls in line with New Mexico's need to develop new business."[5]

According to a memo dated December 6, 1983, from NME Vice President Michael Green to William Simpson, a senior vice president for acquisitions and development, the same Lopez (incorrectly identified as Garcia, but still listed as the director of employment security) had

> indicated that we should rely upon his further investigation of the political scene prior to our retaining legal counsel in the State to assist with our political activity. In addition, Mr. Garcia indicated that an additional contribution to the Governor's campaign fund would be appreciated. Mr. Garcia has been in touch with Steve Dominguez regarding an additional contribution of $5,000. If the disbursement has not been made to date, the question is, should it be made before or after the CON is approved?[6]

When a national bank, Irving Trust Co. of New York City, was earlier faced with a similar "request" from state financial officials for a contribution in the process of attempting to open a branch in New Mexico, it determined that it was being "extorted" and went to federal prosecutors with the information.[7] Not NME.

Instead, subsequent to the memo to Bedrosian, a check for $2,500 was made out from NME to the New Mexico Democratic party, with a cover letter from Bedrosian to Lopez, again pointedly referring to the company's desire to "expand its role" as a health-care company. The cover letter, apparently written by the company's assistant director of government relations, Patti Archuletta, was sent to Bedrosian for his signature along with a memo explaining pointedly that the check was "an investment in the Las Cruces project."[8]

Another $2,000 was donated to the reelection campaign of the Democratic mayor of Santa Fe, Louis Montano. The first mention of this donation came in another December 1, 1983, memo, this time between NME employees Bill Williams and Hal Buck. The heading of the memo, which reads: "Subject: St. Vincent's Hospital, Santa Fe, N.M.," makes it clear that this is no simple "good government" donation. The memo itself requests a check for $2,000 payable to "Mayor Montano's Christmas Roast," and gives by way of explanation the following three reasons:

1. Mayor Montano is supporting NME in acquisition of St. Vincent's Hospital.
2. Mayor Montano has 2 years remaining in his current term, is totally committed and heavily supported in running for mayor.
3. Sam Garcia, Santa Fe County Commissioner, and Elmer Garcia, Chairman of the Santa Fe County Democratic Party, are solidly behind Mayor. This combination is politically very influential in Santa Fe. Santa Fe, as you may recall, is the state capital. These 3 politicians and businessmen are also influential with Governor Tony [sic] Anaya.[9]

If there were any doubts as to NME's willingness to buy political support, they should be dispelled by another internal memorandum dated July 1, 1983, from Bill Williams to Ron Messenger, another NME executive. Writes Williams:

New Mexico is an intensely political state. HCA has attempted to acquire St. Vincent's and failed due to a lack of political support and inside information sources.[10]

Lest NME make the same mistake that he felt HCA had, Williams recommends that the company hire Odis Echols, "the most successful long-time lobbyist in the state." NME did just that, signing a contract with Echols for $18,000.

In its public argument on appeal of the initial denial of a permit to build the Las Cruces hospital, NME claimed Memorial General, in opposing the CON for a new competing facility, was simply trying to preserve a local monopoly over both doctors and patients. It was an argument with merit. But particularly here, where one is talking about a *publicly owned* tax-supported hospital, the idea of a medical monopoly is not necessarily unjustified. After all, the advent of a for-profit competitor not known for its largess where care for the poor is concerned could mean the end of the public facility, if it drew away all the doctors with paying patients (which, as NME internal documents show, was precisely the company's intention). In any event, when its argument failed, NME apparently dangled its substantial assets before the eyes of one of the state's two political parties and a governor with national ambitions, in an effort to get them to overwhelm some clear local opposition.

Although NME's efforts eventually paid off, and it got the permit it wanted, its planned hospital in Las Cruces was never built. Perhaps because of the lawsuit filed by Memorial General and the embarrassing revelations about political contributions, or maybe as a result of the company's late 1986 decision to diversify away from acute-care hospitals, in mid-1987 NME dropped its plans to construct that controversial facility. At that point, Memorial General dropped its suit, too.

No one ever determined that NME's campaign contributions in New Mexico during the 1982–86 period were illegal. The grand jury never handed down indictments in the affair. In any case, as all the money flowing into Washington (and the less noticed but equally influential PAC money at the state level) demonstrates, most money given to influence political decision-making is legal. Whether such behavior is in the public interest is another matter altogether.

Tennessee and HCA

Hospital Corporation of America has fought its share of CON battles, but in Tennessee, where it already has the hospitals it wants, the company in recent years has focused its state-level political activities on the indigent-care issue. Recognizing how state decisions in that area can acutely impact a hospital's bottom line, HCA has also been very active with the National Conference of State Legislatures, a Colorado-based organization that has traditionally served as an ideal lobbying forum for corporate America, bringing together state legislators from every state. In the words of New York State Assemblyman Ed Sullivan, "The NCSL does *some* useful things, but not *many*. Basically, what it does is organize fancy gatherings to let state legislators—not usually a very high-powered group—rub elbows with executives from powerful corporations."

HCA has funded NCSL gatherings, financed lavish hospitality suites at others, and perhaps most significantly, provided the organization with funds to produce an "educational" packet on the issue of indigent care. A video tape and a booklet were produced, titled "Questions and Answers on Indigent Care." The basic presentation seems fair, not blatantly advocating one solution over another. But it does soften up legislators to HCA's argument that one solution *not* to attempt is to tax the hospitals on their revenues as a means of raising funds for indigent care, an approach that has been adopted with some success in Florida.

At the same time, in its home state of Tennessee HCA early on won an important friend, then Democratic state legislator Paul Starnes. Starnes, according to the National Conference of State Legislators was paid by the organization (with HCA grant money) to narrate the HCA-funded tape, and then got paid, again officially by the NCSL but indirectly by HCA, to tour the country with the material, addressing other states' legislators.

Head of the General Welfare Committee of the Tennessee House of Representatives at the time the tape was made, Starnes, who has since left the state legislature, was also an important member of a bipartisan commission set up to explore solutions to the indigent care crisis in that relatively poor state.

HCA may not *run* Tennessee, but, as State Senator Stephen Cohen, a Democrat from Memphis, put it, "In order to get anywhere in the Tennessee legislature, you need to get a legislative leader behind you, and the leadership in Tennessee, for whatever reason, doesn't do things in the area of health care regulation that go against HCA. They don't operate like a steam-roller; they don't have to. They just go to the people that back them. HCA has a network of friends and associates in Tennessee politics that works against any kind of reasonable regulation."

The company's political clout in Tennessee stems from its ownership of 8 of Tennessee's 141 acute-care hospitals (and 5 psychiatric hospitals), including the large and prestigious Parkview Memorial in the capital, Nashville. Furthermore, its spin-off relative HealthTrust, which owns another 12 acute-care Tennessee hospitals (HCA properties until 1988), is essentially the same company where state legislation is concerned. HealthTrust is partially owned by HCA. Indeed, HealthTrust (most of whose executives are HCA alumni) has actually contracted with HCA to do its political lobbying for it. Another 5 hospitals formerly managed by HCA were, in 1990, managed by its second spin-off, Quorum, which is 10 percent owned by HCA. Excluding the Quorum holdings, HCA and HealthTrust together owned or indirectly managed one-sixth of the hospitals in Tennessee, which not only made the two companies major employers in the state, but also gave them representation in many of Tennessee's key counties and election districts. Another one-sixth of the state's hospitals were owned by five other national corporate hospital chains, which have shared interests with HCA where health policy is concerned. Additionally, the top executives of HCA, including the two Frists, are part of the social elite in Nashville, which puts them in frequent contact with the political power-houses in the state capital.

Senator Cohen, in describing HCA's political influence, speaks from experience. In 1987, he says he tried to get the Tennessee state legislature to consider an indigent care bill that would have emulated the Florida approach of essentially taxing those hospitals that are making money (in part by not accepting indigent patients) to finance care for the poor at hospitals that *do* treat them. He claims he could not even get a hearing. Said one lobbyist who was pushing for the measure, "The key people on Starnes's general welfare committee convened a meeting with an HCA lobbyist and Cohen's bill was shot down in a New York minute!"

Buying access, the popular euphemism in politics for buying politicians and their votes, is practiced in every state capital and in Washington, D.C., but it is a particularly easy thing to do in states like Tennessee, where legislators are part-time state employees on minimal salaries, and where the total campaign budget in state-wide races is relatively small. In the 1986 gubernatorial race, the official winner was Democrat Ned McWherter, former speaker of the state House of Representatives. But as far as health care goes, the winner was HCA. The company would have had a hard time losing: It gave over $35,000 to McWherter's campaign, much more than it gave to his opponent. But then, it didn't *have* to contribute much to his opponent, Republican former governor Winfield Dunn. Dunn had *worked* for HCA, as vice president for govern-mental affairs, from the time he left the governorship in 1978 until 1989, and he is still on the board of directors of HCA Psychiatric Company, Hospital Corporation's psychiatric hospitals subsidiary.

The 1986 Tennessee gubernatorial election left those worried about HCA's power in the capital with few options. Recalls one rural legislator, Representative D. E. DePriest, "I know a bunch of doctors—all Republicans—who said they gave money to McWherter because they didn't want HCA to own the governor."

According to records kept by the Tennessee chapter of Com-mon Cause, HCA typically gives roughly equal contributions to legislative candidates from both parties, hedging its bets in each election. But McWherter, in any case, was no disinterested party where HCA is concerned. In 1985, when he was still Speaker of the House, his financial disclosure form on file with the secretary of state listed him as the owner of an unspecified amount of HCA stock. In the legislature, health-care activists assert that he was an obstacle to efforts to deal with the issues of cost containment and indigent care. In 1988, McWherter, with more financial support from HCA, won reelection to the governor's mansion.

A number of key political leaders in the state may also have a long-standing reason for showing a certain sentimental fondness for HCA. Many made a killing by holding stock in Hospital Affiliates when the firm was bought by HCA.

Moreover, conflict-of-interest rules for politicians are notoriously weak in Tennessee. For example, the state's attorney general informed McWherter that his ownership of a number of shares of the Correction Corporation of America, a for-profit prison company modeled on HCA, and including many of the same founding investors, did not constitute a conflict of interest. At the time this opinion was offered, the company was lobbying for a contract with the state to manage its prisons. As long as McWherter's shares did not represent a "controlling interest" in the firm, the state's attorney general said there was no problem under Tennessee's conflict of interest statutes. In other words, the mere fact that a legislator might make some money if his or her stock rose in value because of a legislative decision shouldn't trouble anyone! Other states have stricter standards than this.

In any event, HCA's congenial relationship with the new governor only continues a long tradition. The prior governor, Lamar Alexander, and his wife were also HCA investors, and the man in the governor's chair before Alexander was Dunn, who during his tenure as a vice president at HCA was always addressed in the halls of corporate headquarters as "Governor."

To some extent, HCA's success in Tennessee health politics can be traced to the ineffectiveness of the opposition. There is little in the way of an organized health consumers movement, and poverty activists are less common than in some urban states. Also in Tennessee, as in Washington, the broader hospital lobby, the Tennessee Hospital Association, has more or less done HCA's work for it.

As Nashville legal services attorney Gordon Bonnyman explains, "In 1981, the Tennessee legislature decided to cut back on Medicaid coverage from twenty-one days in the hospital to only fourteen. That had to hurt the hospitals, but the hospital association lobbyist was very forthright. He explained to me that they were 'not going to lobby very hard' against the plan because they

wanted to save their strength for [the] cost containment [battle]."
Since HCA and the other proprietary hospitals take many fewer
Medicaid cases than the state's voluntaries, the question of how
much coverage the state would provide for treating such poor
patients was really more of a not-for-profit issue, but the association let it pass. "It shows they were asleep at the switch,"
concludes Bonnyman. He argues that HCA has been "very
sophisticated" in Tennessee in getting the state's hospital association to do its lobbying work, "by saying it's the hospital industry
against the regulators, when it's really the for-profit industry
against the other hospitals."

The Power of Money and the Power of Ideas

HCA's longer-term investment in health politics also draws
on millions of dollars in research funds from a foundation set up
in 1985 with a grant of two percent of the company's stock. In
1986, HCA presented a $450,000 three-year grant to Vanderbilt
University's Institute for Public Policy Studies to fund a series of
studies on issues of obvious import to the firm. The issues to be
studied included: uncompensated hospital care, medical malpractice, how antitrust laws apply in the health area (HCA was
ordered to divest itself of holdings in the Chattanooga, Tennessee,
region by the FTC, which found it establishing a local monopoly
there),[11] and organ transplantation. Among those receiving the
funds was Frank Sloan, a Vanderbilt University economist who
has received grants in the past from the for-profit hospital industry to study indigent care and relative cost and efficiency issues.
Sloan's reports on those subjects are among the few anywhere to
be even modestly favorable to the for-profit hospital industry,
even though his conclusions aren't always a vindication of the
for-profit industry's claims.

Humana too helps fund policy research. In late 1986, the
Harvard Business School, amid much fanfare, released a study by
a member of its faculty, Professor Regina Herzlinger. In contrast to
most earlier research papers, Herzlinger's purported to prove that
investor-owned for-profit hospitals were both cheaper—when
certain tax subsidies to voluntary hospitals were factored into their
pricing—and better able to achieve "social goals."

When first asked, the school's director of communications,
William Hokansen, had said he "didn't think" any of the hospital

companies were donating funds to the school and that Harvard
had funded the study itself. Only after careful and repeated
questioning did he say, weeks after the study had been widely
reported over the Associated Press wire, that the same year,
Humana had agreed to become a George F. Baker Associate of the
school, with a pledge to donate $10,000 annually toward faculty
research efforts indefinitely. But those funds, he explained, coming from a number of major corporations, are pooled, with the
school, not the donors, deciding how to allocate them among its
faculty.

There is no indication, therefore, that the Humana donation
paid for Herzlinger's and the Harvard Business School's project
directly, and even when a company like HCA or Humana does
award a grant directly to an academic researcher, it doesn't mean
the researcher has been "bought," or would even consider slant-
ing a report to suit a sponsor or donor. But corporate sponsors of
research can and do *seek out* those who are already producing, or
seem likely to produce, favorable studies. As we saw in chapter 7,
when FAHS, the corporate hospital lobby, wanted to prove it was
doing its share of indigent care, it went to the American Enterprise
Institute, a reputable Washington think tank that favors free-
market solutions to social problems. Not surprisingly, it got a
favorable study. In that particular case the report was *so* favorable
that a spokesman at the federation said it was "embarrassing,"
and FAHS opted not to tout it.

Texas and Collective Action
by the Hospital Chains

There are few states where one hospital corporation is so
dominant as Tennessee. In other states, the for-profit hospital
industry operates collectively where politics and public policy are
concerned. In Texas, for instance, in 1989, some 39 percent of the
hospitals were investor-owned. But of 181 for-profit facilities, only
17 each were owned by HCA and HealthTrust, the two largest
companies in the state. Fully 150, however, were owned by
for-profit management companies, large and small. When a joint
task force appointed by the legislature and governor's office
developed a far-reaching plan to deal with the growing crisis of
indigent care in 1986, the for-profit hospital industry (according to
legislative staff members active on the committee) played the lead
role in successfully lobbying to eviscerate the reform package.

Originally back in 1985, the task force's idea was to mandate that each county finance 10 percent of its indigent care if, as is the case in twenty-two counties of Texas, it has no public hospital. The money for this and other parts of the package was to come from a 3-percent tax on hospital operating expenses, a tax that would fall on for-profit and not-for-profit hospitals equally. That idea was opposed by the for-profits, but the Texas Hospital Association, a broader lobby representing all hospitals in the state, while expressing distaste for the idea, didn't mount any strong opposition to it. Those institutions—for the most part not-for-profit—that were providing a significant amount of indigent care services, would after all be the beneficiaries of such a plan, since the tax revenues would be used to reimburse them for such care. Even if they *were*, taxed, the money would just come right back to them. In 1985, Lieutenant Governor Bill Hobby then advanced the idea of a 1-percent tax on *profits*, a levy which would fall most heavily on the corporate sector. At that threat, the for-profit hospitals swung into action and rallied the entire hospital industry against the whole idea of a tax.

The result: no tax at all. In the words of Brian Sperry, staff director of the task force, "They gutted the whole package so it basically doesn't do anything about the problem except make it a little harder for hospitals to 'dump' patients."

What was the role of the for-profit industry in essentially defeating reform? "They were behind the defeat, but they got the THA to do it for them," says Sperry.

Through its members' presence in the Texas Hospital Association, the Federation of American Health Systems in Washington played a central role in reshaping the task force's recommendations, but it carefully avoided taking the limelight. In an article on the successful battle in the May/June 1986 issue of the federation's magazine *FAHS Review*, the Texas Hospital Association is given credit, and the association's president, O. Ray Hurst, is quoted as saying:

> We put together a series of public ads and did some mailings—calling it just what it was—a "sick tax." This didn't make us extremely popular in the legislature, but our hospitals didn't get nailed with such a tax, which I regret to observe some other states have allowed.[12]

The Texas indigent-care tax battle illustrates the for-profit industry's astute ability to maneuver the rest of the hospital industry to its side. It also demonstrates a key advantage the corporate chains individually and as a group hold over the rest of the hospital industry. That is, as a smaller group of tightly managed centralized firms, these companies are readily able to identify their collective long-term national interest even in local situations. Creation of a tax on profits to fund indigent care in Texas would have established a powerful precedent that other states would likely have copied, to the industry's clear detriment. The federation devoted a good deal of time and resources to the battle against an "indigent care" tax on hospital profits in Texas, and against a similar referendum in Arizona, because it knew that defeat of those measures would make legislators in other states less likely to attempt the same approach.

It was never a fair contest. Individual public hospitals, together with those not-for-profits in Texas that are increasingly having to treat the poor, uninsured patients not cared for by the for-profit hospitals (and those not-for-profit hospitals that have adopted the for-profits' approach), were aligned on one side. The FAHS in Washington, for its part, clearly perceived the threat to its members' interest and poured its national resources into a successful fight against such a tax.

Louisville: A Company Town

The for-profit hospital sector may not have a *lock* on health politics in such states as Louisiana, New Mexico, Tennessee, or Texas, but its political clout cannot be denied. Still, for pure political dominance, one would have to look at Humana in its hometown of Louisville, Kentucky. Said one local political wag—a health activist—of Humana's extraordinary control over the affairs of Louisville, medical and otherwise, paying tribute of sorts to the two biggest companies based in Louisville, Kentucky Fried Chicken and Humana, "This town is owned by fast food and hospitals. One gets you sick and the other gets you better, all for a price." Kidding aside, though, interview after interview in Louisville began with an insistence on anonymity and the explanation that "This is basically a company town." So wide is Humana's reach that a member of one public service organization involved with indigent health-care issues explained ruefully, "I can't really go into details with you about how they're [Humana] welching on indigent care promises because Humana helps fund us."

Operating on the National Level

What makes the big corporate chains qualitatively different from other hospitals at the state and local level is their enormous relative size, and their ability to bring virtually unlimited resources to bear for lobbying purposes when it suits a company's, or the industry's, national goals.

At the national level the picture is less clear, since at least for the near future, the for-profit hospital industry, which represents only about one in four of the nation's hospitals, will remain limited in its power. Nonetheless, what it lacks in terms of numbers of hospitals, the for-profit hospital industry makes up for in money and in an ability to focus its efforts.

During the two years leading up to the 1986 off-year congressional elections, the FAHS political action committee, FedPAC, raised and spent $390,000 in contributions to congressional candidates. This made it not the largest but certainly a big-league player in the political influence game (the AMA's and AHA's PACs spent $4.5 million and $400,000 respectively for the same period). In the 1988 congressional elections alone, the federation's PAC shelled out another $200,000, according to its annual report; as with most PACs, the money went essentially to incumbents. Federation Executive Director Bromberg reports that another $200,000–250,000 was slated to be spent by FedPAC on the off-year 1990 congressional campaign, compared to the much larger AHA's $412,000. In addition, the four big hospital firms all have their own PACs. According to the Federal Election Commission, these raised and disbursed a total of $265,000 during the 1988 congressional elections, and by July of 1990, they had spent another $292,000 on the 1990 congressional campaign. Humana alone, according to the FEC, raised and spent over $80,000 on the 1990 Congressional elections. And that doesn't count funds given to state and local political campaigns by the companies.[13] But money doesn't tell the whole story. More significant is the fact that the Volunteer Trustees of Not-for-Profit Hospitals, logically FAHS's opponent on many national legislative issues, is so incapable of focusing its diverse membership that it has no PAC, leaving the field to FedPAC and the less focused political action committee of the AHA. Typically, the not-for-profit hospitals themselves give little or nothing to congressional campaigns.

Although the FAHS lobby in Washington is relatively

small—it has nine professional members there, compared to about forty-five at the AHA's Washington lobby—Executive Director Michael Bromberg is widely and consistently described by congressional staffers, Washington journalists, and even competing lobbyists as running one of the best such operations in Washington. His success is in part the result of money, but, as in the case of the individual states, it also has to do with the for-profit hospital industry's more coherent goals. There appears to be little disagreement on national policy among FAHS members. Says FAHS Deputy Director W. Campbell Thomson, "A key to our spectacular success is that we pretty much have the unified support of our entire membership, where the AHA is torn twenty-one different ways. We also have companies like HCA or Humana to turn to when we need someone to run the numbers to find out how a certain proposal will work out."

A free-enterprise mania has swept Washington since at least the outset of the Reagan administration in 1981, and more probably since the middle of the Carter administration, when *deregulate* first became a watchword. This environment has helped to amplify further the power of the FAHS. The for-profit hospitals reached multinational scale and achieved national prominence at exactly the time when their message—unfettered competition in health care—was what Washington wanted to hear. Through the course of the eighties, the first half of which saw a mushrooming of the for-profit hospital industry across the country, the argument that the government should do less, not more, about health care was just what the doctor ordered for a Congress and electorate suffering from runaway health costs.

The federation's first major role in Washington came in 1978, when it helped fight off the Carter administration's plans for price controls on hospitals and doctors. "Everyone agrees that it was the AMA's dough, the AHA's clout, and Bromberg's brains that beat Carter's cost-containment strategy," boasts Campbell. That formula indicates how the for-profit sector is able to steer health policy in its direction, despite its size.

But the for-profit industry's signal victory was of course its successful lobbying effort to get Medicare shifted over from a cost-plus to a fixed-rate reimbursement system. Recalls a member of the House health subcommittee staff, "The federation basically put together the prospective payment program, with [then Reagan Health and Human Services Secretary Richard] Schweiker. The deal reportedly was that [the government would] keep

return-on-equity payments to proprietary hospitals in Medicare."
Under the return-on-equity system, which only applies by definition to for-profit hospitals, such operations received an additional
fee add-on to each Medicare reimbursement, much as utilities are
guaranteed a rate of return on investment. (Schweiker, on leaving
Washington, joined the board of NME—a good example of how
the health-care industry, like the airlines or transportation industry, has a "revolving-door" relationship with federal regulators
and politicians.)

As Humana's David Jones explains, "We knew it would be
hard for us, but it would be harder for the competition, and
besides, it was better than the alternative," which he suggests was
cost controls. His explanation is supported by FAHS spokesman
Tom Goodwin, who said, "Yeah, we lobbied for DRGs, because
the alternative would have been worse, and we think that we are
better able to compete in that environment."

In other words, while it wasn't saying so in AHA circles, the
FAHS effort was, at least in part, a Machiavellian move intended
to bankrupt the not-for-profit and public competition in hopes of
being able to pick up the pieces. That is in fact what began to
happen in the mid-1980s, when for the first time the chains began
to acquire large numbers of voluntary and public hospitals,
instead of mostly older proprietary hospitals. Seeing the hand-
writing on the wall, many of those not-for-profit facilities decided
to sell out.

In fact, the Medicare reform instituting prospective payment
according to diagnosis related groups (DRGs) turned out to be
pretty painful for the corporate chains as well—a good deal more
painful than they had anticipated—and directly led to the collapse
in the industry's shares on Wall Street in 1985–86. Longer term,
however, the strategy (to the extent that it was intended to
improve the industry's *relative* position) is probably going to prove
to have been sound. In 1988, though the growth of the for-profit
sector was at a virtual standstill, with only 3,000 beds added (a
growth rate of only 2 percent), the sector's *proportional* share of the
national hospital market rose from 18 to 19 percent because of the
declining number of surviving public and not-for-profit hospitals.
By just standing still, the for-profit industry has moved ahead. By
1990 for-profit chains owned outright 21 percent of all the nation's
hospitals.

Right or wrong as a strategy, the for-profit industry's role in
establishing the DRG reimbursement system for Medicare is

testimony to the power of the industry. The for-profits succeeded in pushing through a measure opposed bitterly by the rest of the hospital industry, and by the American Medical Association as well.

The FAHS approach in Washington is more typically of a low-profile nature. "Bromberg tries to avoid having the issue put in terms of for-profit versus not-for-profit," says a lobbyist for another health-related industry who finds himself sometimes in opposition to FAHS positions. "He has incredible access on the Hill, and gets things done for the most part at the stage of staff mark-up of a bill. Where there's an actual vote, and it does become a for-profit/not-for-profit issue, as in the 1986 vote on including return-on-equity in Medicare payments [when Congress, facing a continued crisis in health-care budget outlays, pulled the rug out from under the original DRG deal cut between FAHS and HHS Secretary Schweiker], they lose."

Although the FAHS has been around almost as long as the industry itself—the federation was founded in 1967 and Bromberg became executive director in 1969—its first decade was not terribly auspicious. If people noticed the industry at all in Washington in those early days, most tended to sneer at it as a vile enterprise profiting off the sick. Hard conditions for a lobbyist to work under! But those days in the wilderness have contributed mightily to the federation's later successes in the capital. Unable to strike out boldly for its programs because of adverse public opinion, the industry long ago learned in local battles and in Washington to line up allies and work behind the scenes.

While the ideological sympathies of this still young industry are clearly Republican when it comes to wanting low capital gains tax rates, minimal or no government regulation of health care, and privatization of government services, the industry's lobby has been increasingly allying itself with liberal Democrats. It's Democrats, after all, who vote larger budgets for a mainstay of the hospital industry: Medicare. FedPAC contributions have gone to leading health-care liberals in both houses and contributed, for example, to Democratic "populist" Thomas Daschle's upset 1986 Senate victory over a Republican incumbent in South Dakota. Explains FAHS staffer Tom Goodwin, "We support those people who have an interest in free-enterprise approaches to health care, which usually means Republicans. Increasingly however, the allies of the health-care industry are becoming Democrats, because Democrats support funding for domestic programs such as Medicare, which of course represents 40 percent of total expenditures of hospitals in the U.S. That's why you'll find us agreeing with even Senator [Edward] Kennedy sometimes, and in alliance with the American Association of Retired Persons. It's a tendentious alliance of self-interest, but we're talking with people we've never spoken to before."

It's important to note that by 1986 the FAHS had come out strongly against the Reagan program for increased spending on military programs, and the association's trade publication that year ran a feature article attacking the president's Star Wars program as a "technological brain drain." The federation took no position in the 1988 presidential contest.

The ability to take the long view, to compromise, and to work with sometime foes for specific legislative ends has served the for-profit industry well. The AMA by contrast is used to having its way and has expended a lot of public relations capital fighting unpopular rearguard actions against causes like Medicare and Medicaid. Now, however, the seemingly incongruous alliances FAHS finds itself in may also stem in part from its growing power. Organizations like the American Association of Retired Persons (AARP) and legislators with their own liberal agendas to push are finding it necessary or convenient to begin horse-trading with this increasingly important, and fundamentally conservative, organization.

House health subcommittee chairman Fortney H. (Pete) Stark is no friend of the for-profit industry. The California Democrat once even tried unsuccessfully to legislate jail terms for hospital executives whose institutions "dumped" a poor patient who subsequently died. Stark agrees that the power of that industry in Washington is waxing, but he downplays the implications, saying, "People who get too powerful eventually create their own detractors and enemies. Eventually they'll have to start dealing with the doctors, and then the AMA will really start to fight them, so I'll be able to just sit back and watch. Besides, what makes the auto industry or the phone company so powerful is that on important issues, they have the unions in here with them, representing all those workers. These [hospital] companies are all so determinedly antiunion they lack all that clout."

Most observers, however, don't share such a dialectical view—and as we will see in chapter 9, the corporate chains and their lobbyists have found a way around the problem of not having unions to ally themselves with. Rather than fade away as a political force, it seems more likely that as the industry continues to be a factor in the delivery of health-care services, the corporate chains' influence on the direction of national health policy will increase. For confirmation one need only look at the strains within the AHA, the Volunteer Trustees, and the AMA, which have prevented all three from mounting an effective opposition to the growing shift toward unrestrained marketplace medicine, a shift which shows no sign of abating.

The corporate hospital industry has already demonstrated influence far beyond its numbers for some years in Washington. It has shown in certain states that when it has power, it knows how to use it. As it continues to grow proportionally as a factor in the delivery of health care, we can expect to see it become a major, instead of simply a behind-the-scenes, force in national health politics. Inevitably, that will mean even greater attention in Washington to corporate concerns about profitability, and even less to the issue of equal access to first-rate medical care for all. Anyone who says that there are limits to what the hospital industry can get from Washington because health-care bills can only get so high, should look at the history of military contractors. The hospital industry is just as capable of extorting money from Congress by threatening bankruptcy and collapse of the national medical system as the arms industry has been by threatening a Communist takeover.

Says a staff member in the office of Senator Edward Kennedy, "What we're seeing is a change in political priorities, from one that was a commitment to access to health care for all Americans to the idea of rationing care. And the [corporate] hospitals are riding it. It may turn around, but it'll probably get a lot worse before it gets better."

The for-profit hospital companies didn't create that shift, but they're doing their best to hasten its further development.

9

The Prognosis:
America's Hospitals in Chains

> Historically, government intervention has been both reluctant and deficient. However, the overall structure of the American "medical marketplace" is chiefly defined by government policy—either through the form of positive intervention (financing, direct provision, regulatory policy) or negative intervention (allowing interest groups to shape the marketplace).
>
> —Ben Griffith, Steve Iliffe, and Geof Rayner
> in *Banking on Sickness: Commercial Medicine in Britain and the USA*

Back in 1969, when the investor-owned hospital industry was all prospect and no track record, AMI founder Bob Appel got a call from Jack Massey, HCA's bankroller and a member of the latter company's board of directors. In an interview Appel recalls that Massey said he wanted to "come out to look at us." At that time, HCA only had a few dozen hospitals in a few Southeastern states. AMI for its part then had just a handful of hospitals in California. But Massey and his partner, the younger Frist, already had big plans. "After Massey came out, I remember then young Tommy invited me to Nashville. He personally flew me in his plane to some of [HCA's] sites," says Appel, now retired from the business and from any role in AMI, where he served as chairman until 1979. After what Appel terms the "romancing," he says Frist suggested an historic merger that would create a national hospital firm. "He proposed that we divide up the country"—Appel chuckles—"with HCA covering the eastern part and us taking the West." Appel, a long-time resident of Los Angeles, turned Frist down. "I told him, 'Tom, I don't mind country music, but there's no way I'm going to live in Nashville!'"

Although Frist's premature mating attempt failed, both companies, and a number of others—some of them, like American Medicorp and Lifemark, later absorbed (by Humana and AMI respectively)—proceeded to develop national networks themselves over the next decade. In hard times, as in 1973–74 and later in the 1985–88 downturn, the entrepreneurial captains of this industry lowered their sights and their rhetoric. In periods of expansion, however, all continued to express in some way their vision of a future in which American health care would be in the hands of their own, and perhaps several other, large health-care concerns.

Humana, with its burgeoning captive preferred provider organization (PPO) insurance system, now hopes to become a major national competitor in the health insurance market, and has already worked hard to give itself national "brand name" stature. NME envisions a diversified approach offering "cradle-to-grave" care centered around regional health-care "campuses," and has not dropped those plans even though it experienced a period of consolidation in the late 1980s. And Frist, whose HCA has surely been the most acquisitive of the bunch historically, told me in a 1985 interview, just as he was attempting to catapult HCA into the top ranks of the *Fortune* 500 through a never completed merger with $3.5-billion American Hospital Supply, "I want this company to become the General Motors of health care." Although HCA's merger plan with American Hospital Supply fizzled, and low earnings and takeover fears in the late eighties forced the company to divest many holdings and to go private, Frist remains in charge and his long-range goal remains unchanged. Only AMI, which was taken over in 1989 by an investor group which proceeded with a draconian divestment and cost-cutting program, seems to have given up, at least for now, its founder's dreams of a national market.

The idea of a health care GM, a health industry "Detroit," or several dominant firms for that matter, while appealing to Frist and his industry colleagues, ought to trouble consumers. In the postwar glory days of the automobile industry GM's president Charles Erwin ("Engine Charlie") Wilson gave us the famous line: "What is good for the country is good for General Motors and what's good for General Motors is good for the country."

But "smokestack America" is now in decline. The new economic powers are not companies that make things; instead, they are increasingly the firms that provide some service—banks, communications companies, and of course health-care providers. The nation's economic health has now come to depend on decisions made in the boardrooms of these service-sector firms, so it is a matter of some significance—and some concern—when leaders of those companies begin talking, or acting, just like Wilson.

At least one expert, Charles Craypo, chairman of the economics department at Notre Dame University, sees today's hospital corporations taking charge of national health policy just as yesterday's car manufacturers dictated national transportation policy:

> What has occurred earlier in the automotive and steel industry in America is now occurring in health care. Just as the steel industry consolidated at the turn of the century and the auto industry consolidated in the 1920s, now you're seeing a consolidation of the health care industry, through acquisitions aimed at vertical and horizontal integration. And as a few big for-profit chains come to dominate the industry, as they did in steel and autos, you're likely to see the same kind of behavior you saw develop in those industries—a shifting away from price competition into safer areas like advertising and marketing.

Beds and Cars

Comparing for-profit hospital chains to car factories, as both Frist and Craypo have done in their own way, might seem a peculiar notion, yet consider these parallels:

• Both industries were for the most part started by practitioners—engineers in the case of the car, and doctors, hospital lawyers, and pathologists in the case of hospitals;

- Both eventually caught the eye of Wall Street financiers eager to ride a new growth industry to the top;
- Both grew dramatically, through a process of aggressive acquisition; and
- Both from the outset were, or quickly became, critically dependent upon government subsidy for their success. For just as the automobile industry relied upon heavy public investment in road improvement and highway construction, now the hospital industry must attribute its success to public funds for care of the elderly and to tax subsidies, loan guarantees, and outright public grants for construction and acquisition of facilities.

Over the years, the American automobile industry came to be much more than just another enterprise. It crushed its competition, the private railroads and public trolleys, in order to encourage the use of the car. GM through its National City Lines subsidiary bought and dismantled dozens of extensive urban electric rail systems, including the nation's largest in Los Angeles. Beyond this, the car industry even altered the way we live, helping to create today's suburban sprawls through the promotion of superhighways, and becoming a cornerstone of the American economy.

The corporate hospital industry hasn't yet fundamentally changed the way we live or heal ourselves, but that's what some of its more far-thinking executives like HCA's Frist and Humana's Jones want to do. These corporate leaders have the stars of Detroit in their eyes when they dream of a future that will see health-care expenditures in America passing the $1.5-trillion mark by the year 2000, with hospitals still snaring the lion's share of that total. They are already talking as if their prescription for the nation's health— unrestrained marketplace medicine administered by centrally run, integrated health-care conglomerates—is the answer to problems of cost, access, and quality.

Like the automobile industrialists before them, they are also putting pressure on the competition, driving out of business those private not-for-profit and public hospitals they don't acquire. There have even been rumors—reminiscent of those about GM and the municipal trolleys—that some for-profit hospital management companies sometimes deliberately do such a poor job operating a hospital under contract that the owner becomes desperate to sell the facility. Then the management company offers to buy it. Whether the industry's documented management failures have been deliberate or the result of incompetence, at least one firm that *doesn't* own hospitals has played to suspicions about other management companies' motives. Hospital Management Professionals, of Brentwood, Tennessee, ran an advertisement in the *FAHS Review* saying:

> We have no hidden agenda. We don't own hospitals. We *only* manage. We enhance your census and make you more efficient, while keeping you freestanding. In local control.[1]

One of the largest hospital management companies, prior to its going private, was HCA. But the problem with the theory that HCA might have *deliberately* managed hospitals into the ground the better to buy them is that some examples of the company's poor management practices occurred at facilities it ran under contract in New York, a state where corporate chains are prohibited from owning hospitals. Specifically, HCA was raked over the coals by New York's Department of Health for the condition of a public hospital it managed in Rome, New York. Further, HCA was unceremoniously dumped after three years of managing a public hospital under contract to Green County, outside of Albany. There, the company ran through three managers in as many years, and rang up unprecedented deficits that had to be covered by the county's taxpayers.

Thinking Big

How far can the process of growth and concentration go in the hospital industry? The answer depends upon what time frame is used. Clearly, the corporate chains are not going to take over the nation's entire hospital system tomorrow, after the slump and retrenchment of the late 1980s. But all the companies were on an upswing by 1990. Overall hospital occupancy was starting to rise again, thanks to new hospital-based medical technologies, better understanding of how to handle Medicare patients to ensure maximum profitability, and a steadily growing elderly population. Over the longer haul, as the baby boom population ages and the political power of the senior lobby grows accordingly, hospital companies won't suffer for want of either patients *or* reimbursement for their care. And as their financial condition improves, the same forces that encouraged concentration of hospitals into chains in the boom years prior to 1986—presumed management efficiencies, a desire to establish and control regional markets, a need to show revenue growth—are sure to reassert themselves. What makes this next upturn different from previous ones, however, is that this time around, instead of a bunch of small players, there are several multibillion-dollar companies in place and ready to move.

How big those companies already are can be readily demonstrated with a few numbers. By 1990, even after HCA and AMI had sold off big chunks of their holdings, the industry's old Big Four still boasted sales, or patient revenues, of $15.5 billion. Adding in the revenues of the three spin-off companies, Health-Trust, Quorum Health Resources, and EPIC, brings the total for that year to over $18 billion. With for-profit hospitals accounting for a total of 25 percent of all the nation's 6,000 hospitals by 1990, this group of four (or seven) had become a concentrated core within a larger sector. Hospitals overall garnered some 40 percent of the $650 billion spent in America on health care in 1990, or about $260 billion, according to statistics compiled by the federal Health Care Finance Administration.

Business Week magazine's 1989 list of the nation's 1,000 largest companies ranked by market value gives an indication of how large the hospital companies had become by that year. HCA was number 158 (alongside such corporate fixtures as Amerada Hess, Deere and Company, and Bethlehem Steel); Humana was number 209 on the chart; and all four of the hospital chains were in the top half of the list, even though the shares of three of the four were selling at well below their historic highs (in mid-1989, Humana's were the exception, selling at a three-year high of $31).

What clouds the near-term picture for the industry is uncertainty about the role and level of government funding of health care. For the past few years, with the government tightening the screws on reimbursement to both hospitals and doctors, the hospital sector—profit and not-for-profit—has been struggling. Few observers, however, whether on Wall Street or in the industry itself, expect this situation to continue indefinitely. As Sid Tyler, executive vice president of NME's Hospital Group, explained in a 1989 interview, his firm is not only keeping its large stable of acute-care hospitals, but also is reestablishing a "development unit" to begin acquiring new facilities. "We feel there's going to be a point where they [the government] have to improve reimbursement levels," he said. "If they didn't do that, the private hospitals would simply decide to drop out of the Medicaid program, and the fact is that the municipal and county hospitals in this country simply are not able to handle that caseload. Most of them are already full now." Tyler claims that in 1989, California (one of the more generous states in terms of Medicaid funding) paid hospitals only 35 percent of their costs of caring for poor patients, while Medicare was down to paying about 50 percent of hospital costs. Those figures can be disputed (since they depend in part on what hospitals *say* their costs are), but it is indisputable that hospitals have been forced to get by on reduced reimbursement for care of the elderly and poor. The advantage under such circumstances, as we have seen, goes to those hospitals that can best control the type of patients they admit; i.e., limit the number of those for whom reimbursement is minimal. Where a corporate chain sees a hospital at which it can change the patient mix for the better, there is plenty of room for further expansion.

Explains NME's Tyler, "The days are not gone when we can come in and turn around a weak hospital. What is gone are the days when you could by a *dog* of a hospital and make it work." What NME is doing then, seems to be going back to its roots. "The early concept of the company, as developed by the founders, [Richard] Eamer and [Leonard] Cohen, was to build hospital campuses, with the hospital as a center, and with all other services nearby," says Tyler. "That concept is even more valid today."

While not all the other big hospital firms are publicly proclaiming plans to return to an acquisition mode after several years of dormancy or even shrinkage, it's clear that all expect to renew the process of expansion and concentration as we enter the 1990s. In September, 1990, Humana signed a deal to buy the giant nine-hundred-bed Michael Reese Hospital and Medical Center in Chicago, and its associated 240,000-member HMO, for a reported $75 million in cash plus assumption of $54 million in existing indebtedness. At that time, Tim Moody, a Humana spokesman, commented to me that the company would be "looking for other such opportunities" to establish regional hospital bases for its insurance plan.

The winning bidder for AMI in 1989, IMA Holdings (an investor group headed by the Pritzker family of Chicago, owners of the Hyatt hotel chain, and including former United Aircraft Chairman Harry Gray, takeover attorney Mel Klein, and First Boston, an investment bank), likewise was confident about the potential for growth in the industry. There were no plans announced to dismantle AMI assets, and indeed the high price paid for AMI, a reported $2.14 billion, precluded any attempt to sell off the firm's hospital properties at a profit. The new owners were closed-lipped about their plans, but a further narrowing of the company's focus onto domestic acute-care hospitals appeared to be their game plan. (There were several higher bids made for AMI, but the company's board rejected them, apparently not convinced that the financing was secure.)

After a management buyout of HCA was completed in 1988, HCA began to refocus on its core business: acute-care hospitals.

By 1990, then, all four of the biggest companies were significantly restructured, had paid down their debt loads or were in the process of paying them down, and were ready to begin moving forward again and expanding.

After battling off potential takeovers for several years, AMI's board of directors finally voted in 1989 to look for a friendly buyer. Charles Reilly, a former AMI executive and currently managing partner of Shamrock Investments of Los Angeles, was part of one group that bid unsuccessfully for the firm. "Obviously, I still think very highly of the industry and its growth potential," he explained in an interview later that year. "Sure, there will continue to be pressures to keep costs down, but acute-care hospitals remain and will continue to be the major service industry in the U.S. The hospital is still the core of a high-tech health-care system. It will always be the nucleus of that care. They'll always be subjected to political pressure, but for the same reason that the industry is pressured, it's also protected, given the value we as a society place on human life. Decisions which would dramatically constrain access to technology, or reduce access to care, I think will never be accepted, so there's a safety net under the industry, and it's a substantial safety net."

Where the Growth Will Come From

Despite temporary setbacks that forced the biggest companies to scale back their operations in the mid-1980s, the consolidation of the hospital industry as a whole continued apace. It was just not so visible.

When companies like HCA, AMI, and NME sold off some of their hospitals, for example, things didn't just go back to the way they were a few years before when the companies had been smaller. First of all, the sold units did not become independent hospitals again. Rather, these divested facilities were snapped up at bargain prices by smaller investor-owned hospital chain companies with names like Nu-Med, Gateway Medical Systems, Forum Health Investors, National Healthcare, and AmeriHealth. And where new facilities were concerned, in 1986—not a particularly great year for hospital construction—nearly half of the eighty-five hospitals constructed by the for-profit hospital industry were built by small concerns. In 1988, only NME and AMI of the big four chains were building new facilities: for NME only two, and just one for AMI. Smaller companies, however, were at work on twenty-one new hospitals. In its 1987 Directory of Investor-Owned Hospitals and Hospital Management Companies, the FAHS listed a total of sixty-five such firms, compared to only forty-five two years earlier. The growth of some of those small firms, over the same period that the Big Four, and even some of the mid-sized companies, were languishing or selling off properties, was nothing short of spectacular.

National Healthcare, for instance, owned and managed only fourteen hospitals with a total of 1,542 beds in 1985 (two large managed hospitals accounted for almost half the beds). When the company went public with a stock market offering a year later, it was operating thirty-six hospitals that had a combined total of 3,351 beds (only three were managed facilities, the rest it owned outright). Further, Chairman Stephen Phelps claimed the firm had turned down 150 hospitals that were offered to it.

In 1985, Gateway Medical Systems owned four hospitals with 582 beds. When Gateway went public, also in 1986, it owned six facilities and was negotiating to buy another six from AMI. Over the same period Comprehensive Care went from fourteen to twenty hospitals, while Jupiter Hospital Corporation leapt from just three hospitals in 1985 to seven in 1986, more than doubling its revenues in a year.

Viewed in this manner, the pace of concentration barely slowed in the hospital industry, or in the relative growth of the investor-owned sector. 1986 saw 93 hospitals added to the investor-owned total, bringing it to 1,186 (including 94 outside the U.S.), while the number of voluntary, public, *and* free-standing private hospitals *declined*. While the corporate chains in the three previous years, 1983, 1984, and 1985, added 103, 144, and 138 hospitals, respectively, in 1982, another good year for the industry by all accounts, only 89 hospitals were purchased by the corporate chains. Hence, on balance 1986 was not much different from the prior four years in terms of overall growth of the for-profit hospital industry.

Probably the worst year for the industry was 1988. That year, the number of investor-owned hospitals rose by only three to a total of 1,220, an increase of less than one percent. But because the number of public and not-for-profit private hospitals fell by forty-five that year, the net effect was an increase in the corporate share of the nation's hospitals from 18 to 19 percent.

This new situation, in which smaller hospital companies were doing most of the growing, led some people mistakenly to think that the whole future of the health-care industry had changed overnight. As the FAHS reported in a special 1986 issue of its *Review* devoted to the new smaller firms in its membership:

> Rapid changes, retrenchment and reorganization in the health care industry, especially by the larger companies, have placed new emphasis on the current and future role of the emerging, smaller investor-owned companies in the nation's health delivery system.
>
> In recent years, experts have been predicting that a small handful of companies—possibly 10 to 12 so-called megasystems—would dominate the industry. However, a growing number of smaller hospital and health systems companies have emerged.
>
> Perhaps Tom Peters, the noted management consultant and author of the best-selling book *In Search of Excellence*, puts the newest trend in the health care industry in proper perspective when he advises "to think small—it's a bold idea."[2]

As observers of the industry circa 1986–88, Peters and FAHS were absolutely correct. In the short term, there was a flowering of smaller companies. Of course, there was no guarantee that the environment would continue to nurture new firms, or that those little firms would remain small. But a burgeoning of small firms and a concentration of hospitals into a few hands are not mutually exclusive trends. The former may even be necessary for the latter to happen successfully.

As the hospital business evolves from a growth industry to a concentrated "mature" industry, a new round of mergers, and inevitably business failures, can be expected to narrow the field.

Instead of simply buying hospitals piecemeal, as they often did in the past, the big hospital corporations will now begin buying up entire chains as they did in an earlier growth cycle in the 1970s, perhaps shutting down or spinning off some of their less desirable holdings along the way. In fact, the small competing companies make the growth of the big firms easier. This is because if the smaller firm is in financial trouble at the time of sale, the larger buyer may well pick up dozens of hospitals at a fraction of the cost it would have required to buy or build the properties separately. And, of course, in the process of "rescuing" a troubled firm, the buyer can shut down "uneconomic" hospitals with much less of a public relations cost than could the original owner. After all, the fault lies with the troubled small firm. All the big firm is trying to do is rescue the operation. The small hospital companies actually may perform a "weeding out" function for the bigger firms, by making initial determinations about the viability of particular hospitals.

William LeConey is an investment banker with Liberty Street Capital who saw the potential of the hospital business early. He followed the industry for Merrill Lynch before moving to Liberty Street and continues to watch it closely. In 1986, after the fall in share value suffered by the Big Four firms, he said, "I think we're still headed towards the 'super-med' idea, but the lesson of the last year or so is that it won't happen overnight. Give it five or ten years. Then you're going to see a lot of acquisitions." At the beginning of the century's final decade, that prediction still looks pretty sound.

How the Future Hospital Industry Will Look

Bigness is in the cards, but there are a number of possible scenarios, all involving further concentration in ownership of hospitals:

• One possibility would be the development of vertically integrated systems of hospitals and insurance plans on the model of Humana, perhaps with the addition of free-standing surgi-centers and clinics, hospitals and nursing home operations. This scenario would represent a combination of the Humana and NME strategies.

• A second scenario would be the takeover of the hospital chains by larger firms in the health industry (insurance or pharmaceutical companies, for instance).

• A third possibility would be the takeover of hospital companies by major employers, like GM or IBM. There was, for instance, some talk in 1986 among Wall Street analysts of GM interest in HCA, though both companies denied it. McDonnell Douglas owned a big chunk (17 percent) of Republic Health, a second-tier hospital firm, but sold its holding to a management group that bought the company in 1986.

None of these scenarios can be discounted, but they are not all equally likely to happen. Whether the industry stays largely independent, as it has been for the first two decades of its growth, or falls under the wing of larger firms in other industries depends much upon the response of the largest companies to the short-term challenge of declining hospital use and tighter reimbursement schedules. Stock prices will probably rise and discourage takeover bids if tough restructuring, in the form of reductions in bloated management staffs and divestment of unprofitable hospital holdings, can effect good returns while occupancy stays around 50 to 60 percent. (After all, with the baby boomers beginning to age, occupancy isn't likely to fall much further, and indeed since 1988 it has been slowly rising again.) External factors, such as a rise in interest rates or a recession—hospitals are more or less recession resistant, and even countercyclical to some extent—could also help existing firms remain independent.

In any event, the leadership of the largest companies seems anxious to avoid takeovers, and among the top companies, only at AMI have outsiders forced out existing management. The managements at the other three major companies have taken steps to make takeovers less easy—reducing indebtedness, improving price/earnings ratios, and even, in the case of HCA, going private. But things could conspire against them. As Humana's David Jones said in late 1986, when asked about the possibility of a takeover of Humana, "It won't happen if I can help it, but if the market [for hospital stocks] keeps weakening, who knows what will happen?"

The prediction that large employers will eventually buy up the for-profit chains (giving a whole new meaning to the term *company doctor*!) rests on the assumption that since health care is a major uncontrollable factor in these giant companies' labor costs, they will decide to gain control over it by internalizing the whole system. It is certainly true that American industry has been crippled in the international marketplace by employee health costs (since in other countries, the state covers most of the bill) and has been casting about vainly for ways to control them. In 1988

Chrysler paid $5,950 per employee in health benefits (or about $700 per car built), according to Walter Maher, director of employee benefits. Chrysler claims that the comparably low per vehicle cost of health-care benefits in Japan ($246), Germany ($337), and France ($375) helps explain the success of imported cars in the U.S. market. Of course, not all U.S. corporations pay such large health benefits to their workers. Indeed, many smaller firms only offer minimal benefits, and none to part-timers (which is one reason the number of uninsured Americans is so high). But overall, the fact remains that U.S. corporations, through employee health benefits packages, pay roughly 25–30 percent of the nation's health bill, according to the Washington Business Group on Health. This organization, composed of 180 of the nation's biggest firms, is attempting to develop some kind of national health plan to control those costs or to shift them from the corporation to the taxpayer.

During the 1980s, most U.S. employers responded to rising employee health-care costs by attempting to shift some of the expense back onto their workers. With health costs for employees rising during that decade at a 10–15 percent clip annually, the battle over who would pay became one of the major strike issues in unionized companies. In nonunion companies the shift was simply imposed, by making employees pay part of their premiums, increasing deductibles, or eliminating first-dollar coverage for such things as prescriptions and office visits. Still, there are limits to how much of those costs even the most assertive managements can shift onto employees before low morale, lost productivity, and inability to hire qualified people start to cost them more than health benefits ever did.

Could owning company hospitals be a solution? Probably not. The main problem with this idea is that the expense side of hospital operations can be pared only so far before quality of care starts to be threatened. This means the company that bought a hospital system would be gaining only minimal savings on existing labor costs in return for assuming what by all accounts is a very complex and labor-intensive subsidiary operation. In addition, for most of the potential buyers, there is no synergistic connection to hospitals of the type that might make them an interesting or attractive sideline for other business reasons. (It's worth noting here that Kaiser Permanente, the nation's largest HMO operation, began in the 1930s as a health plan for employees of the Kaiser Steel company, a West Coast steelmaker with smelters that were located in many areas, particularly in the Northwest, where health-care facilities were poor or nonexistent. For Kaiser, having a company-owned hospital system was once a progressive and cost-effective answer. Eventually, however, the company found it necessary to spin off the health-care operation.)

At first glance, the second scenario mentioned above seems most likely: the insurance industry buying up the hospital companies. The large hospital companies themselves have all toyed with the idea of creating their own insurance subsidiaries, though only Humana has stuck with this strategy. At least one knowledgeable observer of the health industry, physician/businessman Dr. Stanley Wohl, has argued that the hospital industry is only a pawn in the larger scheme of the insurance industry. (He notes that insurance company executives sit on most hospital companies' boards of directors.)

Wohl explains, "The key to the whole health-care system is the insurance industry. They want very badly to get their hands on the hospital system, since they can use health insurance as a loss leader for their much more profitable life insurance business. What's happening is that the whole health system is being crunched into ten or twelve large systems, with the large insurance companies in the background. What they want to be able to do is offer a full-range insurance package to the big employers like IBM and GM, taking the business away from Blue Cross, and then they'll use health insurance as a way of getting in the door to sell their life insurance plans."

What this theory has going for it primarily is the enormous size of the industry's major firms: Equitable Life Assurance (which once had a joint HMO-style venture with HCA), Aetna (which teamed up with the Voluntary Hospitals of America), Prudential, Metropolitan Life, and INA/Cigna. All are multibillion-dollar operations and are relatively large in comparison to the hospital companies. But there are other factors to consider that argue against the idea, and it's hard to find anyone in either the hospital or insurance field on Wall Street who's betting on such a future for either industry.

Dan Kollin, a hospital industry analyst with Goldman Sachs, a major investment banking firm, says, "I'd say Wohl's prediction is off the mark. INA had a hospital management subsidiary— Hospital Affiliates—and sold it off. I haven't seen any insurance company be successful in running hospitals. Anyway, the hospital industry is having a tough time. Why pay for something you get for free? As long as the hospitals have surplus beds, they'll have to make them available at below cost."

From the other direction, Herbert E. Goodfriend, first vice president for research at Prudential-Bache Securities and a leading insurance industry analyst, says, "I don't see insurance companies taking over hospitals. In point of fact, the two businesses operate at cross purposes—hospitals want to increase utilization, and insurance companies want to reduce it. And so far, in the experiments at merging the two functions together, the failures have been notable. Management too is a problem. They're two entirely different corporate cultures."

Of course Wall Street analysts can be wrong—they certainly were a few years ago in seeing the hospital industry as a no-lose investment—and Wohl may be correct. For instance, if Humana succeeds in proving that vertical integration of hospitals and insurance plans works—and the company's success is already hard to dismiss—the major insurance companies will most likely start taking another close look at companies like HCA, AMI, and NME, or at a constellation of smaller regional hospital chains.

Who's in Charge?

What *can* be said with some certainty about the hospital industry is that however it grows, whether independently or as part of a larger conglomerate system, control over health-care issues will increasingly pass from the patient (to the extent that patients ever controlled their own care), the collective populace (in the form of the government), and the physician to the managers of a few large enterprises. This has been the story of American industry, and there is no reason to suppose the health-care industry, late to consolidate but making up for lost time, will follow a different script. As Wohl explained to me, "The basic issue remains that fewer and fewer people are owning all the hospitals, and with vertical integration, the whole control over health care has gone over to the people who control all aspects of the system. My personal point of view is that it's a loss for the consumer, because they're losing the right to go where they want—and the whole 'cost savings' thing is a hoax. Maybe GM's saving on health costs, but it's coming out of the workers' pockets."

Curiously, in all the debates about how to control soaring

health costs in America, this issue of popular versus corporate
control over medicine has gotten left out. It is a serious omission.

In their 1985 research paper titled "Health Care for Profit: The
Impact of Investor-Owned Health Care Chains on Workers and
Communities," Notre Dame's Professor Craypo and coauthor
Mary Lehman of Cornell University's School of Industrial and
Labor Relations wrote:

> The historical experiences of key manufacturing and
> service industries following their consolidation . . . are
> both instructive and ominous in this regard. Steel, auto,
> telephone and other such consolidated industries were
> profitable, rapidly growing sectors of the economy in the
> decades after they had been centralized by enterprising
> corporate organizers and financiers, just as health care is
> today for the investor-owned systems. But the dominant
> firms became productively complacent; they continued to
> extract predictable rates of return from declining facilities
> and were quiescent in the face of mounting foreign
> competition. In the end they scaled back . . . activities
> in traditional product lines and diversified into other
> businesses, abandoning the secondary firms and commu-
> nities that depended on the basic industries. The eco-
> nomic and social costs that resulted from this collapse are
> now being paid.

They added:

> There is nothing to prevent [the new health-care
> companies] from exploiting the ongoing profit potential
> in American medicine and then moving on to some other
> commodity after events have changed enough to make it
> an unattractive investment, leaving in their wake an
> industry which has been "milked" and forcing the pro-
> vision of basic health care services back onto the public
> sector.[3]

It is worth recalling Humana's 1973 explanation, recounted in
chapter 2, for choosing a new corporate name. Humana executives
told the company's shareholders the intent was to select a name
that would not preclude new directions, should these someday
prove more lucrative than hospitals. Indeed hospital chains large

and small have already closed down a few unproductive "assets." While such a move can be easily justified from a standpoint of strict economic efficiency, that kind of argument wins little applause in a neighborhood that once had a hospital and now has none.

Defenders of corporate medicine have long argued that the chains were unlikely to leave communities stranded. After doing this a few times, the argument went, the chains would presumably find it much harder and more costly to enter other community markets. And until recently, it was true that this enlightened self-interest on the part of the chains ensured a careful search for responsible buyers for divested facilities. But as plant closings in the manufacturing sector in the 1980s have demonstrated, the opposite behavior pattern is perhaps more likely. By simply shutting down an operation that either isn't getting desired support from a community in the form of tax breaks or is confronted with union workers unwilling to grant wage concessions, a company can frighten other communities and groups of employees into doing its bidding. The truth probably lies somewhere in between. In a period of rapid expansion through acquisitions, a company will probably take care to be a good corporate citizen in the event of a hospital sale or closing; but as the industry moves into a period of consolidation—"shakeout," in Wall Street parlance—the hard-line approach will prevail.

HCA was always a particularly responsible chain when it came to divestiture, at least until 1986. Then, as times got harder, the company stopped worrying about niceties. Never mind that in buying up scores of rural community hospitals across the Southeast in the early days, Frist and members of the company's acquisition department used as a sales argument the company's size and "staying power." When it became necessary for competitive reasons to make the company leaner and meaner in 1987, Frist quickly dumped over half his hospitals. He set them adrift on a raft constructed of sodden debt instruments—a company financed with over a billion dollars in "junk" bonds and floating-rate bank debt. (In May 1988, the new company's securities were rated B-3 by Moody's Investors Service and CCC+ by Standard & Poor's, hardly confidence-inspiring classifications.) With what must have been a touch of sarcasm or irony, Frist named this new assemblage of hospital "losers" HealthTrust. As the new company's chairman, chief executive officer, and president, R. Clayton McWorter (no relation to Governor Ned McWherter of Tennessee)

has said the HealthTrust hospitals will be "no-frills" operations
with reduced services. And many of these will be unloaded again,
probably into the hands of even less secure entrepreneurial firms.
Some will inevitably be abandoned altogether. As McWorter told
the *Wall Street Journal* in 1987, "It's amazing what you'll do when
your back is to the wall and you're highly leveraged." He added,
"When I get up in the morning, I don't have to worry about the
board or the founder. I just think about the lenders."[4]

No mention of communities here. As a matter of fact, the
whole story of how the HealthTrust divestment was conceived, as
related by Frist to the *Wall Street Journal* in November 1987,
suggests that the fate of those communities figured very little, if at
all, in the operation. As the *Journal* tells the story:

> . . . last February, he [Frist] was high above the
> Atlantic on a flight bound for Europe when it hit him that
> his company was in need of "radical surgery." On the
> ground, he found a phone and called his chief financial
> officer, Roger Mick, to tell him he had two weeks to
> develop a plan to get rid of half the company's hospitals.
> For years the operative word had been growth; now it
> was streamline.[5]

Now the hospitals HCA surgically transplanted into Health-
Trust were not, strictly speaking, sinking the company. In fact,
only 3 of the 104 hospitals "sold" to HealthTrust were actually
losing money, according to HCA. The rest just weren't making the
15 percent return that was HCA's corporate standard. The lesson
here, therefore, is that no community with a corporate hospital is
really safe from the risk of reduction in needed services, or even
an outright closing, at the whim of management.

In an interview in the *FAHS Review*, Sidney F. Tyler, executive
vice president of NME's hospital group, made it clear that when it
comes to divestment, it isn't just dying institutions that are
scuttled or set adrift. In 1986, NME unburdened itself of eight
hospitals (it sold them to two small for-profit companies) when the
company's stock fell on hard times and earnings fell to $85 million
from $150 million the year before. In explaining NME's sudden
decision Tyler said:

> This is not to say that these particular hospitals did
> not have some growth prospects. But they did not fit our

style of management or the profile we would like to see for our medical staff. By that, I mean the staff may not be as cohesive and forward-looking as is necessary for the hospital to be a strong competitor in the future. In addition, the hospital may require a lot of capital in future years, and we may not get an acceptable return on that investment, especially with uncertainties of the Medicare capital issue. So these are some of the factors we look at in assessing the hospitals we want to keep, and those we want to divest.[6]

In the same edition of the magazine, HCA's Vice President for Acquisitions and Development Joseph D. Moore explained his firm's equally sudden divestment of eighteen hospitals following a stock slide and earnings drop (this was a year before the Health-Trust spinoff):

In divesting hospitals, what we are trying to assess is this: Given the resources we have as a company, does it make sense to continue with that investment? We have to consider not only how it is operating currently, but also what the future will be for that particular facility . . . So the hospital doesn't necessarily have to be losing money for a divestiture to occur.[7]

In other words, what Tyler and Moore seem to be saying is that if doctors in a community resist corporate directives regarding patient mix and treatment methods (the real meaning of the term "not forward-looking"), if a community doesn't seem to be growing rapidly, if the local economy is in decline, or if a hospital work force is trying to unionize, watch out. That hospital may soon be on the auction block or closed.

The Implications of Corporate Dominance

Few people bothered to examine the implications of the wave of corporate mergers in the early part of the century, or to consider what the long-term social impact of almost universal automobile ownership would be on American society, until long after the nation's cities and rail transportation systems had been irreversibly gutted. Similarly, today little attention is being given to the impact on the nation's health system of the takeover of acute-care hospitals by a few giant companies. Instead, observers, particularly in academia and government, tend to obfuscate the issue by suggesting that there is no real difference between not-for-profit and for-profit hospitals, or by noting that the corporate chains still own only a relatively small segment of the entire industry. (People were saying that when the chains had only 10 percent of the market. Now they have over 21 percent, and over 25 percent if chain-managed facilities are counted in the total.)

On the first point, as most physicians will readily point out, as others in academia have demonstrated, and as common sense suggests in looking at such loosely affiliated groupings as Voluntary Hospitals of America and even many of the more centrally run religious chains, there *are* fundamental differences between not-for-profit and for-profit hospitals, independent or chain. As we saw in the case of hospital/physician relationships and in the case of treating the poor, these differences are being reduced, but it is not because they are moving toward some middle ground. Rather it is because to survive, much less grow, the not-for-profit hospitals must become like the for-profits by joining chains, creating for-profit subsidiaries or joint ventures with physicians, insurers, and the like. To the extent that not-for-profit hospitals fend off the growth of the for-profits, it will be because, to paraphrase an old Pogo cartoon, "They met the enemy, and it was them." This need to copy the for-profits may in fact explain why it is the not-for-profits that are seemingly in the lead in devising the kinds of joint-venture for-profit operations with physicians that most concern those worried about medical conflicts of interest. Because they are not-for-profit by law and as such are constrained from running at a profit, they have to design creative ways to do through subsidiary joint-ventures what the for-profits can do in a much more straightforward fashion.

On the second point, the relatively small percentage of the total hospital market owned by investor corporations, the fact is that already the largest for-profit chains are more powerful than their share of hospital ownership might suggest. In 1983, the four largest for-profit chains' revenues of $8.8 billion represented one fourth of the total revenues of 147 of the largest chains of profit and nonprofit hospitals in the country, according to Notre Dame's Professor Craypo. That same year, HCA alone controlled 40 percent of the beds owned and managed by the thirty largest for-profit, investor-owned hospital chains. By 1988, while HCA's share of total beds was down, the four biggest chains, together with their two big spin-off companies, HealthTrust and EPIC, had total revenues that were double the 1983 figure and had further enlarged their share of total hospital chain revenues.

According to Craypo, it isn't necessary for these largest firms to have actual ownership of most of the nation's hospitals and related health-care systems (though some knowledgeable observers see them owning 50–60 percent of the nation's hospitals in another decade), in order for them to dominate the industry. "An industry is considered to be concentrated when the largest four firms together have more than half the sales," argues Craypo. At that point, these "lead firms" can, like IBM in computers or General Motors in automobiles, "develop industry standards on product pricing and levels of production" and "shape the industry's distribution and marketing, production technologies, product quality and design," while maintaining "a degree of control over their economic environment that smaller rivals do not possess."

Health care, moreover, is different from automobiles and steel in a way that actually makes it *easier* for a few firms with a much less dominant national presence to dictate the terms of competition. For the most part, health care is a locally produced, locally delivered "product." This almost unique aspect of the industry is too often ignored in discussions of corporate power in health care, but it goes a long way to explain an otherwise peculiar phenomenon: the way the not-for-profit hospital sector everywhere has aped the for-profits' behavior.

Even in New York State, where publicly traded, investor-owned hospitals are still not permitted, most hospitals are increasingly being run in a much more "businesslike" fashion, with marketing and amenities becoming important, even at financially strapped institutions. How could one attribute this profound change in behavior to the existence of a corporate sector that only represents some one in four of all hospitals? Of course, amendments in the way government reimburses hospitals for Medicare have had an impact (something the chains had a hand in), but that's only part of it.

The answer is that in many places across the country, those same chain hospitals have represented a much larger segment of a local or regional market. We saw earlier how AMI at one point owned three of the four hospitals in San Luis Obispo, California, and three of five in the wider county region, and how from that position of economic dominance it was driving the local public hospital into the ground. We saw another case where the same company's hospital in Gonzales, Louisiana, was bankrupting the local public facility. There was also the tale of Tampa General Hospital, which the local community was forced to completely restructure and renovate because Humana's new Women's Hospital was drawing away all the lucrative middle-class births. Costly construction at taxpayer expense of a new obstetrics wing at Tampa General surely made the old hospital look much nicer, but it probably did little to improve the actual quality of care, which was reportedly already first-rate by all accounts.

These and many other local exercises in corporate market power are not lost on hospital managers and local communities anywhere in the country. Even in jurisdictions with no for-profit hospital, most independent and not-for-profit hospital chain facilities responded to real or perceived threats from for-profit hospitals by imitating their behavior: bringing in professional managers and marketing experts, embarking on expensive remodelling or rebuilding programs, tightening up on providing charity care to indigents.

The local nature of much hospital care in America enhances the market power of the corporate chains in another way, too. As we saw in Kansas, the administrators at Wichita's Wesley Medical Center were so worried about the ability of any big chain buyer of one of the city's two troubled Catholic charity hospitals to undercut Wesley in a price war that they jumped the gun and sold their own facility first, to HCA. This was no case of paranoia. The corporate chains *are* aggressive competitors (though not always on price so much as in the buying of physician practices or in advertising). And their local hospitals *do have* staying power, thanks to virtually unlimited backing from national headquarters. Just as the major petroleum refiners have been able to drive independent retailers out of business on specific street corners by selling gas under cost, corporate hospitals can essentially spend local rivals into the ground, particularly when they are up against an unaffiliated competitor.

As Walter Adams, distinguished professor of economics at Michigan State University and coauthor with James Brock of *The Bigness Complex,* explained in an interview, "Concentration rates are important in determining the potential for monopolistic behavior in the case of firms with national markets, but in the case of health care, you have essentially local markets, and there, it's much easier for firms with a much smaller market share to control markets. Take dairy products. Nationally, the top four companies control only 20–25 percent of the market, but in specific local markets they are dominant, and you get anticompetitive behavior."

Furthermore, one thing that works *against* successful monopolistic practices in something like dairy products, namely the relatively low cost of entry into a market for new competitors, is absent in the case of hospital care. If a dairy market becomes *too* noncompetitive in terms of price, someone is bound to enter it with a lower-priced product line, thus destroying the monopoly or oligopoly. But in the case of hospitals, at least within a local area, the cost of entry is enormous. This too works to the advantage of the corporate chains, which are almost always in the position of being the newcomer to a local market. As such they are able either to buy in at fire-sale prices or, if they think a market has the potential to be sufficiently lucrative, they can use their national assets and access to inexpensive capital to build. The cost to a large national hospital corporation of entering a local market is relatively small: a few million dollars for a company with revenues of several billion. (A corporate chain, faced with a big tax bill on profits, might even welcome the new cash outlay as a deduction from pretax earnings, a consideration not even available to a not-for-profit.) On the other hand, to an existing free-standing hospital faced with the arrival of corporate competition, that kind of money, or even the cost of just modernizing an existing facility, is large, potentially debilitating, and often out of reach entirely.

Of course, another corporate chain would find the entry costs in a given market similarly easy to meet. But it is another peculiar aspect of this industry that, by the admission of most of its own top executives, there are very few cases where the for-profit companies have gone head-to-head in competition. "You're right that we have not been competing with each other except in a few cities," says Charles Reilly, who until 1986 was in charge of development at AMI. "Where we competed with each other was in buying existing hospitals." As hospital executives readily explain, once one company establishes or gains control of a hospital in a local market, the other firms, which may have made competing offers for the facility, tend to look for greener pastures to exploit. As AMI's past president Walter Weisman put it in the

November/December 1986 issue of *FAHS Review*, "Health care companies will be seeking potential [market] niches rather than attempting to 'nudge over' existing strong operators."[8]

Should the industry eventually evolve into a relatively small number of vertically integrated firms, each having hospitals, patient feeder systems of clinics, and a package of insurance and HMO plans (whether owned or part of some kind of joint venture arrangement), the competitive picture will be mixed. There may be direct competition among those firms, but the pressures and incentives for them to compete with restraint will be similar to those operating in other concentrated industries. And some aspects of vertical integration, such as combining traditionally antagonistic operations—namely hospitals and insurance—are fundamentally anticompetitive. It removes the insurance industry as a factor in pressing hospitals to keep costs down and doctors to keep admissions to only those necessary. At the same time, it contributes to oligopolistic practices by further raising the ante for would-be entries into a market. Any new competitor, in other words, would have to have sufficient capital from the outset to own all the components of a vertically integrated operation in a region, not "just" a hospital.

That the hospital industry aspires to market control and the resulting kind of "gentlemanly" competition, as practiced in such industries as autos, steel, or textiles, is indisputable. Before the industry was hit by the DRG system in 1985, FAHS's executive director Michael Bromberg talked grandly of the entire health-care industry, predicting that it would be dominated a decade hence by "ten or twelve large firms." He clearly expected several hospital companies to be among them. AMI's Weisman spoke only slightly less grandly of a similar number of "influential" firms. Frist, besides consciously aiming at General Motors as a model, has long boasted of the advantages of bigness in promoting his company to potential acquisition targets and to hospital boards considering whether to hire HCA as a manager. While these companies may have a measure of influence well beyond their size, with three in ten hospitals in corporate hands (counting leased and managed facilities), by 1991 it is unlikely that they will continue being relatively minor players in the larger hospital industry, or even in the broader corporate line-up, for long.

For one thing, all the major companies have their eyes on what is potentially the biggest plum in the field of health care:

contractual arrangements to provide care to large captive populations, whether these be the employees of national corporations, government employees, military dependents, or even welfare populations. To do this, they need to have facilities in all major population centers, and to either own or have some affiliation or joint venture arrangement with a health insurance firm. None of the companies is in a position to do this yet because none has facilities in place to provide full national coverage. All are, however, clearly interested in the idea. On the government side, the Pentagon has been experimenting with contracting out hospital care for its massive military dependents population, and during the next decade it is likely to put care for that group out to bid. HCA admits to following that project closely. Humana is probably doing likewise and has already, through its insurance subsidiary, contracted for the care of entire county work forces in Florida and other places where it has a major presence.

Humana has also gone in a major way for the elderly patient "market," and has become the nation's largest HMO for Medicare patients. In that role, the company has provided an object lesson in what's wrong with the whole concept of capitated care.

The way Medicare HMOs work is that a company sets up an HMO plan which people on Medicare may opt to join *instead* of Medicare. The patient, in theory, gets first-dollar coverage of all ailments at no charge or for a small annual fee, while the government, relieved of the costs of Medicare for that patient, pays a flat fee—really an annual insurance premium—to the private HMO. In this way, at about $475 a head, Humana during 1990 raked in nearly $650 million in tax dollars for its largest such program, the 177,000-member Humana Gold Plus Plan in Florida.

But the Gold Plus Plan, and other Humana Medicare HMO plans outside Florida, have also proved to be problematic for patients and care-givers alike, according to government insurance regulators and the Federal Department of Health and Human Services. In a four-part series of stories in October 1990, a team of investigative reporters for the Ft. Lauderdale, Florida *Sun-Sentinel* disclosed that over five thousand complaints had been lodged involving the Humana plan, many of them for unconscionably long delays in making payment, or worse, refusal to authorize treatment for serious medical problems.[9] The company was also cited in 1988 by federal auditors for "improper marketing activities." Specifically, some members of the company's sales force, which works on commission ($60 a head for new enrollees), have been found to be signing up new elderly enrollees without explaining that they would lose their Medicare coverage, or that they might be required to use Humana facilities for their treatment. Indeed, the paper reported that some Humana Gold Plus Plan cards contributed to the confusion by having the subscriber's now useless Medicare card printed on the reverse side.[10]

Humana claims it has made improvements in its system, including the delegation of complaints to an outside agency for resolution and the running of criminal background checks on all new sales agents, but the problems continue, according to state and federal regulators.[11] And in a capitated system where a private company's profit is determined by how much under its set annual per-person fee it can provide care to an ailing and elderly population, it's hard to see how problems and abuses won't continue. Nonetheless, with the nation's health bill reaching the crisis stage, capitated care plans are gaining support in Washington regardless of the popular attitude toward them.

Also working in the corporate chains' interest is the fact that governments, whether state or federal, prefer dealing with large entities. The increasingly complex bureaucracy and red tape of the Medicaid and Medicare reimbursement systems is handled far more easily by large central offices than by the personnel and equipment at a single hospital.

How dense and costly the paperwork has become was illustrated by David White, executive vice president and chief operating officer at Community Health Systems, a nine-hospital corporate chain based in Houston. In an interview published in the July/August 1989 issue of the *FAHS Review*, he said that the personnel required to deal with billing and government red tape

> proliferate now to the extent that hospitals that used to
> have wings filled with bedrooms with patients in them,
> now have administrative offices in those locations. They
> are now filled with the non-clinical administrative side of
> the business.[12]

As Joseph Califano, Health Education and Welfare Secretary in the Carter administration, writing later in his new position as chairman of Chrysler's health care committee, noted in an April 12, 1989, *New York Times* op-ed piece:

> America's health care system is the world's most
> expensive to administer. The proliferation of efforts to

track and screen for abuse every patient, procedure and
prescription has made it more important for doctors and
hospital administrators to master accounting and regulatory manipulation than to master medicine.

Even Los Angeles County Hospital, one of the largest public
hospitals in the country, was having a difficult time keeping up
with the Medicaid paperwork in 1977–78, when I was covering
that beat for the *Los Angeles Daily News*. The county was, in fact,
losing millions of dollars a year through failure to meet deadlines
on submission of patient billing paperwork. And the paperwork
flood has only gotten worse in the intervening years, according to
the L.A. County Health Department.

No one, including the for-profit industry's cost-conscious
executives, enjoys having to deal with all that paperwork, but the
big home offices of centralized operations like NME or Humana
are certainly far better equipped to handle it than small local
hospitals. This places the big firms at a clear competitive advantage.

There is, incidentally, an enormous irony to the paperwork
involved in America's Medicare and Medicaid programs. In countries with fully nationalized health-care systems, like Sweden,
Great Britain, and Canada, paperwork is minimal. It is precisely
because costs are so high in our system of marketplace medicine
that regulatory control—and the accompanying paperwork designed to prevent fraud and abuse—abounds. As one Canadian
hospital executive reportedly told a public health researcher at
Harvard, "We have one or two back office people at the hospital to
handle patient billing—and another roomful to take care of the bill
for treatment of the occasional American tourist!"

Finally, and equally important as an inducement to growth
and consolidation, it is the very nature of investor-owned enterprises that they must grow to maintain their share price. Rare
indeed is the investor today who buys a stock because of the
dividend it pays. Rather, investors tend to buy speculatively,
looking for increases in share value. And as Shamrock Investments partner and former AMI executive Charles Reilly observes,
"When corporations are publicly owned, they have an obligation
to grow, and that means more concentration, because it's easier to
grow by concentration."

There will be pauses in that process, as in 1973 and the
mid-1980s, and no doubt another "shakeout" sometime in the future.

However, just as we have seen the concentration of the hospital industry continue right through hard times, the long-term trend assuredly is for further growth and consolidation.

Political economist Professor Uwe E. Reinhardt commented this way on the issue of local control versus concentrated corporate control: "All these years Americans have wanted local control of health care, but increasingly it will be dominated by national chains, sitting in Louisville, Nashville, and Beverly Hills, and making health policy for the entire nation. I'm not at all unfavorably disposed to this vertical integration, though. It makes economic sense. We Americans have reimbursed the health-care industry as only a drunkard would do, but we have been so cheap about funding the infrastructure we forced the hospital industry to go to the private sector to raise funds. If you do that, sooner or later you have to turn them into a business. There's no evidence that the for-profits are more efficient or cheaper. What they *are* good at is getting money—from Wall Street and Zurich and Singapore. There's no point in bashing them now for that."

Corporate Hospital Power

While Reinhardt says he doesn't fear the growth of for-profit medicine on economic grounds, he does express concern about the hospital industry's growing *political influence*. Although for-profit hospital corporations are only relatively small players nationwide in terms of number of beds or share of the nation's medical bill, the industry has been remarkably successful in getting its way in a Congress enamored of free-enterprise ideology, as passage of DRG reforms for Medicare illustrated in 1983. "The Federation of American Health Systems is the most successful lobby in Washington," he reports.

We have seen earlier how the industry is now able to influence the political environment for its economic benefit in states where it is a significant player in the health-care field. Just as the giant auto and steel companies did before it, it will likely exercise the same power in the future in Washington, where national health policy is determined.

Because the for-profit hospital lobby has had to learn, as a relatively small special interest in Washington, to play the game of coalition building, it is well suited to power politics. As demonstrated in the preceding chapter, the industry's lobby at the national level and its larger firms in selected states have been adept at presenting issues in ways that bring the not-for-profit and public hospitals on board. At the very least it has been able to defuse potential opposition from those sectors.

So far the industry, bitterly antiunion, has barely tapped that well-spring of political power: the labor movement. Such industries as steel and automobiles long ago learned to play jobs against pollution controls and an end to import restraints. But turning to rank-and-file workers for lobbying assistance will not be easy for the hospital companies. The for-profit health-care industry as a whole has a strong antiunion record, surely best exemplified by the nursing home giant Beverly Enterprises. In 1987 this for-profit nursing home chain earned the dubious distinction of being singled out by the Reagan administration's National Labor Relations Board (NLRB)—no small feat—for a whopping one thousand violations of workers rights. The hospital companies, for their part, have for years studiously avoided acquisitions of hospitals that had labor pacts. As a result there are almost no unionized for-profit hospitals. And the various unions that represent hospital workers have had almost no success to date organizing any of the companies' facilities.

Despite this antilabor tradition, the industry has recently recognized the potential for such political alliances. Besides, it has another potential ally that the auto industry has rarely been able to harness—the consumer/patient. As Humana's Jones put it in an interview, "You're increasingly going to see us being advocates of better government funding for the poor and the elderly."

In fact, despite not having unions to ally itself with, the FAHS is nonetheless now trying, with some success, to use hospital industry employees to press Congress in the interest of the companies. In its September/October 1987 issue of *Review* magazine, distributed to all its member firms, the trade association prominently quoted released Beirut hostage and career hospital administrator David Jacobsen as saying, "The pendulum of health budgeting can be swung back if an army of volunteers from your hospitals is willing to 'enlist' in the service of a new political force."[13]

Just such a strategy has permitted the defense industry, with plants and military bases in every congressional district, to win ever larger budgets, even as the Cold War was ending. With hospitals in every state, many of them mainstays of local economies, the hospital companies are in an excellent position to emulate the defense industry. Nor does a poor record of labor relations preclude the hospital corporations from seeking political alliances with their employees. After all, the auto and coal industries are hardly paragons of good labor relations. Yet even though the United Auto Workers and United Mineworkers are among the most militant unions in the country, both the auto and coal industries have managed to bring the organized workers and their leaders into common cause on many issues, such as import quotas, clean air or mileage standards, and acid rain legislation.

The for-profit hospital industry has already demonstrated how its own version of this strategy will work. The 1988 FAHS annual report, in a section on a grass-roots campaign to "protect Medicare," included the following statement:

> All across the country, hospitals are actively reaching out to their elected representatives.
>
> For example, in New Orleans, two NME affiliated hospitals sponsored a televised "Medical Awareness Forum," in which the local U.S. representative and several civic, political and business leaders discussed the hospital payment crisis.
>
> An HCA hospital in Roanoke, Virginia, packed a bus full of employees and drove to the steps of the U.S. Capitol in Washington, D.C., to demonstrate against Medicare budget cuts. Humana hospitals distributed tabloid newspapers explaining the significance of the Medicare shortfall to patients, employees and local residents. A red campaign button, emblazoned "Medicare: No More Cuts!" was first developed by a Humana hospital and endorsed by the Federation. To date, we have distributed more than 25,000 of the buttons to hospital workers and friends all across the U.S.

This "grass roots" effort was conceived by Humana and organized by the FAHS to prevent massive cuts in Medicare funding during the first year of the Bush administration. The idea was to use hospitals as a base for community organizing. But because the hospital industry organized the protests, the message was not to maintain health *coverage* for the elderly. Rather, it was to maintain *reimbursement rates* to the hospitals for that coverage—a subtle but important difference that demonstrates who was using whom in this coalition.

Humana Public Affairs Vice President George Atkins, the brains behind the campaign, explains what happened:

> It started with a conversation [FAHS Executive Director Michael] Bromberg had with a member of Congress. He was talking with him about how the cuts in Medicare would hurt hospitals, and the Congressman told him, "Mike, I believe what you're saying, but I don't get but three letters on this from home." When Mike told me about this, I realized it was true, and I started wondering what we could do here at Humana to motivate all our people.

Atkins worked fast. He recalls:

> Phase one was to develop a program for our own people, and then, realizing that we were a small part of the universe, we moved out into the community to any group that was interested: Rotary Clubs, senior centers. What we had to do was give our employees the ammunition. We developed the message: "No More Cuts" in Medicare, and put it in a framework that was understandable. We got top corporate management and all the hospital managers and sales people involved. We then went on a training program. We got everyone to write Congress, and we invited all our local candidates to a hospital. It was a ripple effect kind of thing.

Atkins says that FAHS spread the program to all the federation's member companies and eventually to the broader American Hospital Association. "The real key was coalition building," he says. Humana and many other hospital companies even handed out brochures to Medicare patients, urging them to write to Congress with the "No More Cuts" message.

One member of Congress, whom Atkins wouldn't identify, complained about the notes, saying, "If you don't quit having people send me those red cards you haven't *seen* cuts yet!" But Atkins laughs, "We kept them coming to his office, and in the end he voted with us!" The culmination of the campaign was a nonbinding "sense of the Congress" resolution (basically a Congressional spine-stiffener) calling for "No More Cuts." The results:

The Bush administration's proposal for over $5.5 billion in Medicare cuts was trimmed to under $2.3 billion.

"Hospitals used to just roll over on issues like this," says Atkins. "Now we're working as an industry." Next on the agenda, says Atkins, is "health-care *system* reform," which he said will have to deal with the issues of access, Medicaid, and costs. An emboldened corporate hospital sector can be expected to push for reforms in its own interest in each of these areas, and what they seem to want is not universal access on the model of most of the national health systems in the rest of the industrialized world. Rather, most corporate hospital executives look forward to a kind of tiered care.

Here's how it was described to me in 1986 by F. Scott Gross, then head of NME's hospitals division:

> I think a two-tiered hospital system is inevitable, in fact, I think it will be three tiers, based not on quality of care delivered, because that will be the same. The tiering will be: the medically indigent, who will be cared for by the private sector under government contract on a bid basis—and it's going to become socially acceptable for those services to be provided bare bones; economy class—same quality but slightly better amenities, again probably on a capitated basis under contract with employers; and full price, for people who want the private room and the gourmet meal. It will be like on an airplane—equally safe for everybody, but more comfortable for some than for others.

This picture is radically different from the current American system of health care, particularly in terms of the value system upon which it is premised. The idea is that no longer should everyone be "mainstreamed" into a common medical system. Instead, different classes of patients will be steered into different medical systems and to different doctors, based on their income levels or insurance coverage. Yet with all eyes focused only on cost, no one—consumers, legislators, or even physicians—seems to notice that the system we thought we had is completely changing under our feet.

When the auto industry was in its infancy—even when Henry Ford was mass-producing Model T's—few people thought of Detroit as a powerful "special interest" in the making. Yet by the

1960s and 1970s, this auto industry would be able to stall indefinitely serious efforts at emission reduction, improved gas mileage, passenger safety, and even crash resistance standards. That's not to mention its success in getting the government to establish import restraints on foreign cars, restraints which, by one estimate, cost U.S. consumers an extra $16 billion over a four-year period. The same might be said of a government-protected and subsidized energy industry that led American consumers down the garden path of nuclear energy, at even greater cost and risk to health and safety. Now, a new corporate empire is growing, talking all the time about the need to let market forces have sway, but planning already to control those forces through economic and political power.

In 1986, the National Acadamy of Sciences published its major study of for-profit medicine. The report, *Implications of For-Profit Enterprise in Health Care*, looked into almost every aspect of the new corporate hospital industry, but it studiously avoided issues of political power. As one participant in the study, Katherine Somers, laments, "With representatives of the for-profit hospital industry on the committee, it was guaranteed that we wouldn't address that kind of thing."

Somers, a member of the committee and scholar-in-residence at the institute who with six others signed a letter of dissent when the study was published, says, "A problem with our report was that we didn't really address political issues at all. We didn't assign any special studies even though it is an important point. It's too bad. Clearly, large institutions have more clout, but we couldn't demonstrate that—and we couldn't risk being called anecdotal."

In their minority statement, which was published as part of the final report, the dissenters wrote: "We would have little to gain, and possibly much to lose, if for-profit corporations came to dominate our health-care system."[14]

A brave new world of marketplace medicine is upon us. If corporate health-care interests are allowed to grow at the expense of public and community hospitals, while the FAHS and its allies proceed to shape the message about health-care issues that legislators get, that brief statement by Somers and her colleagues may become the most memorable sentence in the National Academy of Sciences study.

10

Controlling the Market and Our Health-Care Destiny

In a way, we're kind of like a utility.
— Thomas Frist, Jr., Chairman
HCA

There is no practical way to regulate the economic oligarchy of autocratic, self-constituted and self-per-petuating groups. With all their resources of interlocking directors, interlocking bankers and interlocking lawyers, with all their power to hire thousands of employees and service workers throughout the country, with all their power to give or withhold millions of dollars' worth of business, with all their power to contribute to the campaign funds of the acquiescent or to subsidize the champions of the obdurate, they are as dangerous a menace to political as they are to economic freedom.
— Felix Frankfurter, in a 1936 memorandum
to Franklin Roosevelt urging break up
of the power trust of energy-holding
companies

Medical care, in all societies, is deeply and irretriev-ably political. Nowhere is there anything approaching a pure marketplace in medicine. . . .
— Ben Griffith et al.,
in *Banking on Sickness*

Is health care, and in fact first-rate health care, a right?

The dramatic changes taking place in the health-care industry today make this a fundamental question facing American society. Most modern industrial countries, as well as many less developed countries, have decided that health care should be considered a right. At least in theory, the same held true in America from 1965 to about 1980. Today, however, it is a right in neither practice nor theory. As Walter Weisman put it in a 1987 interview, a year before resigning as president of American Medical International, "I don't believe that health care can be seen as a need the way water, food, or housing is a need."

Is that a fair assessment? In a way, yes. A person denied water would die in days. Denied food, one would last only slightly longer. The homeless may suffer for years, but they are in imminent danger of death in the case of a cold snap. Without medical care, on the other hand, a lucky person might live to a ripe old age.

Viewed another way, however, health care is entirely different. The absence of food or shelter is a condition that compels a person to act to remedy the situation, by finding a job, finding a relief organization, or turning to friends. But people with limited resources let medical insurance lapse and even insured people, who only have to pay a portion of their medical bill, postpone going to a doctor when the first signs of a medical problem surface. In good or even reasonably good health, they ignore the issue, while continuing to pay rent and food bills. When a problem does develop, it is all too often beyond the ability of friends and local charities to solve it; that calls for the resources of a major medical institution. Furthermore, health-care problems typically present themselves suddenly, often rendering the victim incapable of the vigorous efforts necessary to obtain assistance. The result: Poor men in places like Tampa, Florida, unable to raise the money for a hernia repair operation, must live crippled by pain until either the local public hospital decides it needs some teaching fodder, or a needlessly strangulated gut produces a life-threatening medical emergency.

Of course we Americans have even tiptoed around the idea of declaring access to food and shelter a human right, setting up subsidized housing and food stamp programs, but then making access to them difficult. It is only education that we have unequivocably declared to be a right, in part because we realize that unlike food and shelter, failure to obtain a basic education is only recognized as a problem by an individual when it's too late, and in part because it is in everyone's interest to have an educated citizenry.

Interestingly, in both ways, medical care closely resembles education. But as things stand, we have the for-profit hospital industry promoting its philosophy that health care is *not* a right, or that even if it is a right, it is not private industry's responsibility. Meanwhile, both state and federal governments are concerning themselves exclusively with the matter of controlling the *costs* of health care, all the while extolling the virtues of the marketplace. Under these circumstances, needless suffering and inexcusable infirmity are likely to continue and to increase in this land of unrivaled wealth, resources, and medical expertise. Indeed, it is because of this nation's private-sector approach to health care that America, alone among the modern industrial democracies, is seeing a troubling decline in immunization rates for some easily preventable childhood diseases, as parents are told they must pay for the shots, or as the public clinics where they could get such vaccinations cheaply are closed down by city, state, and federal governments. Similarly, it is only in America, among modern nations, that hospitals and individuals are faced with bankruptcy because of the AIDS epidemic. In countries with state medicine, a health crisis like AIDS merely means that taxes for everyone rise a little to fund the health-care system adequately.

At the same time, our own narrow focus on cost cutting may not even solve the problems it is intended to solve. But that should be no surprise. To think otherwise would be a triumph of hope over experience.

Congress, prodded by consumer activists, moved in the late 1970s and early 1980s to deregulate the airline industry. Its intent was clearly to encourage the founding of many small competing companies that would, the theory went, lead to lower fares and better service. There was certainly no intention of fostering a merger-and-acquisition binge that, by 1986, would see six giant companies controlling 84 percent of the business. One of them, Texas Air, was among the very upstart firms that deregulation initially encouraged. Yet here we are with a worse concentration in the airline industry today than we had before deregulation, but without the restraining hand of government regulation on fares and routing decisions. And the prospect by all accounts is for less competition and higher fares in the near future.

Similarly, when the U.S. Justice Department and a federal

judge broke up the nation's biggest monopoly, AT&T, the intent was to introduce competition to communications in order to reduce rates and improve service. The result has instead been to make both benefits contingent upon the size of the customer. Big business users of phone services have experienced major rate cuts and benefited from enhanced service from competing firms. But individual customers, only two years after the dissolution of AT&T, have seen overall phone bills rise 20 percent, according to the Consumer Federation of America. Service, meanwhile, once a hallmark of the Bell system, has become a national joke.

Such tales of market-oriented reforms gone wrong in modern America are legion. In its December 22, 1986, issue *Business Week*—the trade magazine of free market advocates—ran a cover story with the headline "Is Deregulation Working?" The subhead read: "True, Prices Have Fallen. But the Top Players May Stifle Competition." In industry after industry, the article by Chris Welles disclosed that after initial rate cuts to at least some customers, the main result of reduced government regulation was a lupine competition: Already established large firms gobbled up smaller competitors and drove others out of business, often via predatory pricing. The hope that government regulatory agencies would prevent such moves toward concentration by acting in the interest of smaller competitors, particularly in the early stages of deregulation in a particular industry, proved vain. The large players were able to exert their historic political influence in relevant offices of the Federal Communications Commission, the Federal Aviation Agency, the Departments of Transportation and the Treasury, the Federal Reserve, the Interstate Commerce Commission, and in Congress, Welles wrote.[1]

It now seems that the same story is about to unfold in medicine, where a similar effort is underway to use the marketplace to reform an admittedly noncompetitive and overly expensive industry. The goals are again laudable at least in part, but as in the case of other industries, the reality is proving to be something different from what was intended.

When health-care reformers pushed for the creation of Medicare and Medicaid programs in the 1960s, the clear intent was to open the doors of private physicians and private hospitals to those classes of people long excluded from first-rate care: the elderly, the infirm, and the poor. To a great extent they accomplished this admirable goal, "mainstreaming" a large segment of the population that in the past was left with second-class medical care or no care at all. But the unintended side effect was to enrich the nation's hospitals and physicians beyond anyone's wildest dreams, thereby encouraging health-care entrepreneurs like the Frists, Jones, Cherry, Eames, Bedrosian, Appel et al. to devise new ways to exploit the situation.

Now Washington is trying to control the problem of health-care inflation by promoting free-market competition in the industry. No one, with the exception of some doctors and hospital managers, would argue against doing something to reduce the nation's health bill. But so far, there is no convincing evidence that costs are being brought under control by any of these efforts. And in their attempt to address the cost issue, the new "cost-cutter" reformers in Congress and the White House are creating another set of problems: reduced access to quality care for the poor and elderly, reduced independence of judgment for the physician, and reduced freedom of choice for the average patient. Ultimately, they are creating a new center of concentrated corporate power, this time in health care, to join the pantheon of similar centers of power in energy, surface transportation, aviation, chemicals, agriculture, and publishing, to mention a few.

The implications of this development are far-reaching. Some radical thinkers, for instance, have tended to view current developments as just another proverbial "swing of the pendulum." As one self-described advocate of nationalized medicine (temporarily employed as a government relations expert by one of the corporate hospital chains) explained almost glibly, "All this corporate medicine will eventually lead to a reaction and demands for access for all, which will result in some kind of nationalized medicine."

The problem with this dialectical theory, however, is that it ignores the new power of the diversified health services companies. It is unlikely that any foreseeable government in Washington would attempt radical reform of the health-care system entailing the expropriation or elimination of several multibillion-dollar corporate entities. Instead, as talk of nationalized medicine again enters the political agenda, it inevitably involves some accommodation with those firms that allows them to continue to operate, providing care at least to the wealthier members of society. Yet such dual systems are doomed to failure. As the Thatcher government in Great Britain has demonstrated, when the upper and upper-middle class are allowed to use a private health system— one which, by the way, is composed largely of hospitals constructed and sometimes still run by U.S. firms like Humana and

HCA—government support for the public system becomes inadequate, quality of care and service suffers, and the system collapses.

Another possibility would be for the "nationalization" of health care, with the corporations actually handling the delivery of all care under contract to the central government on a bid basis. In other words, large hospital chains, or insurance groups, or a combination of the two, would bid for the right to act as giant HMO plans under contract to the government to serve some distinct geographic group. As thousands of elderly Florida residents who turned in their Medicare benefits in return for the siren song of membership in a Medicare HMO run by Humana learned, such a "solution" can mean a reduction in health care services, frustration and delay in getting treatment, and ultimately even potentially bankrupting bills for emergency treatment the plan refuses to cover. Such a future for American health care would greatly profit the participating companies and would amount to corporatization, not nationalization, of the system. (In 1988, the Thatcher government proposed this very idea for Great Britain, but quickly withdrew it after it was denounced even by members of the ruling Conservative Party.)

The point is that today, any realistic effort to confront the problems posed by the establishment of marketplace medicine must take the existence of giant, powerful national health services corporations into account. Short of a revolution, at this stage they probably aren't going to vanish from the scene any more than Exxon or General Motors is.

I do not mean here, however, to suggest that the more radical proposal of an American national health-care system based on either the Canadian or some other model ought to be dropped. At the 1987 annual convention of the American Public Health Association, where the theme was Healthcare: For Profit or for People?, a lively debate was held on the subject of a campaign for just such a system. Some argued for a kind of "incrementalism," while others said that approach had already been tried in the form of Medicare, Medicaid, and cost controls, and had failed. This latter group wanted an all-out mass campaign for national health care on the Canadian or Swedish model. On the objective evidence of both those nations' experience, in terms of availability of care, quality of care, and cost, this is clearly the best solution for America too.

In 1991, at the request of the House Committee on Government Operations, the General Accounting Office issued a report on the Canadian health system and concluded that, if it were imposed immediately on the U.S., lock, stock and barrel that year, "the savings in administrative costs alone would be more than enough to finance insurance coverage for the millions of Americans who are currently uninsured."[2] Further, it stated that "There would be enough left over to permit a reduction, or possibly even the elimination, of co-payments and deductibles . . ." The net savings of converting to a Canadian-style system would be $3 billion in year one, the report said, with future years showing further cost savings.[3]

Poll after poll has demonstrated over the years that a majority of Americans quite understandably *want* some form of socialized medicine. (Indeed, it's difficult to think of another issue where the public has so broadly wanted something and the government has so willfully ignored that demand.) And by 1991, a campaign for a "single-payer" system modeled on Canada's was underway. Spearheaded by a group of doctors, Physicians for a National Health Program was beginning to line up the unified support of several major labor unions for a political campaign that they felt would take years to realize. Said national co-coordinator Dr. Steffie Woolhandler, "I used to think that they'd come up with another half-way measure to co-opt the national healthcare movement, but now I don't think they can. The health industry interest groups—the AMA, AHA, insurance industry groups and the rest—all disagree and have driven the political system into gridlock. Meanwhile, as costs rise, the idea of a single-payer plan is gaining currency." Woolhandler's long-term analysis may be accurate, but even if it is, such a campaign ought not to preclude pressing for measures designed to limit the current abuses of the developing corporate system of health care. To fail to do so would leave the field to the health-care industry for the critical years of its consolidation, which would make it even more difficult to control or reform. This becomes particularly important now that some major corporations like Ford and Chrysler have themselves begun pushing for some kind of ill-defined "national health system."

The for-profit hospital industry, perhaps more acutely than other segments of the medical-industrial complex, has recognized the threat posed by talk of national health care and what Woolhandler and other advocates of such a government-run program call a single-payer system. Writing in the Federation's 1991 Annual Report, Patricia A. Davis, the new FAHS president and senior vice president in Humana's health-care division, called on the for-profit hospital industry to:

> . . . encourage participation in our ongoing "grass roots" political campaign by our primary audiences—most importantly, you, the membership; the medical professionals who are affiliated with our hospitals, and the product suppliers and others with whom the hospital industry relates.

She warned:

> Unless we work diligently to overcome it, those who favor a monolithic, nationalized scheme will succeed in persuading the public that our inaction is sufficient grounds to force us from the scene.[3]

The same federation document offered a "Ten Point Plan" to reform the national health-care "system." Five of those ten points involved shifting more costs directly onto workers and patients or restricting their freedom of choice in obtaining medical care. Three others called for providing more money to hospitals and health-care *providers*.[4]

If, as many people believe, health care ought to be considered a right, it becomes necessary to establish mechanisms to ensure the proper behavior of private hospital companies (or, should they become subsidiaries of larger companies, of their parent firms). Market incentives alone cannot do this.

Some such mechanisms already exist, though they may need to be dusted off and reworked. Certificates of need have long served to provide communities with a bargaining position to win at least some concessions from hospital owners and managers. The concept of "health systems agencies," which acted on those permit applications, was flawed not as an idea, but in practice. The problem was that the agencies—appointed as they were by local and state government leaders—tended to be dominated by doctors and hospital administrators, whose main interest was simply protecting existing health-care power centers in a community. The failure of most HSAs to represent the health consumer shouldn't condemn the system, though.

What is needed is not to scrap CONs, as state after state has done over the past decade. This action, solidly backed by the for-profit hospital companies, just succeeds in turning hospital siting, construction, and expansion into a vast commercial free-for-all, over which no one but corporate boards of directors has any say. Rather, the whole trend should be reversed. Instead of being scrapped, local health-system agency boards should be made truly democratic by mandating that they be representative not just of health providers but of health consumers, including the poor. Better still, they should be made into elected instead of appointed bodies. If it is appropriate for local communities to have real control over education through elected local school boards, surely it is equally appropriate for them to control their health-care destiny in a similarly democratic way.

Such revitalized agencies, far from having their authority reduced, should have it augmented. At present, there is nothing to stop a hospital company from deciding, based on the evaluation of corporate bureaucrats in some distant headquarters office, that the profitability of a local hospital unit is inadequate to satisfy shareholders, and that in the interest of improving the parent company's bottom line, it should be shut down, or even turned into a weight-loss clinic or detox center. An HSA with enhanced powers might be able to approve or reject such a decision before it could happen.

This would require little in the way of new legislation, since hospitals currently require operating licenses. And all state licenses come with conditions attached. Limits on freedom to close down operations would just be another condition. Similarly, should the parent company want to divest a hospital, selling it to another firm, the community should have veto power over an unacceptable buyer, and the right to take over the property if it is mismanaged or bankrupted.

Industry executives talk soothingly of the need for a "rationalization" of health care, a euphemism that means some 30 to 50 percent of the nation's hospitals need to be closed down. It may well be that the nation is "overbedded," but leaving the marketplace to determine which beds will disappear is sure to be traumatic and unfair to hundreds of local communities. Especially vulnerable will be areas where the local hospital is not only an important health resource but is also the main employer.

In their booklet *Health Care for Profit*, economist Charles Craypo and coauthor Mary Lehman note that between 1974 and 1981 more than two hundred hospitals in the American Hospital

Association "disappeared," and by 1982 another 160 were considered "financially depressed."

On this point they observe:

> Centralized decision-making by chain managers has been less concerned with day-to-day operations than with location, investment and procedural policy. But the latter are crucial to the type and availability of health care services in particular communities. At the extreme, they determine whether a given area or population has both affordable and quality care. At the least, they determine whether it keeps pace with or falls behind national trends and standards. Furthermore, centralization abolishes local health care markets and exposes them to national and ultimately even international capital markets; the plant and equipment needs of local hospitals are no longer judged on their own merits and according to local financial resources. They are compared with competing subsidiary hospitals and the parent company's alternative investment opportunities and credit sources. Funds can just as easily leave a community as come into it under these conditions. It all depends on priorities within the inventor-owned chain.[6]

When HCA's Thomas Frist, Jr., suggested to me that hospitals resembled utilities, he only meant to say that they were essential to society. But neither Frist nor any of his competitors is anxious to see society do to health care what it did to the utilities—assert public control over them. There were, of course, two reasons for the regulation of utilities as established in the New Deal. One was the fact that water, power, and communications are essential to the well-being of a community. The other is that utilities are, by nature, monopolistic. The cost of laying two entirely redundant networks of water mains in a city, or two electric power grids through a region, would be so great that no amount of resulting competition could compensate. The answer in America has been to permit the private operation of such industries as monopolies, but to submit these private enterprises to public regulation, so as to keep services up to certain standards and rates within line.

How different are hospitals in this regard? On the first count—the one alluded to by Frist—they would seem to be equally essential. Just as it needs gas, electricity, water, and telephones, every community needs quality medical care at an affordable price. On the second count, there would seem also to be a good analogy. Hospitals are extremely expensive institutions. According to various studies, the cost of buying or building a hospital is at least $100,000 per bed. Over the short term, with an overabundance of hospital beds, the purchase cost at least may decline marginally, but longer term, as health care becomes increasingly technological, that figure can be expected to rise, not fall.

Does it make economic sense to have two hospitals in a community when one would suffice to serve its population? Consider the fairly typical case of a small city, where there may be a public hospital serving the poor and several private hospitals catering to the insured middle and upper class. Collectively, these facilities are probably operating at the national average of about 50–65 percent occupancy, though any one of them could serve all the population. What will happen? Charges at those several institutions will be set at levels necessary to balance the books and turn a profit, except at the public hospital used primarily by the poor, where taxes will be raised as needed to keep it afloat (unless the local voters decide, as many have, to cast their needy neighbors adrift by closing or selling the public hospital).

In theory, by letting the market work, this situation should be resolved as one hospital in such a community garners all the business and the others close down. But will that actually happen? If a community has strong feelings about caring for its less fortunate, it may decide to keep the "inefficient" public hospital running whatever the costs. Or if that facility is shut down, two essentially redundant private facilities may both be kept open by setting prices artificially high and competing for patients on the basis of other considerations: amenities, specialties, et cetera. In either event, total health costs to that community will not be as low as they should be.

If, as executives of all the hospital companies are fond of asserting, health care is essentially a local or regional business, it makes little sense to concentrate it into the hands of a few national corporate entities as they are doing. If that is the inevitable direction of the industry in a free market, the policy answer is to empower communities to control the local health-care environment as much as possible.

But local empowerment alone is not enough. Local authorities are no match for unrestrained national, much less multinational, corporate power. As countless multistate or multinational corporations have demonstrated, it is relatively easy to gain concessions from even the most alert and suspicious local citizenry by playing communities off each other. The company need only dangle before each the carrot of new jobs or tax revenues or services and brandish the stick of loss of the same. It is thus necessary that national policies also be adopted to limit corporate medical power.

What might these be?

One obvious answer is to develop a tough antitrust approach that addresses some of the special characteristics of the health-care industry, something that has not been done consistently to date. Because this industry is developing in such an unusual fashion, with a few relatively large firms and myriad "mom-and-pop" local or regional facilities, standard textbook definitions of market dominance will lead to little or no antitrust enforcement. To the extent that markets for hospital care are local, looking at a company's national market share, or even its regional share, also misses the point. A lone hospital in a rural area is by definition a monopoly. But there are monopolies and there are *monopolies*. As we noted in the case of Las Cruces, New Mexico, when that hospital is a public facility, it is answerable to the community and cannot properly be called a monopoly. When it is a not-for-profit facility, even if in an association like Voluntary Hospitals of America, it is a monopoly, but does have a local board that is at least subject to local pressure. If it is an independent proprietary hospital, it again is a true monopoly, but still its owners and managers have to deal with their neighbors. When a corporate chain owns the same facility, however, the situation is qualitatively different. Now there is a monopoly position in the local market, and the major decisions on pricing, operations, and long-range growth and investment are being made at some distant headquarters, while profits are siphoned out of the community.

Antitrust statutes do not currently address such *political* distinctions very well. They should.

The same might be said of the tendency toward vertical integration of the industry. Humana's model of a company owning both hospitals and insurance plans represents the complete elimination of at least one layer of competing market forces. Absent are the conflicting interests of the hospital company, trying to fill beds, and the insurance company, trying to keep patients' hospital utilization and medical bills down, which have worked to some extent in the interest of both society and the patient. Even in the HCA/Equitable joint-venture model, the fact that both the insurance giant and HCA owned 50 percent of the resulting venture reduced, if it didn't totally eliminate, that healthy conflict. Likewise, as hospital corporations attempt to tie up physician referrals by buying physician practices, entering into joint-venture arrangements with doctors groups, or signing up such groups in profit-sharing PPO or HMO plans, another source of healthy conflict beneficial to the patient in terms of quality assurance and cost control is lost.

Once established industry-wide, such vertically integrated systems will make it increasingly hard for new entrants to shake up cozy noncompetitive arrangements, something economists consider an important aspect of preventing monopoly behavior. There will be few new entrants indeed if the minimum size for successful competition in health services becomes ownership of enough hospitals to enter into a group health insurance joint venture and assets sufficient to buy physicians away from competing established institutions. Hospital companies will establish regional networks of secondary and primary care facilities around centrally located tertiary-care teaching hospitals. This system will become the basic unit of investment—to be tallied in hundreds of millions of dollars—for entering the integrated health-care business. Once that happens, there probably will be no more new competitors, just as there have been no new auto makers of any consequence in over half a century because of the enormous entry costs.

Even if vertical integration offers some advantages in terms of efficiency (and this is questionable), perhaps in this industry the disadvantages are important enough that it simply ought not to be allowed. Already, the Board of Medical Licensure in Kentucky has decided to challenge the growing links between that state's seven thousand physicians and its hospitals. In a letter sent in late 1986 to all physicians in the state, the board warned that it would discipline any physician who entered into an agreement to send patients to a hospital that the board found to be, in effect, financially supporting the physician. "The relationships are becoming so involved that it's hard to tell whether doctors are independent practitioners or hospital employees," said board Chairman Dr. Royce Dawson, in explaining the move, reportedly the first of its kind in the nation.

Doctors' profit-sharing and joint-venture arrangements with hospital companies so resemble kickbacks that eventually some kind of regulation or prohibition might be expected. But no one is likely to fuss much about the tie-ins between insurers and hospitals. In my view, these ought to be just as troubling, if not more so. When Humana began its insurance operation, its then Group Health Division Director Henry Werronen said the goal was keeping costs down. "The key to keeping insurance costs down is controlling hospital costs," he explained, "since sixty cents on every health insurance dollar goes to the hospital and only thirty cents to the doctors. And who's in a better position to control hospital costs than the hospitals?" In fact, however, what Humana did to make its insurance plan work was to put the screws on the doctors, by limiting their options in treating patients, in effect shifting the ratio of the consumer's dollar even *more* in favor of the hospital.

Another national measure that might be taken to regulate the increasingly market-oriented corporate health-care system would be to license the management and owners of corporations in this field. The logic of such licensing is simple. Doctors have been licensed for a century because society felt that their life-and-death power over patients required some assertion of public control over their behavior. By all accounts, including those of many hospital company executives themselves, the recent trend toward corporate medicine has shifted much of that physician's power over life-and-death medical decision making to the hospital and the insurer. Instead of hospitals being just physician workshops and insurance companies being just paymasters, hospital managers and insurance executives now tell doctors how much and what kind of care they can give their patients, and how much they can expect to earn. More broadly, they decide what kind of health care will be available to entire communities. Ought not such "practitioners" of medical care be similarly regulated by the state? Requiring that a hospital corporation's top executives and perhaps board members obtain and maintain a state license would do much to ensure that they would not abuse their growing power in the interest of profits for shareholders. To do so could mean losing the ability to run the company.

After all, stockbrokers like Michael Milken or Dennis Levine are licensed by the government, in their case by the federal Securities and Exchange Commission. If a broker violates the trust of investor clients, he or she can be barred by the SEC from dealing in securities. Why shouldn't such strictures be applied to hospital executives who are dealing with patients' actual lives and health?

A further important reform would be to end hospitals' self-monitoring through the Joint Commission on Accreditation of Healthcare Organizations. Instead state or federal bodies would conduct annual, unannounced spot inspections. This would have the salutary effect of making information about hospital operations public—something the JCAHO has always studiously avoided. A free-market approach to health care is ludicrous if, as is now the case, consumers have only the information hospitals choose to provide to them. Since any state or federal regulatory body would have its members appointed by elected officials, this would also make government more directly accountable for the quality of acute health care in America than it is today.

Finally, of course, if all such efforts are tried and fail, the health-care industry may follow the pattern of other capital-intensive industries in America, becoming concentrated into a few megacorporations. In that case, there will remain the possibility of treating it formally as a kind of utility. The appropriate state or federal agency would determine standards for treatment, charges, capital investment, and rates of return to shareholders for each company in the industry. Given the dismal performance of public service commissions in protecting ratepayers in most states, this would be an unfortunate option to have to pursue. The New York Public Service Commission is so bad at this primary responsibility, for instance, that a state consumer affairs agency, and often a consumer affairs representative from the state attorney general's office, has to challenge its every rate decision!

The health services corporations, led by the hospital industry, say health care is a locally or at most regionally defined market. But they are nonetheless trying their best to turn it into a commodity, the same anywhere in the country. Companies like AMI, NME, Humana, HCA, and even smaller firms like Republic or National Healthcare are trying to establish name recognition for their care. A Republic nose job or a Humana heart transplant are not far off, it would seem (even if a Humana *artificial* heart no longer seems in the cards). Nor is a strictly segmented, multitiered system of care that will see the rich getting treatment full of options and amenities, the middle-class getting good quality "managed" care with some of the amenities but few of the options, and the poor with none of the above, and perhaps not even with quality "managed" care.

It need not be that way. But so far, an obsession among government and academic policymakers with short-term cost control and an ignorance among consumers about what it means to turn cost-plus medicine, with all its failings, into free-market medicine have prevented any regulation of this fast growing and faster changing industry. On the contrary, deregulation of the industry continues apace.

As industry critic Dr. Arnold Relman says:

> If and when the for-profits take over a very large part of the system, the public will be dependent on policies that are made in corporate boardrooms for the benefit of shareholders rather than by responsible people in the community and the health-care community. It's really a question of whether Wall Street or Main Street makes these decisions. To say that the public wants it to be Wall Street because they're not objecting to what's been happening is to believe that people want McDonald's to decide what's best for the nutrition of the American public.

The imponderable in all this is the reaction of the public when it finally does start to realize that there are trade-offs for the amenities some of them have come to take for granted. Will anyone tolerate a staggering $1.5-trillion national medical bill in the year 2000? Will employees accept health plans that don't pay for everything they're used to, or that make them go to certain places and use certain doctors? Will the majority accept dramatically lower standards of care for the less well-off minority? Will communities tolerate the writing-off of their towns' health system by large hospital or health-care corporations headquartered sometimes a continent away? Will doctors accept de facto employee status? Will patients remain loyal when they discover their doctors answer to two masters—their customers and the hospital?

It is still too early in the game to answer such questions with certainty, but it's a safe guess the answer to most will be no. We Americans spend more on medical care, both in the aggregate and as a percentage of our incomes, than any other society, but our attitude toward hospitals and even physicians remains ambivalent at best. In recent decades, American health consumers have rebelled at various aspects of corporate medicine, most notably the lock the major drug companies developed on prescription drugs, which was broken by legislation designed to open the way for generic drugs. And a variety of surveys show many of us to be absolutely suspicious of large corporations of *any* kind.

It is clear, though, that public demand for some control over the growing corporatization of health care must materialize soon. Otherwise, what economists soothingly call the "rationalization" of the existing system may go so far that the idea of a decent system of public health care will, like the erstwhile public trolly-car system in Los Angeles, be lost forever and impossible to replace. The final question may then be: Even if the American people object to the results of marketplace medicine, will we be able to do anything about it?

NOTES

Preface

1. Grant, James P., *The State of the World's Children 1990*, Oxford University Press (for the United Nations), 1990. p. 75.
2. Lindorff, Dave, "The Venture 100: Getting Ready for the Recovery," *Venture*, May 1983, Vol. 5, No. 5, p. 38.

Chapter 1

1. Health Care Finance Administration, 1990 statistics on health insurance coverage of the population.
2. Health Care Finance Administration statistics.
3. Federation of American Health Systems, and Health Care Finance Administration.
4. "Study Shows Hospital Profits Actually Rose 14% in First Year of Medicare Fixed-Payment System," *Los Angeles Times*, November 26, 1985, p. 2.
5. Pear, Robert, "Hospital Profits on Medicare Rise Under a System to Control Costs," *The New York Times*, March 29, 1987, p. 1.
6. Bean, Ed, "Latest Survey Shows Hospital Charges Increasing Far More Quickly Than CPI," *Wall Street Journal*, January 6, 1988, p. 17.
7. Kramon, Glenn, "Insurance Rates for Health Care Increase Sharply," *The New York Times*, January 12, 1988, p. 1.
8. Easterbrook, Gregg, "The Revolution in Medicine," *Newsweek*, January 26, 1987, p. 40.
9. Department of Health and Rehabilitative Services, *State of Florida Medicaid Survey*, 1990.
10. Phillips, Carolyn, and Mills, David, "Humana Hopes Artificial-Heart Project Will Make Its Name a Household Word," *Wall Street Journal*, November 19, 1984, p. 23.

11. Office of the Actuary, Health Care Finance Administration, *National Health Expenditures Projections, 1986-2000,* published in 1990.
12. Relman, Arnold S., "The New Medical-Industrial Complex," *New England Journal of Medicine,* Oct. 23, 1980, p. 963–70.
13. Steiber Research Group, *1990 National Hospital Advertising/Marketing Expenditures Fact Sheet,* Steiber Research Group, Chicago.
14. *1991 Annual Report,* Federation of American Health Systems, Washington, D.C., p. 18.

Chapter 2

1. *1991 Annual Report,* FAHS, *op. cit.,* p. 22.
2. *ibid.,* p. 21.
3. Luecke, Pam, "Golf Game Set Foursome on a Course to Success," *Courier-Journal,* May 5, 1985, p. A10.
4. "American Medicorp Sues Bank for Its Role in Humana Tender Bid," *Wall Street Journal,* October 20, 1977, p. 33.
5. "Hospital Concern Uses Meeting of Analysts to Score Oppenheimer," *Wall Street Journal,* February 2, 1973, p. 20.
6. "Oppenheimer Fires Analyst Who Leaked a Report on Hospital Management Stocks," *Wall Street Journal,* December 13, 1972, p. 5.
7. *1991 Annual Report,* FAHS, *op. cit.,* p. 18.
8. Pascale, Catherine McDonald, "National Healthcare Inc. (OTC-NHCI)," Bear Stearns, New York, May 22, 1986 report.
9. Mariann S. Mashburn et al. vs. National Healthcare, Inc. et al., in U.S. District Court for the Middle District of Alabama, Southern Division. Civil Action No. 87-D-70-S, filed March 25, 1987, p. 44.
10. "National Healthcare Says Judge Approves Settlement of Suit," *Wall Street Journal,* March 10, 1988, p. 26.
11. Gregory, Ed, "Hospital Giant Rapidly Curing Its Built-In Ills: HealthTrust Shocks Wall Street," *Tennessean,* December 4, 1990, p. 1E.

Chapter 3

1. "Healthcare Advertising Roundtable," *Healthcare Advertising Review,* Lancaster, Vol. III, No. 2, March-April 1987, p. 6.
2. Steiber Research Group, *op. cit.*
3. "Auxiliary News: Forgetting Self, Remembering Others," *Caring,* Communications Department, National Healthcare, Inc., Dothan, Vol. II, No. 2, Summer 1986, p. 7.
4. American Medical International, Inc., Final Order, Federal Trade Commission, Docket No. 9158, July 3, 1984, p. 54.
5. Memo from FTC Initial Decision, Docket No. 9158, July 27, 1983, p. 75.
6. Jones, David, "Questions and Answers," from the 13th Biennial Institute Hospital and Health Care Administration Alumni Association, School of Public Health, University of Minnesota, October 16, 1985, as published by Humana, Inc.
7. Committee on Implications of For-Profit Enterprise in Health Care,

Bradford Gray, Study Director, *For-Profit Enterprise in Health Care*, National Academy Press, Washington, D.C., 1986, p. 191.

8. Committee on Implications of For-Profit Enterprise in Health Care, Bradford Gray et. al., *op. cit.*, p. 138.

Chapter 4

1. Brinkley, Joel, "Plan for Cutting Hospital Costs by Rewarding Doctors Draws A.M.A. Fire," *The New York Times*, September 24, 1985, p. A24.
2. *ibid.*
3. *ibid.*
4. Kirchner, Meriam, "Will You Have to Join a Hospital Chain to Survive?" *Medical Economics*, November 25, 1985, p. 164.
5. Starr, Paul, *The Social Transformation of American Medicine*, Basic Books, New York, 1982, p. 162.
6. *ibid.*, p. 177–8.
7. Gorman, Kit, 'What's Up Doc? Hospitals' Recruitment Causes a Stir," *New Orleans City Business*, March 3–16, 1986, p. 1.
8. Kinkhead, Gwen, "Humana's Hard-Sell Hospitals," *Fortune Magazine*, Nov. 17, 1980, p. 76.
9. Gorman, Kit, *op. cit.*, p. 1.
10. Humana Hospital West Hills memo from Medical Executive Committee to All Members of the Medical Staff, November 14, 1985.
11. Gorman, Kit, *op. cit.*, p. 1.
12. Jones, David, "Questions and Answers," *op. cit.*
13. The Council on Ethical and Judicial Affairs, *Current Opinions*, American Medical Association, 1989, p. 32.
14. *ibid.*, p. 30.
15. Shortell, Stephen M., "Physician Involvement in Hospital Decision Making," *The New Health Care for Profit*, ed. Bradford Gray, National Academy Press, Washington, 1983, p. 79.
16. Committee on Implications of For-Profit Enterprise in Health Care, Bradford Gray et al., *op. cit.*, p. 211.

Chapter 5

1. Hull, Jennifer Bingham, "Road to Recovery: How Ailing Hospital in South Was Rescued by a For-Profit Chain," *Wall Street Journal*, January 28, 1983, p. 1.
2. Habersham County Grand Jury 1984, *Grand Jury Presentment*, 1984, Habersham County, Georgia.
3. Eamer, Richard, "Nonprofit vs. profit: What data do you see? For-profits are measurably more efficient: corporation executive," *Modern Hospital*, April 1971, p. 116.
4. Johnson, Richard L., "Data show for-profit hospitals don't provide comparable service: consultant," *Modern Hospital*, April 1971, p. 116.
5. *1981 Annual Report*, Federation of American Health Systems.
6. Putka, Gary, "Heard on the Street: Big Hospital Chains Continue Healthy

Showing Even As Limits on Medicare Costs Appear Certain," *Wall Street Journal*, March 11, 1983, p. 55.

7. Booz, Allen & Hamilton, Inc., "Comparative Economic Performance Among Tennessee's Proprietary & Not-for-Profit Hospital Sectors," Hospital Alliance of Tennessee, Nashville, December 1984, p. 1.

8. "Proprietary Hospital Charges to Blue Cross/Blue Shield of North Carolina Subscribers, 1983," Blue Cross/Blue Shield of North Carolina, Raleigh, 1985, p. 6.

9. Pattison, Robert V., "Response to Financial Incentives Among Investor-Owned and Not-for-Profit Hospitals: An Analysis Based on California Data, 1978–1982," in Committee on Implications of For-Profit Enterprise in Health Care, *op. cit.*, p. 190.

10. Renn, Steven C., Schramm, Carl J., Watt, J. Michael, and Derzon, Robert A., "The Effects of Ownership and System Affiliation on the Economic Performance of Hospitals," *Inquiry*, Fall 1985, Vol. XXII, p. 231.

11. Teitelman, Robert, "The SuperMeds: Bent on stitching together a family of hybrid health-care giants, Wall Street just might drown its patients in red ink," *Financial World*, June 10, 1986, p. 26.

12. "Florida Cost Containment Survey of 1983," State of Florida Department of Health, 1985.

13. Committee on Implications of For-Profit Enterprise in Health Care, Bradford Gray et. al., *op. cit.*, p. 93.

14. Joint Legislative Health Care Planning and Oversight Committee, *Health Choices*, South Carolina Division of Research and Statistical Services, 1988.

15. Murray, Frank, "More Means Less," a letter to the editor, Las Vegas *Review Journal*, June 14, 1985.

16. "Building on Success: A Statement on American Health Policy," *1989 Annual Report*, Humana, Inc., 1989, p. 6.

17. Ahlquist, Gary, and Greene, Andrew, "Hospital Mergers: Cure or Disease," Booz, Allen & Hamilton, Inc., 1989, p. 1.

Chapter 6

1. Phillips, Carolyn, and Mills, David, *Wall Street Journal*, *op. cit.*, p. 23.

2. *ibid.*, p. 23.

3. *ibid.*, p. 23.

4. "Heart Pioneer Resigns," Associated Press, *The New York Times*, June 25, 1988, p. 7.

5. Altman, Lawrence K., "Health Care As Business: Experts Ask Whether Emphasis on Profits Could Dilute the Ideal of Medical Research," *The New York Times*, November 27, 1984, p. 1, and Altman, Lawrence K., "Doctors Prepare for New Attempt to Replace Human Heart Today," *The New York Times*, November 25, 1984, p. 1.

6. Scott, Janny, "Artificial Heart: Furor Blurs Horizon for Dr. DeVries," *Los Angeles Times*, January 4, 1987, p. 1.

7. Jones, Rochelle, *The Supermeds: How the Big Business of Medicine is Endangering Our Health Care*, Charles Scribner's Sons, New York, 1988, p. 8.

8. Altman, Lawrence, *op. cit.*, *The New York Times*, November 25, 1984, p. 1.

9. Butterfield, Fox, "Proposed Sale of a Hospital by Harvard Is Raising Fears," *The New York Times*, September 4, 1983, p. 24.

10. Starr, Paul, *op. cit.*, p. 435.
11. Lewis, Irving J., and Sheps, Cecil G., *The Sick Citadel: The American Academic Medical Center and the Public Interest*, Oelgeschlager, Gunn & Hain, Publishers, Inc., Cambridge, 1983, p. 223.
12. Egdahl, Richard H., "The Involvement of For-Profit Chains With Teaching and Research Institutions," in Southby, Richard McK. F., and Greenberg, Warren, *The For-Profit Hospital: Access, Quality, Teaching, Research*, Battelle Press, Columbus, 1986, p. 19.
13. Lewis and Sheps, *op. cit.*, p. xvii.
14. Berliner, Howard S. and Burlage, Robb K., "Proprietary Hospital Chains and Academic Medical Centers," November 1985 paper presented at the Annual Meeting of the American Public Health Association.
15. Gray, Bradford, et al., Committee on Implications of For-Profit Enterprise in Health Care, *op. cit.*, p. 149.
16. *ibid.*, p. 148.
17. Jones, David, "Visions of Medicine," *Massachusetts Medicine*, March/April 1986, p. 24.
18. Stewart, Kay, "U of L's Swain Wins Praise for Changes in First Six Months," *Courier-Journal*, September 18, 1981, p. B1.
19. *ibid.*, p. B1.
20. Gil, Gideon, "Panel to Probe State Payments to Humana for Indigent Patients," *Courier-Journal*, April 16, 1991, p. B1.
21. Lawson, Gil, "Humana Denies Getting Double Pay for Indigent Care," *Courier-Journal*, April 25, 1991, p. B1.
22. King, Mike, "Medical Equipment U of L Didn't Get Led to Conflict," *Courier-Journal*, May 9, 1985, p. 1.
23. King, Mike, "Trial Marriage With U of L Has Resulted in Both Spats and Successes," *Courier-Journal*, May 9, 1985, p. 1.
24. Gil, Gideon, "Hospital Reroutes Some Emergency Patients," *Courier-Journal*, September 22, 1987, p. 1.
25. Norton, Wilma, "Hospital Is Forced to Close Emergency Room 5 Hours," *Courier-Journal*, January 6, 1984, p. B2.
26. Waitzkin, Howard, "Deciding Against Corporate Management of a State-Supported Academic Medical Center," *New England Journal of Medicine*, November 13, 1986, p. 1299.
27. Lewis and Sheps, *op. cit.*, p. 209.
28. Gray, Bradford, et al., Committee on Implications of For-Profit Enterprise in Health Care, *op. cit.*, p. 150.
29. Berliner and Burlage, *op. cit.*
30. Lewis and Sheps, *op. cit.*, p. 59.

Chapter 7

1. Burton, Thomas Ray, Sworn Affidavit in Franklin Circuit Court, 1983.
2. Frye, J. R. "Buck," Assurance of Voluntary Compliance, Franklin Circuit Court, June 30, 1983.
3. Plake, Sue Thornton, ed., *Task Force on Indigent Health Care, Final Report*, State of Texas, 1984.

4. Relman, Arnold, "Can We Afford Health Care as a Commodity?," *Technology Review*, April 1984, p. 13.
5. Tolchin, Martin, "Hospitals Use Charity to Fend Off Tax Collectors," *The New York Times*, July 15, 1987, p. 15.
6. Relman, Arnold, *op. cit.*, p. 13.
7. Belkin, Lisa, "Hall County Journal: Town Revives a Hospital and Itself," *The New York Times*, December 5, 1988, p. 16.

Chapter 8

1. Testimony of Joseph Reina in Edwards trial, U.S. vs. Edwin W. Edwards, et al., Criminal Action No. 85-078, Section E(1), U.S. District Court, Eastern District of Louisiana, District Judge Marcel Livandais, October 23, 1985, p. 92.
2. Ward, Leah Beth, "Anaya Seeks to Halt Federal Investigation," *Albuquerque Tribune*, March 28, 1986, p. A1.
3. Memo from Joseph Rosenfeld to William Simpson, September 24, 1983, National Medical Enterprises, Exhibit 86 in Memorial General Hospital vs. National Medical Enterprises et al., U.S. District Court for the District of New Mexico, No. CIV-85-0248C.
4. Letter from John Bedrosian to Dan Lopez, December 1, 1983, Exhibit 29 in Memorial General Hospital vs. National Medical Enterprises et al., U.S. District Court for the District of New Mexico, No. CIV-85-0248C.
5. Letter from Michael R. Ferien to Toney Anaya, c/o Dan Lopez, June 17, 1982, Exhibit 12 in Memorial General Hospital vs. National Medical Enterprises et al., U.S. District Court for the District of New Mexico, No. CIV-85-0248C.
6. Memo to William T. Simpson from Michael H. Green, National Medical Enterprises, December 6, 1983, Exhibit 6, in Memorial General Hospital vs. National Medical Enterprises et al., U.S. District Court for the District of New Mexico, No. CIV-85-0248C.
7. Affidavit of Thomas W. Gillespie, Special Agent, FBI, December 4, 1984, in re. Toney and Elaine Anaya vs. United States of America, U.S. District Court, District of New Mexico, CIV-86-1094, Government Exhibit 41.
8. Memo from Patti Archuletta to John Bedrosian, National Medical Enterprises, December 20, 1983, Exhibit No. 24, in Memorial General Hospital vs. National Medical Enterprises et al., U.S. District Court for the District of New Mexico, No. CIV-85-0248C.
9. Memo from Bill Williams to Hal Buck, National Medical Enterprises, December 1, 1983, Exhibit No. 19, in Memorial General Hospital vs. National Medical Enterprises et al., U.S. District Court for the District of New Mexico, No. CIV-85-0248C.
10. Memo from Bill Williams to Ron Messenger, National Medical Enterprises, July 1, 1983, Exhibit 20, in Memorial General Hospital vs. National Medical Enterprises et al., U.S. District Court for the District of New Mexico, No. CIV-85-0248C.
11. Federal Trade Commission Docket No. 9161, filed October 30, 1984, Initial Decision, Judge Lewis F. Parker, p. 90.
12. "Hurst: THA Striving to Make Laws Work, Ready to Fight Any Revival of

'Sick Tax'," *Federation of American Health Systems Review,* Washington, D.C., May/June 1986, p. 43.
13. Selected list of receipts and expenditures (1989-90), Federal Election Commission, June 18, 1991.

Chapter 9

1. Healthcare Management Professionals advertisement, "Why Does This Horse Look a Lot Like a Zebra?," *FAHS Review,* November/December 1986, p. 41.
2. "A Special Report: Emerging Health-Care Systems: The Number of Companies Grows; Megasystem Idea Fading?," *FAHS Review,* November/December 1986, p. 16.
3. Craypo, Charles and Lehman, Mary, *Health Care for Profit: The Impact of Investor-Owned Hospital Chains on Workers and Communities,* Dept. of Labor Studies, Pennsylvania State University, University Park, PA, 1986, p. 68.
4. Bean, Ed, ". . . While Big Debt Burden Forces Head of Former Units to Set Priorities," *Wall Street Journal,* November 17, 1987, p. 52.
5. Bean, Ed., "A Lighter Load for Hospital Corp.'s Frist," *Wall Street Journal,* November 17, 1987, p. 52.
6. "A Special Report: Emerging Health-Care Systems: The Number of Companies Grows; Megasystem Idea Fading?," *op. cit.,* p. 17.
7. *ibid.,* p. 17.
8. *ibid.,* p. 17.
9. Schulte, Fred; McVicar, Nancy; and Bergal, Jenni; "Medicare HMO Fails Some Patients," *Sun Sentinel,* October 21, 1990, p. 1.
10. Bergal, Jenni; Schulte, Fred; and McVicar, Nancy; "Enrollment Errors Cause Uncertainty," *Sun-Sentinel,* October 22, 1990, p. 1.
11. McVicar, Nancy; Schulte, Fred; and Bergal, Jenni; "In the Cross-Fire," *Sun-Sentinel,* October 23, 1990, p. 1.
12. White, David, "Hospital Operations Execs Focus on Human Resource Needs: Radical Change Is Needed in Management," *FAHS Review,* July/August 1989, p. 23.
13. Jacobsen, David, "Spotlight: Hostages to the Deficit," *FAHS Review,* September/October 1987, p. 16.
14. Gray, Bradford, et al., Committee on Implications of For-Profit Enterprise in Health Care, *op. cit.,* p. 205.

Chapter 10

1. Welles, Chris, "Is Deregulation Working? True, Prices Have Fallen. But the Top Players May Stifle Competition," *Business Week,* December 22, 1986, p. 46.
2. Nadel, Mark V., ed., "Canadian Health Insurance: Lessons for the United States," General Accounting Office, GAO/HRD-91-90, June 4, 1991, p. 3.
3. *ibid.,* p. 7.
4. *1991 Annual Report,* FAHS, p. 3.
5. *ibid.,* p. 15.
6. Craypo, Charles and Lehman, Mary, *op. cit.,* p. 66.

GLOSSARY

AHA The American Hospital Association, trade and lobbying organization for the hospital industry.

AMA The American Medical Association, a trade and lobbying organization for physicians.

AMI American Medical International. The first corporate hospital chain, founded in 1960 by Uranus Appel in Los Angeles. Now headquartered in Dallas, Texas. Chairman is Robert W. O'Leary, former CEO of Voluntary Hospitals of America.

CON Certificate of need. CONs are permits required by some states to construct a hospital or to purchase costly diagnostic or medical equipment, such as a CAT-scan device or lithotriptor.

DRG Diagnosis-related group. When Congress reformed the Medicare program, it established 477 categories of ailments and ordered that every patient in the Medicare program be assigned to a category before being admitted to a hospital. A set reimbursement amount was established for each DRG. If a hospital treats a patient for less than the set amount, it keeps the difference. If the treatment costs more than the allowed figure, the hospital has to assume the loss.

EPIC EPIC Health Group is an ESOP spinoff of 36 hospitals which AMI unloaded in 1988, shortly after the formation of Health-Trust by HCA, for similar reasons: The hospitals were dragging down company profits and share values. Chairman is Kenn S. George.

301

ESOP   Employee Stock Ownership Plan. A legal arrangement which
              technically allows employees to own their own company by
              having their shares held in trust. In practice, most ESOPs are
              more of a tax avoidance scheme than a true form of "worker
              management."

FAHS   The Federation of American Health Systems is the for-profit
              hospital industry's own trade and lobbying organization. Fed-
              PAC is its Washington-based political action committee. Origi-
              nally called the Federation of American Hospitals (FAH).

HCA   Hospital Corporation of America. Founded in 1965 in Nash-
              ville, Tennessee, by a father-son team, Thomas Frist and
              Thomas Frist, Jr., along with Jack Massey of Kentucky Fried
              Chicken fame, it was for many years the largest hospital chain
              in America. Currently chaired by Thomas Frist, Jr.

HealthTrust   An ESOP spinoff of 104 mostly smaller rural hospitals that was
              formed in 1988 when HCA decided to get rid of its least
              profitable holdings to help fend off a possible unfriendly
              takeover of the parent company. Chairman is R. Clayton
              McWorter.

Hill-Burton   A program created in Congress in 1946 to provide funds to
              build hospitals across the nation.

HMO   Health Maintenance Organization. A prepaid health plan
              which ensures that members who use the HMO's clinics and
              doctors, and who go to specific hospitals either owned by the
              HMO or having a contract with it, will have all their bills paid
              in full or almost full. HMOs generally offer the patient the least
              freedom of choice.

HSA   Health System Agency. A regional planning organization com-
              posed of appointed officials who are charged with planning to
              meet an area's health-care needs and with considering the
              merits of applications for CONs by medical organizations. Once
              present in every state and region, HSAs have been eliminated
              in most states in recent years.

Humana   Founded as Extendicare, a nursing home chain, in 1962 by two
              Louisville, Kentucky, attorneys, David Jones and Wendell
              Cherry, Humana is currently a hospital company and health
              insurance company. Its chairman is David Jones. Cherry died in
              1991.

IPA   Independent Practice Association. Essentially the doctors' an-
              swer to the competition of HMOs and PPOs. Instead of
              working for an HMO, an association of doctors agrees to care
              for IPA member patients for a set annual fee.

Medicaid   This is the health insurance program for the poor, or at least for those whose family income, after adjustments, falls below a level of slightly more than the federal poverty guideline. The rate of reimbursement for Medicaid is set by the states, some of which make it so low that most doctors and hospitals avoid treating Medicaid patients.

MediCal   The name for California's version of Medicaid.

Medicare   The federal health insurance program for the elderly and the disabled.

NME   National Medical Enterprises. Long the most diversified of the major corporate hospital chains, with holdings of nursing homes, psychiatric hospitals, specialty hospitals, and medical equipment firms, NME was founded in 1965 by three Los Angeles attorneys, Richard Eamer, Leonard Cohen, and John Bedrosian. Eamer remains the company's chairman.

PCN   Primary Care Network. The insurance industry's answer to competition from HMOs and PPOs. In a PCN, doctors agree to handle member patients at reduced fees (typically 80 percent of customary fees for Blue Cross PCNs), and patients agree to select a participating primary care physician to act as a "gatekeeper" who will decide when they need a specialist or hospitalization. PCNs tend to offer more freedom of choice than HMOs or PPOs though the "gatekeeper" approach can be stricter than in some PPOs.

PPO   Preferred Provider Organization. A network of hospitals and independent physicians who have staff privileges at those hospitals. The buyer of PPO insurance gets full or close to full coverage as long as he or she uses those physicians and goes to those hospitals. PPOs offer wider choice of physician, but not of hospital.

Index